CHINESE SHORT STORIES
OF THE TWENTIETH CENTURY

GARLAND REFERENCE LIBRARY OF THE HUMANITIES
VOLUME 1496

Chinese Short Stories of the Twentieth Century
An Anthology in English

Edited and Translated by
Zhihua Fang

Garland Publishing, Inc.
New York and London
1995

Library of Congress Cataloging-in-Publication Data

Chinese short stories of the twentieth century : an anthology in English /
translated and edited by Zhihua Fang.
      p.   cm. — (Garland reference library of the humanities ; vol.
1496)
Includes bibliographical references.
ISBN 0-8153-0532-X (alk. paper)
1. Short stories, Chinese—Translations into English. 2. Chinese fiction—20th century—Translations into English. I. Fang, Zhihua,
b1963– . II. Series.
PL2658.E8C485 1995
895.1'30108—dc20   95-22414
                                                              CIP

Printed on acid-free, 250-year-life paper
Manufactured in the United States of America

FOR YE XIANMEI, MY MOTHER, AND FANG PEIYUAN, MY FATHER

Contents

Acknowledgments

It is a pleasure to express my gratitude to Dr. Willard Bohn, Dr. Douglas Hesse, and Dr. Curt White, who read an earlier version of these translations and offered valuable suggestions and advice. I also owe thanks to Dr. William Woodson and Dr. Richard Dammers, who encouraged and motivated me in my work. I would especially like to thank Dr. Irene Brosnahan, who not only read my translations, but also checked them against the original Chinese texts for accuracy and faithfulness. I am truly grateful to Dr. Susan Rusinko for her reading and appreciation of my translations, at a time when she was already extremely busy with her own books. To Dr. David Gould, I want to express my thankfulness for his reading and commenting on my trans-lations. My thanks also to Adrienne Makowski, who worked as production editor on this book.

Lastly, I owe a great debt of gratitude to Dr. Ray Lewis White, without whose inspiration, support, and guidance, this project would have never progressed this far and this well.

Introduction

For a long time, Chinese literature has been a fascination for a great number of people in America. The fascination comes not only from people's admiration for world famous Chinese classics, but also from people's deep interest in the splendid works of many modern Chinese writers.

In modern Chinese literature, as in most other modern literatures, fiction has grown to be the dominating genre for the literati and the flagship of modern creative writing. And in modern Chinese fiction, the short story seems to have played a role, both in literature and sociopolitics, that may be unequaled in any other modern literature. To understand the unusual dominance of the short story in modern Chinese literature, one needs only to take a quick look at the significant body of works of Lu Xun, the greatest Chinese writer in the twentieth century, and the multitudes of short stories that came into being in the late 1970s and early 1980s in China. For complex cultural, political, and economic reasons, the short story seems to be the genre that has stolen the spotlight from the novel in modern Chinese fiction.

The deciding factor in the rise of the short story in modern Chinese literature, it seems to me, is the social and political involvement that the dominating writers of short fiction have intended in their works. Before the twentieth century, although there had long been a desire in Chinese men and women of letters to rule the world through their pens and a tradition to designate their writings as the vessels of moral teachings, almost all (except Confucius and a few others) realized their worldly aspirations through direct involvement in politics or administrative work, not through writing. At the arrival of the twentieth century, however, many Chinese intellectuals, finding commercial writing for literary magazines and newspapers more alluring and lucrative than endless administrative work, discovered the means through which their voices could be heard and their political opinions noted. Well-educated and enlightened Chinese intellectuals rushed to the world of fiction, bringing with them not only the hope of making a decent living through entertainment but also the ever-so-noble ideal of curing social ills, cultural diseases, and political malevolence. Hence, fiction writing boomed by the turn of the century in the once dominantly poetic China. Because of the lack of a large middle class in China in this century, because of the lack of extensive education in the population, and for other political and economic reasons, short stories, instead of novels, were made easily available and became widely read. Thus, as the short story became the more popular choice of fiction in twentieth-century China, national sensations could be easily stirred by certain short stories, as in the cases of "The Diary of a Madman" (1918) by Lu Xun and "The Class Teacher" (1977) by Liu Xinwu, and writers of short stories could become household names overnight in the politically volatile and socially unstable land of the dragon.

To help others to appreciate the works of the best Chinese fiction writers, I have translated and compiled in this text a collection of eight of the best Chinese short stories written in this century by various writers in different periods. This collection represents the finest of Chinese short fiction in that these stories not only reveal the amazing talent of these writers, but also their social, cultural, and political inquiries, which have won for the short story the limelight in modern Chinese literature. To understand the stories better, let us take a brief look at the history of twentieth-century Chinese literature.

For the purpose of this introduction, I arrange the literary history of twentieth-century China into five periods. This arrangement is based largely on historical and cultural considerations rather than on convenience in literary inquiries. This arrangement, however, also reflects my consideration and firm conviction that a scholar will benefit the most when he or she studies twentieth-century Chinese literature in close scrutiny of Chinese history, Chinese society, and Chinese culture in the twentieth century.

1897–1916	Literary Clashes on the Western Front
1916–1949	Freedom in Chaos
1949–1976	Suffocation and Search for Survival
1976–1989	Revival of a Spirit
1989–present	Decline of the Written Word

Many literary critics tend to overlook the period just before 1916 in Chinese literature. Sometimes this period is denigrated and trivialized. But to understand the origin of Chinese literary works in the first few decades of the twentieth century, one has to study the period of Chinese literary history between 1897 and 1916, the period of the "New Fiction." When Western gunboats were forcing China to open its doors for fair or unfair trade and other exchanges, the weak and corrupt Qing Dynasty initially resisted for fear of change and then finally acquiesced in humiliation when confronted with superior Western military power. Relying on their military superiority, Western countries asked for or simply demanded autonomous concessions in certain coastal Chinese cities, such as Shanghai and Guangzhou (Canton), which were walled off from the rest of those Chinese cities and were basically free from Chinese law. When many of these humiliating concessions were well established at the turn of the century, some educated and patriotic Chinese took advantage of those concessions and used them as a means of protection to engage in antigovernmental activities, among which was the publication of books, magazines, and newspapers openly attacking the corrupt and cowardly Qing government. Spearheaded and stimulated by such magazines and newspapers, publications in the whole country gradually became more fearlessly political (mainly antigovernment), and, in such a time of rapid social and political changes, Chinese literature, although still producing a great deal of insignificant works of all kinds, suddenly began to flourish with a political and nationalistic zeal as fiction gained unprecedented popularity among the people. More important to note, political and social concerns of Chinese writers, which had existed for thousands of years, were to be further developed not only in poetry, essays, and historical writings, but also in the once-despised fiction, as the political and social consciousness continued to grow in the works of such prominent writers as Li Boyuan, Wu Yanren, Cheng Duxiu, Lu Xun, Mao Dun, Guo Moruo, and many others. In the meantime, Chinese intellectuals came into touch with Western literatures and realized that there was much to learn from them. As more foreign literature was translated, Chinese writers often modeled their writing after Western literary works. In their contact with Western literatures, Chinese writers gradually found some new qualities in their own writing: They were shifting further away from classical Chinese in their writing and were using more vernacular Chinese; they learned to use many new techniques in their writing, such as the first-person narrative, which was now put into use more often than the traditional third-person–omniscient (the storyteller mode); and, instead of presenting extraordinary people, they also came to write, as Charles Dickens did in his works, about the common people, detailing their typical problems and their ordinary daily lives. All these new developments, although naive and quite superficial in most cases, would eventually lead to the mature writings produced by Lu Xun and others in later years. Without this period of new growth by the New Writers (writers in the New Fiction movement), the years of literary greatness would not have followed in the 1920s, 1930s, and 1940s.

Yet, at the turn of the century, although voluminous literary works were either translated or created, especially in the commercialized and Westernized Shanghai, Guangzhou (Canton), and Hong Kong of the time, modern Chinese literature was still awaiting the clarion call of Lu Xun's "The Diary of a Madman," which was published in 1918 in the May issue of *New Youth.* Before the publication of "The Diary of a Madman," however, a cultural and literary revolution dubbed the "New Culture Movement" had already been launched by two prominent figures in Chinese literature, Cheng Duxiu and Hu Shi, along with others, when they published numerous articles detailing what the new direction should be for Chinese literature. Cheng Duxiu lived in Japan for a while, and Hu Shi studied at both Cornell and Columbia. Returning home with their revolutionary ideas, they started in 1916 and 1917 to call on Chinese writers to abandon their traditional ways of thinking and writing and to adopt in their writing fresh ideas and new subjects, to become more concerned with social problems of the time, to gain more knowledge of the common people, to abandon classical Chinese for vernacular Chinese, and to be more practical and realistic instead of complacently and sickeningly romantic. It was a call for total change, and it was a call that Lu Xun heeded well in "The Diary of a Madman." From that point on, a new tradition was formed by the alliance of a whole generation of brilliant Chinese writers led by Lu Xun. Out of this revolution came a multitude of great works produced not only by Lu Xun, but also by Mao Dun, Ba Jin, Ye Shengtao, Shen Congwen, Lao She, Xu Dishan (author of "Spring Peach"), and many others. In twentieth-century Chinese literature, this period is commonly regarded as the most significant and fruitful. The writers did not have total freedom, but since the 1911 Revolution, which overthrew the Qing Empire and ensured the founding of the Republic of China in the following year, there was freedom enough in those chaotic and traumatic times to allow the resilient Chinese writers to produce powerful, mature, and valuable works that probably will never cease to be great and significant.

In the first half of this century, the freedom that Chinese writers more or less cherished for a continuum of more than thirty years was by no means a fair-weather condition guaranteed by any constitution or bestowed upon them by the authorities. In fact, they fought for it, died for it, and took good advantage of it, all due to the chaos in a young republic which became gradually oppressive when it was overrun with corruption and constantly threatened with dismantling factors, such as the vicious warlords, the rebellious peasants, the communist insurgence, imperialist foreign intervention, and a backward and deteriorating economy. As the Republic of China tried to tighten its grip on its dissidents all over the country, prominent writers like Lu Xun and Mao Dun were occasionally regarded as a threat to the government; some were arrested, hunted down, and prosecuted; some ran over to the small Chinese Communist territories for safety and a better future; some simply took to hiding when they knew the government was after them. At certain times, even Lu Xun, the most famous writer of the time and the century, had to either live in the Japanese concession in Shanghai or move his residence frequently for fear of being a target on the government's blacklist because he either participated in some illegal political activity or wrote certain articles attacking and insulting the government.

As noted earlier, a certain freedom for writers had already existed before the founding of the Republic of China. There were three major reasons for the creation of such freedom that existed even before this century. One obvious reason was the introduction of Western ideology along with Western technology to China, infusing the country with democratic ideas. Second, when new Western ideologies were introduced, new intellectuals hastened their nationalistic fight against the Qing Empire by using their most powerful weapon, the pen. Third, as noted earlier, there existed humiliating concessions to foreign powers in China in such cities as Shanghai, Guangzhou, and Hong Kong. In such concessions, or blocks of a city that were zoned off "in loan" to foreign countries, Chinese law did not apply and the foreign countries ran them as if they were their own territories. Many newspapers and magazines were registered with the concessions or even published in the concessions, over which the Qing Empire largely had no legal authority even if the newspapers and magazines made a bold attack on the highest government. But the works from that period are now of limited significance, because the "New Fiction" of the time was still in the stage of finding its own form and purpose. Most writers of the time were still learning various new writing skills from the West, and even a new punctuation system was still being formed out of Western punctuation systems. The most valuable products of this period were works attacking the dying Qing Dynasty, especially the works by such famed writers as Li Boyuan, Wu Yanren, Zeng Pu, and Liu Tieyun. These devoted novelists fearlessly and tirelessly exposed the traditional Chinese government as they knew it and their works are still widely read in China today. Yet, the early years of the twentieth century were soon to witness the rise of a different kind of fiction in China, the fiction that is known as the "Mandarin Duck and Butterfly Literature," works dealing mostly with love affairs and romantic matters; very often, these works are looked upon as aesthetically superficial and morally corruptive, although they touched on certain important social issues. To a large extent, later writers like Lu Xun fought against and criticized such fiction, from which their own works drastically differed. Nonetheless, these works and writers of the "Mandarin Duck and Butterfly Literature" paved the way for later writers in more ways than those later writers knew or would like to admit, especially in the use of vernacular Chinese, in the adoption of some Western ideology, and in the development of certain important writing techniques.

Freedom for Chinese writers was to change for the better after the weak Qing Empire fell to the revolution of the Chinese Nationalist Party led by Sun Yat-sen. Although there has always been a totalitarian or even fascist control over the country by different people in the reign of the Republic of China, especially Chiang Kai-shek, the Chinese Nationalist Party, which governed the Republic, never learned the controlling techniques of the latter-day Chinese Communist Party; on the contrary, the Republic was somewhat influenced by Western democracy and sometimes inadvertently allowed the publication of certain literary works, magazines, and newspapers; besides, the power was not centralized in the early stages of the Nationalist Party rule—warlords were still fighting over territories; generals like Yuan Shikai and Zhang Xun even made successful attempts to establish short-lived new empires. In the fragile and unstable Republic, many antigovernment works were therefore often easily printed in a society that was merely halfheartedly or nominally devoted to freedom of speech. It almost seemed that the Nationalist Party at the time acquired only the skills to go after a piece of work after the damage had already been done, probably mainly at times when the government officials felt their image was terribly damaged or that their totalitarian rule was in danger of derailment.

It was in such conditions that many great works of literature were written and published. Four of the eight stories discussed in this book are chosen from this period, which is an adequate representation of not only the number of stories published during this period but also the quality of all short stories of this period. These stories, like most other stories of the time, are painfully realistic, for, to most Chinese, the first half of the century was a time when the whole nation was desperately seeking a new direction in a hostile and bigger world that was no longer centered around the Chinese empire. With bitterness, writers like Lu Xun, Mao Dun, Ba Jin, and Xu Dishan made self-examinations of the nation and the culture, reaching far back into history and looking deeply into contemporary society. In their works, they question the backwardness and the weaknesses of China; they show the world the sufferings of the powerless little people at the bottom of Chinese society; they hope to wake up the nation from its slumber of apathy; and they wish for China a brighter future than what they saw and could even foresee. It was only natural that these works would threaten and weaken the foundation of the Nationalist Party's rule at the time, because many of the works directly, if the writers could get away with it, or indirectly attacked the government of the time. Thus, it was also understandable, as the Chinese Communist Party would later gloat over and continuously publicize, that most of these writers would stay in mainland China when the Chinese Nationalist Party fled the mainland and retreated to the island of Taiwan in 1949. Hence, the link between Chinese literature and Chinese society in this period was inevitably close, which should be self-evident in the first four stories in this collection.

From the founding of the People's Republic of China until 1976, under the reign of Mao Zedong and the Chinese Communist Party, writers on the mainland had little freedom and their creativity and talent were largely suffocated. First-class writers, such as Mao Dun and Ba Jin, who had published many volumes of novels and stories, ceased to produce decent works after 1949, with the possible exception of Lao She, who wrote such popular plays as *The Tea House* in the 1950s. Writers in Taiwan in this period were not in much better shape. No work from this period is represented in this collection due to the length and nature of this book. This decision should not, however, be interpreted as any neglect of the works produced during this period in either the People's Republic of China (the mainland) or the Republic of China (Taiwan), for I have read many stories from this period by writers from both sides of the Taiwan Strait who have often amazed and touched me. Many of the works in this period of time in both the Republic of China and the People's Republic of China are worth extensive study. For example, a highly notable novel published in China during this period was *The Brilliant Sunny Sky*, published by Hao Ran in 1964. In it, one can easily detect the writer's skillful command of the Chinese language and his creative talent, but no one will be fooled into believing that it was not propagandistic, for the whole novel is based on a series of accolades for the Chinese peasants' struggle for a socialist style of collective farming. Therefore, whereas no work from this period has been chosen for this collection, the period is itself worth extensive literary study and research, especially if one has a strong belief in and makes good use of Bakhtin's dialogic theory to conduct detailed explorations into the complex linkage between politics and literature in a chaotic totalitarian state.

A second period that was rich in short story production and high in literary value started in 1976, not long after the death of Mao Zedong, the man who ruled China for decades with as much control as he could muster until the day he died. While only history will have the capacity to judge Mao Zedong, I nonetheless think his death signaled liberation for a generation of Chinese writers. While the two early and best-known short stories, "The Class Teacher" and "The Wound," were not published until 1977 and 1978, the atmosphere in which Chinese writers could even contemplate works of such a subversive nature was created in 1976, when Mao died and his wife was arrested along with three other core hard-line leaders of the country—the so-called "Gang of Four." The other four stories collected in this text are powerful and wonderful creations of this period. Among other causes, what made the works of this period influential is simply that the writers became the organ through which millions of Chinese uttered the pains and sorrows suffocated and suppressed for almost thirty years by a totalitarian rule. The echoes that millions of Chinese found in these works of their own painful and tormented cries were transformed into respect and admiration for these writers, many of whom became household names.

Even though the decline of Chinese literature was already in the making in the late 1980s, the Tiananmen tragedy in 1989 simply put an end to all possibilities of a revival of the written word. At one time in the late 1970s and early 1980s, literary works could cause sensations throughout the nation and writers were the envy of the country for their sociopolitical influence and for their resulting financial success. As the country became commercialized and industrialized, their financial success diminished in comparison to the huge profits that business people quickly reaped. What made it worse for Chinese writers was the rapid rise of television in the 1980s and the subsequent decline in sales of literary magazines. When I visited China in the summer of 1990, I was surprised to see no *Xiaoshuo Yuebao* (Fiction Monthly) around; it once used to be one of the most popular fiction magazines in China because every month it presented an authoritative selection of the best short stories of the previous month from the literary magazines all over the country. During the late 1970s and early 1980s, to many college students and literarily inclined people, to read *Xiaoshuo Yuebao* or similar magazines was a monthly ritual. But in a society rapidly transforming its state-controlled economy into a capitalist supply-and-demand system, the lack of sales shut the magazine down. Actually, starting as early as 1985, no longer could people expect the kind of sensations caused by such stories as "The Wound," "The Class Teacher," or "The History of Manager Qiao Taking Over" in the late 1970s and early 1980s. Some scholars simply declared the death of politically and socially important subjects as the leading cause in the decline in Chinese fiction. Replacing subject matter as the central concern in Chinese fiction were the polished use of language and the probing into people's inner worlds, which made fiction writing in China take on the characteristics of most American fiction in this century. Chinese literature in the few years between the late 1970s and the early 1980s went through a period not unlike what American literature went through in the first half of this century. And it is not hard to understand the rapidity of its development, for after 1976 China took a crash course in Western capitalization, made its sharp turn to commercialization, and experienced the television boom in a matter of ten years in the late 1970s and early 1980s.

The late 1970s and early 1980s were a golden age for Chinese writers, who were instant literary giants in a world almost devoid of television (television hours were short; television programs were simple, didactic, and informative; all television stations were strictly controlled by the government; and it was still taboo to air advertisements on Chinese television in the late 1970s). In this short and happy revival of a free spirit in Chinese fiction, different literary schools were formed in China, such as the "Literature of the Wounded," "Reform Literature," "Literature of Root Seeking" (Xungen Wenxue), and "Literature of the Countryside," or "Literature of the Folk Culture," and so on. Even after the Tiananmen tragedy, writers from some of these schools still regularly write and publish works of great originality and creativity, even under the strict control of the government, although all the works carefully steer away from any serious discussion of political issues and concerns. Yet, nowadays, especially after the government tightened its control on all publications following the 1989 Tiananmen student movement, that period from 1976 to 1989 often invokes in Chinese people nostalgic reflections of those fourteen years when there was increasing freedom for the men (and women) of square Chinese characters (not letters) and when literature had unimaginable power and influence in people's lives and in the state's affairs. It was a magic, romantic, and wondrous time that will never be again.

For better understanding of the stories, it would be beneficial to place them in historical and cultural perspectives. For American readers, it would also help to take a comparative view of the history of both China and America in the twentieth century. To give the reader a historical view of the major developments in twentieth-century China and America, a comparative timetable of major historical events follows:

	China	America
1900		
1911	Xinhai Revolution	
1929		The Big Crash
1937	Japanese Invasion	
1937–45	Anti-Japanese War	
1941		Pearl Harbor
1940s	The Second World War	The Second World War
1946–49	Civil War (The Liberation War, tens of thousands of deaths)	
1951	Korean War	Korean War
1954–75		Vietnam War
1957–60	The Great Leap Forward (at least 30 million deaths due to human-made famines)	
1966–76	Cultural Revolution (tens of thousands of deaths)	
1989	Tiananmen tragedy	

A quick glance at the main events in the history of the two nations would quickly reveal one very important fact: China in this century has had a much more traumatic experience than has America. Many might disagree by stressing the traumatic nature of the atrocities in the United States, such as the Big Crash in 1929, the Japanese bombing of Pearl Harbor, the inner-city riots, the Vietnam War, and so on. To Americans, these historical periods or events were indeed tragic and painful and should never be overlooked or forgotten. Yet, when compared to the violent events in twentieth-century China, the events in America seem minor. Just the famines and natural disasters in China in the first half of the century alone could help put the problems in China into perspective. There were droughts and floods that affected millions of Chinese and destroyed tens of thousands of lives at a single time. At one time, the Yellow River, the third longest river in the world, flooded and drowned tens of thousands of people and left millions homeless. Also, beginning in the late 1880s, China was also in a constantly warring state. Initially there were peasant rebellions and wars against foreign invaders. Immediately following the bloody Xinhai Revolution, there was also the "Second Revolution" launched in 1912 against Yuan Shikai, a general turned dictator who snatched power from the Chinese Nationalist Party. After Yuan Shikai was finally overthrown, warlords in different provinces started wars against each other for control of territories; meanwhile, there was the never-ending battle between the budding Chinese Communist forces and the Chinese Nationalist army. Before those wars were over, the Anti-Japanese war began, putting the Chinese people deeper into the quagmire. No sooner was the Anti-Japanese War won than the Civil War (or "The Liberation War," as it has been called by the Chinese Communist Party) broke out, lasting for a devastating period of four years, and finally in 1949 ending in the Communist control of the mainland and the Nationalist retreat to Taiwan. Right after the People's Republic of China was founded, the country found itself massively involved in the Korean War, in which both China and America played major parts on opposing sides. In these devastating wars, millions of lives were lost; tens of thousands of families were torn apart; cities, communities, and lands were violently ravaged; and an ancient civilization with a long continuous history and rich culture became deeply scarred both mentally and physically.

But the natural disasters and wars were by no means the only destructive agents at work. After 1949, when the Civil War ended and the People's Republic of China was founded, Mao Zedong, the head of the Chinese Communist Party, launched two campaigns that would last years and cost millions of human lives. One was an economic catastrophe called the Great Leap Forward, which was a naive and ambitious economic plan that turned disastrous. In 1957, feeling the urge to catch up with Western industrialized countries, China decided to speed up its economic progress by rearranging its industries and expanding its industrial constructions, simply using all means possible or impossible to fulfill the dream of producing enough steel, machines, and grain to inflate quotas in order to appear to be a prosperous and industrialized country. The truth, however, was that the factories and the farmers were never able to produce enough to fulfill the quotas set by the government. Thus schemes were created to meet the quotas. In agricultural production, tons of rice were reportedly harvested on one tiny mu (about 0.16 acre) of land. In steel production, most factories were too small and were equipped with backward technologies while facing insufficient supplies of raw materials. Therefore the farmers all over the country were called upon to build their own steel smelting "factories" and use whatever metals they could find at home as the supplies to produce "steel." In such a sad hoax of biblical proportions, the honest and hopeful peasants felled even their fruit trees to be used as fuel and smashed even their pots and woks to turn them into "raw materials" for steel production. At the same time, people were forced by zealous government officials to report ten times more grain than they could ever hope to harvest. So they had to go hungry, their grain and other agricultural products having been collected by the state to prove the "bumper harvests." Although no detailed records about the population were kept for this period, the rough calculations reported by experts in China later showed that over thirty million people might have died from starvation or other causes during the three years of "The Great Leap Forward."

In some of the stories in this collection, writers have positioned this maddening and tragic period of Chinese history as the partial background of their stories. No sane Chinese who have witnessed or know of that part of their history would ever look upon those years without a shudder.

In order to help the reader better appreciate the stories and understand the writers, I have prefaced each story with a brief introduction to the writer. While these introductions do not offer exhaustive biographical information, I intend mainly to construct for the reader a historical setting in which the story can be situated. I hope the reading will not only be entertaining but also enlightening, assisting the reader to gain insight, which may not be available otherwise, into a culture and literature. I also hope that this collection will heighten Americans' interest in Chinese literature, modern or classic, because there is in it a vast treasure to be discovered and cherished. It will be pleasing to me if the reading of these stories and other Chinese literary works should, in one way or another, facilitate in many Americans better understanding of a people and culture that once seemed distant and mysterious.

BIBLIOGRAPHY

Bakhtin, M. M. *The Dialogic Imagination*. Ed. Michael Holquist. Tr. Caryl Emerson and Michael Holquist. Austin: University of Texas Press, 1981.

Chang, Sha Sha. "Structural and Cultural Problems in Translating between Chinese and English." *Translation Perspectives II: Selected Papers, 1984–1985*. Ed. Marolyn Gaddis Rose. Binghamton, NY: Translation Research & Instruction Program, SUNY, 1985. 54–61.

Cheng, Gek Nai. "Late Ch'ing Views on Fiction." Dissertation Abstracts International 43: 1 (1982). 172A.

Chow, Rey. "Mandarin Ducks and Butterflies: A Response to the 'Post Modern' Condition." *Cultural Critique* 5 (1986–87): 69–93.

Deeney, John J. *Chinese-Western Comparative Literature Theory and Strategy*. Hong Kong: Chinese University Press, 1980.

Duke, Michael S. "A New Romantic Generation? Young PRC Writers of the Post-Mao Era and the Romantic Tradition in China." *Tamkang Review* 15 (1984–85): 464–83.

Eoyang, Eugene. "Audiences for Translations of Chinese Literature." *The Art and Profession of Translation*. Ed. T. C. Lai. Hong Kong: Hong Kong Translation Society, 1975. 125–41.

Hoffman, Frederick J. "The Voices of Sherwood Anderson." In *The Achievement of Sherwood Anderson*. Ed. Ray Lewis White. Chapel Hill: University of North Carolina Press, 1966. 232–44.

Galik, Marian. "The Concept of 'Positive Hero' in Chinese Literature of the 1960s and 1970s." *Asian & African Studies* 17 (1981): 27–53.

Hegel, Robert E., and Richard C. Hessney. *Expressions of Self in Chinese Literature*. New York: Columbia University Press, 1985.

Ho, Koon-ki T. "The Application of the Structuralist Approach in East-West Comparative Literature: Problems and Prospects." *Tamkang Review* 14 (1983–84): 297–324.

Hsia, C. T. *A History of Modern Chinese Fiction*. New Haven, CT: Yale University Press, 1971.

King, Richard O. "A Shattered Mirror: The Literature of the Cultural Revolution." *Dissertation Abstacts International* 47: 3 (1986). 905A.

Kinkley, Jeffrey C., Ed. *After Mao: Chinese Literature and Society, 1978– 1981*. Cambridge, MA: Council on East Asian Studies, Harvard University, 1985.

Kubin, Wolfgang, and Rudolf G. Wagner. *Essays in Modern Chinese Literature and Literary Criticism*. Bochum, Germany: Brockmeyer, 1982.

Larson, Wendy Ann. "Autobiographies of Chinese Writers in the Early Twentieth Century." *Dissertation Abstracts International* 46: 4 (1985). 986A.

Lee, Leo Ou-fan. "Contemporary Chinese Literature in Translation—A Review Article." *Journal of Asian Studies* 44 (1985): 561–67.

————, Ed. *Lu Xun and His Legacy*. Berkeley: University of California Press, 1985.

Lei, Da. "A Turbulent Low Ebb." *Fiction Selective* (Xiaoshuo Xuankan) 2 (1989): 103–10.

Leung, K. C. "Literature in the Service of Politics: The Chinese Literary Scene since 1949." *World Literature Today* 55 (1981): 18–20.

Link, Perry. *Mandarin Duck and Butterflies: Popular Fiction in Early Twentieth Century Chinese Cities*. Berkeley: University of California Press, 1981.

Liu, Ts'un-yan, and John Minford. *Chinese Middlebrow Fiction: From the Ch'ing and Early Republican Eras*. Hong Kong: Chinese University Press, 1984.

Louie, Kam. "Youth and Education in the Short Stories of Liu Xinwu." *Westerly* 26 (1981): 115–19.

Louis, Winnie Laifong L. "The Fiction Image of Post-Mao Youth: A Thematic Study." *Dissertation Abstracts International* 48: 9 (1988). 2340A.

McDougall, Bonnie S., Ed. *Popular Chinese Literature and Performing Arts in the People's Republic of China*. Berkeley: University of California Press, 1984.

Shen, Dan. "Literary Statistics and Translation—With Particular Reference to English Translations of Chinese Prose Fiction." *Dissertation Abstracts International* 49: 2 (1988). 255A.

————. "Objectivity in the Translation of Narrative Fiction." *Babel* 34 (1988): 131–40.

Shih, Vincent Yu-chung. *The Literary Mind and the Carving of Dragons: A Study of Thought and Pattern in Chinese Literature*. Hong Kong: Chinese University Press, 1983.

Spiller, Robert E. et al., Eds. *Literary History of the United States*. New York: Macmillan, 1968.

Sun, Cecil Chu-chin. "Problems of Perspective in Chinese–Western Comparative Literature Studies." *Canadian Review of Comparative Literature* 13 (1986): 531–47.

Tam, King-fai. "Publications in Chinese on Chinese–Western Comparative Literature Studies." *Tamkang Review* 11 (1981): 431–36.

White, Ray Lewis, Ed. *Sherwood Anderson's Memoirs*. Chapel Hill: University of North Carolina Press, 1969.

Yang, L. Y. Winston, and Nathan K. Mao, Eds. *Modern Chinese Fiction: A Guide to Its Study and Appreciation*. Boston: Hall, 1981.

Yang, L. Y. Winston, and Curtis P. Askins, Eds. *Critical Essays on Chinese Fiction*. Hong Kong: Chinese University Press, 1980.

Yuan, Haoyi. "Survey of Current Development in the Comparative Literature of China." *Cowrie* 1: 1 (1983): 81–125.

————. "Survey of Current Development in the Comparative Literature of China." *Cowrie* 1: 2 (1984): 75–94.

CHINESE SHORT STORIES
OF THE TWENTIETH CENTURY

CHAPTER 1

"The Diary of a Madman" (Kuangren Riji)

Lu Xun (1881–1936)

Introduction to the Author

Lu Xun is the nom de plume for Zhou Shuren. His original name, however, was Zhou Zhangshou, but was changed to Zhou Shuren, which has long been regarded by his scholars as his real name. While Lu Xun is a household name in China, his other names are much less known.

Lu Xun was born in 1881 into a large but financially and socially declining family in the city of Shaoxin in Zhejiang Province. His grandfather was a learned scholar in the Royal Academy, but his father never achieved nearly as much, either in academic learning or social status. By the time Lu Xun was a young child, his family was already in poor financial shape due to his father's various illnesses, such as tuberculosis. Lu Xun would later remember the degrading experience of going to a pawn shop in town to exchange family valuables for money. But fortunately, both Lu Xun and his brothers were still able to go to school, and Lu Xun and one of his two brothers even received advanced education due to their hard work and the support of relatives and friends.

To understand Lu Xun's works, a good knowledge of his family background is indispensable, because many of his stories came directly from his family life in Shaoxin and the people he grew up with. For many years, under the rule of either the Republic of China (when he was considered a dangerous dissident) or the People's Republic of China (when he was lauded as a literary giant), Lu Xun's family life was only partially revealed or discussed; and there was not much talk of his flamboyant grandfather, his arranged marriage to a woman whom, oddly, he neither loved nor officially forsook, or the fact that he was really raised by his stepgrandmother when he was a child. Even now, there is not much written about these aspects of his and his family's life. Since the Chinese people have much pride in Lu Xun as the greatest Chinese writer in this century, it might be considered a disgrace or at least a discourtesy to display a great man's dirty laundry.

Such information about his family life, however, is quite pertinent to our reading of his stories. In this and the next two stories, the introduction will offer some important and relevant information about Lu Xun's life, because without a fairly thorough knowledge of his family life, both when he was a child and as an adult, one may not fully understand or explain certain characteristics in many of Lu Xun's works, such as his deep sympathy for women and his evident distaste for traditional Chinese scholars.

In 1902 Lu Xun went to Japan as a government-sponsored student to study medicine, first in language classes in Kobun Institute in Tokyo and then in a medical college in the city of Sendai in the north. According to his description in the emotional and vivid preface to his first collection of short stories, *Call to Arms*, he became painfully aware of the Japanese prejudice against then weak China. Eventually he was to return to China without completing his college education. Although the exact details may still be unclear, Lu Xun explains that, one day in class in Sendai, he was outraged to see a film in which a Chinese was caught as a spy for the Russians in the Russo-Japanese War. As this Chinese was being executed, the other Chinese looked on apathetically. While the Japanese students in the classroom cheered, Lu Xun made up his mind that the cure for the downtrodden Chinese was not modern medicine, but something else. Yet, after he left the medical collage in Sandai, he was to stay in Tokyo for some time before he went back to China in 1909. During his stay in Tokyo, he read widely, wrote some, translated some works into Chinese, and participated in various literary activities.

When he returned to China, he published in 1909 a collection of translations, entitled *A Collection of Foreign Stories*. Later he wrote in classical Chinese a short story called "Remembrances," a work which is now seldom regarded as part of his canon. His occupations after his return to China were mainly teaching at various high schools or colleges and serving as an official in the government. He spent much of his spare time collecting copies of old Chinese calligraphy and reading old Chinese books. On the literary and political fronts, he was rather inactive, for he had largely lost faith and hope in the Chinese people, especially after a failed attempt to find enough compatriots in Tokyo to launch a literary magazine before he returned to China. After the May Fourth Movement in 1919, he joined the editorial board of the influential literary magazine *New Youth* and became active in the New Literature Movement. But he remained for a long time an unknown figure until in 1918 he published "The Diary of a Madman," a short story detailing the fantasized world of a madman in the form of a diary. The story took the country by storm and established Lu Xun's place in Chinese literature.

In his lifetime, he published only two slim collections of short stories. Later he published some historical stories which he retold using various sources. He never wrote or even attempted to write a novel, possibly because of two important factors, among others. First, his serious writing did not begin until he was in his forties (he died at fifty-five), so he had little or no time for a novel in addition to writing short stories. Second, he became a public and political figure after the publication of "The Diary of a Madman." Having assumed the role of national conscience, he felt an obligation to devote much of his time to contemporary social and political issues. Therefore, in his later years of failing health and busy social activities, he wrote little more than "zawen," a unique kind of short essay in which he mostly discussed contemporary social and political issues. In these essays, he tirelessly and bitterly attacked the social ills, national problems, and governmental policies of the time. Being a writer who started to write stories in order to wake up the complacent nation, Lu Xun became disappointed and disillusioned later in life about the progress in China and probably thought that the "zawen" essays would be a more effective and powerful tool. While Lu Xun's "zawen" essays have become as much a part of the treasures in Chinese literature as his other works, it is his short stories that deserve the attention of any student in Chinese literature.

The Diary of a Madman

[1918]

Two brothers, whose names I will keep anonymous, were both good friends of mine in high school; but after a separation of many years we gradually lost touch. Some time ago, I happened to hear that one of them was seriously ill, and, as I was going back to my old home, I went out of my way to call on them. I saw, however, only one of the two brothers, the one who told me that the sick person was his younger brother. "I appreciate your coming such a long way to see us, but my brother recovered some time ago and has gone to a place to take up a temporary government position." Then, laughing loudly, he produced two volumes of his brother's diary, saying that, from these, the condition of his illness in the past could be seen and that there was no harm in showing them to an old friend. I took the diary home and read it through, and I found that the writer had suffered from some sort of "paranoia." The language was rather jumbled and incoherent, and there were many bizarre statements; he did not give any dates either. Only the colors of the ink and the styles of the writing were not the same, so I knew that it was not all written at one time. But, among the writings, there were also certain sections that were not altogether disconnected, and I have made out a copy to offer it for medical research. Of the mistakes in the language, not a single word was altered; only, although the names are all those of country folks, unknown to the world, and of no importance, they have all been changed. As for the title, it was chosen by the patient himself after his recovery, so I did not change it. Written on April 2, the Seventh Year of the Republic.[1]

1

Tonight, very good moonlight.

It has been thirty years since I last saw it; so today when I see it, my mind is extraordinarily refreshed. I begin to realize that, for the past thirty years, I have been in the dark; but I must be extremely careful. Otherwise, why should the Zhaos' dog have looked at me twice?

I have reasons to fear.

2

Tonight there is no moonlight[2] at all. I know this is a bad omen. This morning when I walked out of the door cautiously, Zhao Guiwong had a strange look in his eyes: as if he were afraid of me, as if he wanted to harm me. There were seven or eight others, putting their heads together to discuss me in a whisper, but they were also afraid of me seeing them do that. All the way, the people were like that. The most vicious one among them opened his mouth and smiled at me once. I then turned cold from head to heel, knowing that their arrangements had all been made already.

I was not afraid, however, and continued on my way. A group of children in front of me were also discussing me, and the look in their eyes was just like that in Zhao Guiwong's and their faces, too, were ghastly pale. I thought, What grudge could these children have against me to make them behave like this? I could not help calling out, "You tell me!" But then they ran away.

I wonder what grudge Zhao Guiwong has against me, what grudge the people on the road have against me; only twenty years ago, I kicked Mr. Gu Jiu's[3] old ledger books once, and Mr. Gu was very unhappy. Although Zhao Guiwong does not know him, he must have heard talk of this and decided to avenge him. He is conspiring against me with those people I met on the road. But then what about the children? At that time, they were not even born, so why should they stare at me strangely, as if they were afraid of me, as if they wanted to hurt me? This really frightens me, puzzles me, and makes me feel broken-hearted.

I see. This has been taught to them by their fathers and mothers!

3

I can't go to sleep at night for a long time. Everything should be studied before one can understand it.

Those people, some of them have been pilloried by the county magistrate; some have been slapped in the face by the local gentry; and some have had their wives taken over by a bailiff, or their parents driven to suicide by creditors; in those times, their faces never looked as frightened and fierce as they did yesterday.

The strangest thing was the woman on the street yesterday spanking her son, saying, "Little devil! My anger won't go away till I bite you several times!" But her eyes were looking at me. I gave a start and was unable to hide it; then those people with livid faces and long fangs all burst into laughter. Old Fifth Chen[4] hurried forward and forcefully dragged me home.

When he dragged me home, the members of my family all pretended not to know me; the look in their eyes was exactly the same as that of the others. When I went into the study, they then locked me in as if to coop up a chicken or a duck. This incident has left me more bewildered about what is going on.

A few days ago, a tenant of ours from Wolf Cub Village came to report the failure of the crops and told my older brother that a big villain in their village had been beaten to death; then several people dug out his heart and liver, stir-fried them in oil, and ate them so as to increase their courage. Once when I interrupted, the tenant and my brother both looked at me several times. Only today do I see that the look in their eyes was exactly the same as that of those people outside.

Thinking about it, I turn cold from the crown of my head to the heels of my feet.

They can eat human beings, so they may not spare me.

You see, the woman's words of "bite you several times," the laughter of those long-toothed people with livid faces, and the tenant's story the other day are obviously secret signs. I have realized that in her speech all was poison, hidden in their laughter were all daggers, and their teeth, white and glistening in rows, were tools to eat people.

When I think of myself, although I am not a bad man, ever since I kicked the Gu's ledgers, it is now just hard to say. They seem to have other thoughts that I completely cannot guess. Besides, once they get upset, they will call anyone a bad character. I also remember that when my older brother was teaching me to write persuasive essays, no matter how good a man was, if I made some contrary arguments, he would mark them with several circles.[5] Whereas if I made some remarks to excuse the bad guys, he would say, "Crafty hand in rewriting history, out of the ordinary." How can I possibly guess what, indeed, their thoughts were? Especially when it is a time when they want to eat people.

Everything requires careful study before one can understand it. In ancient times people often ate human beings; that I still remember, but not quite clearly. I opened the history book to look this up, but this history book had no chronology, and scrawled on each page were the words "Virtue and Morality." Since I could not sleep anyway, I looked at it carefully for half the night, and then from in between the lines of these words I saw some other words; the two words written over the whole book were "Eat people!"

All these words written in the book and all the words spoken by our tenant are staring with their strange eyes at me with a broad smile.

I am also a man. They now want to eat me!

4

In the morning, I sat quietly for a while. Old Fifth Chen brought in the meal, a bowl of vegetables, a bowl of steamed fish; the eyes of the fish were white and hard, and its mouth was open, just like those people who want to eat people. After a few servings with the chopsticks, I could not tell whether the slippery pieces were fish or men, so I threw them all up.

I said, "Old Fifth, tell my brother that I feel quite suffocated and want to take a stroll in the garden." Old Fifth did not answer, went away, and, after a moment, came back to open the door.

But I did not move and figured how they would treat me, knowing that they would not loosen their grip on me. Sure enough! My older brother led in an old man and slowly walked over; the old man's eyes were filled with a vicious gleam, but he was afraid that I could see it, so he lowered his head toward the ground and secretly looked at me from the side of his glasses. My older brother said, "You seem very well today." I said, "Yes." My older brother said, "Today I have invited Mr. He[6] to come over and give you a diagnosis." I said, "All right!" Actually, I knew quite well that this old man was the executioner in disguise! It was nothing more than pretending to check my pulse in order to see if I was fat or lean: For this contribution, he would be given a share of my flesh to eat. I was nonetheless not afraid; although I do not eat people, my courage is greater than theirs. I held out two fists to see how he would start his job. The old man sat down, his eyes closed, measured my pulse for quite some time, and remained motionless for quite a while; then he opened his ghostly eyes and said, "Don't think wildly. Recuperate quietly for a few days, and you will be all right."

Don't think wildly and recuperate quietly for a few days! Recuperate till I become fat, so they can naturally have more to eat; what good will it do me? How can it be "all right?" The whole lot of them want to eat men, but they are so secretive, trying all they can to cover it up and not daring to do it outright. It really could make me laugh myself to death. I could not hold it back, so I started to laugh out loud and was very happy. I myself knew that in this laughter there was plenty of courage and righteousness. Both the old man and my brother turned pale, awed by my courage and righteousness.

But the more courage I have, the more they want to eat me to acquire some of my courage for themselves. The old man stepped out the door, and, before he had gone far, he said to my older brother in a low voice, "To be eaten at once!"[7] My brother nodded. So you are involved in it, too! This big discovery, though as if unexpected, had also been expected: The accomplice in eating me is my older brother!

A man-eater is my older brother!

I am the brother of a man who eats men!

I will be eaten by men, but I am still the brother of a man who eats men!

5

These few days I have been thinking with a concession: even if that old man is not an executioner in disguise, but a real doctor, he is still an eater of men. In the book called "Herbs something," compiled by their founder Li Shizhen, it was clearly written that men's flesh can be boiled to eat;[8] can he still claim that he does not eat men himself?

As for my older brother, I am not being unjust to him either. When he was teaching me the books, he told me himself it is permissible to "exchange sons to eat."[9] And once in discussing a bad man, he said that not only did the fellow deserve to be killed, he should "have had his flesh eaten and his skin slept on." I was still young at the time, and for quite a while my heart beat wildly. That story our tenant from Wolf Cub Village told the other day about eating a man's heart and liver did not surprise him at all; he kept nodding his head. It is evident that his heart is just as cruel as before. Since it is permissible to "exchange sons to eat," then anything can be exchanged and anyone can be eaten. In the past I simply listened to his explanations and let it go at that in confusion; now I know that when he was giving me those explanations, not only was there human fat at the corners of his lips, but his whole heart was filled with the intention of eating people.

6

Pitch dark. I don't know whether it is day or night. The Zhaos' dog has started barking again.

The murderous heart like that of a lion, the timidity of a rabbit, the cunning of a fox . . .

7

I know their method; they would not kill me outright, nor would they dare, for fear of disastrous consequences. So they have all conspired with each other and set traps everywhere, to force me to kill myself. One might recognize much of it if one takes a look at the behavior of the men and women on the street a few days ago and my brother's actions these last few days. It would be best to take off my belt and tie it on the beam to hang myself tightly; they would then not be blamed for murder, but they would have realized their dream and they would naturally give out a kind of whimpering laughter in great delight. On the other hand, if a man dies of fears and worries, though that makes him somewhat thin, that could still win their nod of approval.

They would only eat dead flesh! I remember that some book says there is a thing called hyena, whose eyes and looks are both quite ugly; it often eats dead flesh; it even chews very large bones into pieces and swallows them down into its stomach; the mere thought of it makes one feel afraid. Hyenas are related to wolves, and wolves belong to the dog family. The other day the Zhaos' dog eyed me several times; it is obviously in the plot, too, as their accomplice and they have already made their arrangements. The old man was looking at the floor, but that could not fool me.

The most pitiful is my older brother. He's a man, too. So why isn't he afraid? And why is he plotting with others to eat me? Does force of habit blind a man to what is wrong? Or has he lost his conscience and is knowingly committing a crime?

In cursing man-eaters, I started with him; to dissuade man-eaters, I shall start with him, too.

8

Actually such reasoning, by now, they should have already understood. . . .

Suddenly someone came in. He was only about twenty years old and I did not see his features very clearly. His face was wreathed in smiles and he nodded to me. His smiles did not seem genuine. I then asked him, "Eating human beings, is it right?" Still smiling, he replied, "This is no famine year; why would one eat human beings?" I realized at once he was one of them, who like to eat humans; and so my courage increased infinitely and I persisted with the question:

"Is it right?"

"What makes you ask such a thing? You really can . . . tell a joke. . . . It is very fine today."

"It is fine, and the moon is very bright. But I want to ask you: Is it right?"

He did not think so, and muttered in reply, "No. . . ."

"No? Then why do they even eat them?!"

"No such thing. . ."

"No such thing? They are eating men now in Wolf Cub Village; also it is even written in the books, in fresh red ink."

His face then changed, dark as black iron. He said with a stare, "Maybe there are such things, and this is the way it has always been. . . ."

"The way it has always been, would that make it right?"

"I refuse to talk with you about all this; all in all, you shouldn't talk about it. You are wrong to talk about it."

I leapt up and opened my eyes wide, but the man had vanished. I was soaked with sweat. He was much younger than my older brother, but, even so, he was one of them. He must have been taught by his parents. And I am afraid he has already taught his son; that is why even the children look at me so fiercely.

9

Wanting to eat men, yet at the same time afraid of being eaten themselves, they all eye each other with rather deep suspicion, gazing at each other in despair. . . .

How comfortable life would be for them if they could rid themselves of such obsessions and go to work, walk, eat, and sleep with ease. This is only a threshold, a juncture. They could be fathers and sons, brothers, husbands and wives, friends, teachers, enemies, and even strangers, bound into a group, discouraging each other, impeding each other, and would not take this step even if they had to die.

10

Early this morning, I went to look for my older brother. He was standing outside the door of the family room looking at the sky; so I walked up behind him, standing in the doorway, and said to him with exceptional poise and politeness:

"Brother, I have something to tell you."

"Go ahead then." He turned his head quickly toward me, and nodded.

"I only have a few words, but I find it hard to say them. Older brother, probably all primitive people in the beginning ate a little human flesh. Later on, because their thinking became different, some of them stopped eating people and tried hard to do what was right, so they became humans, became real human beings. But some still ate people—just like reptiles, some of which have changed into fish, birds, monkeys, and finally humans. But those who make no effort to do what is right are still reptiles. When those who eat people compare themselves with those who don't, how ashamed they must be. Probably much more ashamed than the reptiles are as compared to monkeys.

"Yi Ya boiled his son for Jie and Zhou to eat;[10] that is the old story. But no one expected that since the creation of heaven and earth by Pan Gu,[11] men have been eating each other, from the time of Yi Ya's son to the time of Xu Xilin,[12] and from the time of Xu Xilin down to the man caught in Wolf Cub Village. Last year, a criminal was executed in the city, and a man with tuberculosis soaked a piece of bread in his blood and sucked it.

"They want to eat me, and, of course, you can do nothing about it single-handed; but why must you join them? As man-eaters, what aren't they capable of? If they can eat me, they can eat you as well; members of the same group can still eat each other. But if you will just turn around, change yourself right away, then everyone will have peace. Although this has been going on since the beginning, today we can make a special effort to do what is right, and say that men-eating is not permissible! Older brother, I believe you can say that. The day before when the tenant wanted the rent reduced, you said it was not permissible."

At first, he only smiled coldly, then a murderous gleam came into his eyes, and when I spoke of their secret, his whole face turned pale. Outside the gate stood a crowd, among whom were also Zhao Guiwong and his dog, all craning their necks to peer in. I could not see some of their faces, as if they were masked with cloths. Some were nonetheless long-toothed and had livid faces, smiling with their mouths closed. I recognized them as one gang, all humans who eat humans. But I also knew that their thinking was quite different among themselves. One kind of these people thought that since it had always been so, people should be eaten. One kind knew they shouldn't eat people but still wanted to, and were afraid other people might tell their secret. So, hearing what I said, they became even more angry, but they still smiled their tight-lipped, chilling smiles.

At this moment, my brother also revealed his vicious look, and cried out loudly:

"Get out! What's there to see in a madman!"

At this time, I realized another part of their cunning. They were not only unwilling to change their stand, but had already made arrangements; they had prepared the label of madman to put on me. In the future when I am eaten, not only will there be no trouble, but people will probably be grateful to them. When our tenant spoke of the villagers eating a bad character, it was the same method. This is their old trick.

Old Fifth Chen also walked in with a flaring temper. How could they shut my mouth? I insisted on warning this group of people:

"You can change, change from the bottom of your heart. You should know that in the future there will be no place for man-eaters in the world.

"If you don't change, you may all be eaten by each other. Even if you had a lot of children, they would be eliminated by real people, like hunters kill wolf cubs!—like reptiles!"

Old Fifth Chen drove everybody in the group away. My brother had also disappeared to some place I did not know. Old Fifth Chen advised me to go back to my room. It was pitch dark in there. The beams and rafters were all shaking above my head. After shaking for a while, they grew bigger and piled up on my body.

The weight was so great, I could not move. They meant for me to die. However, knowing that the weight was false, I struggled out, sweating all over. But I still had to warn them:

"You must change at once, change from the bottom of your heart! You must know that there will be no place for man-eaters in the future. . . ."

11

The sun has stopped coming out. The door does not open. Everyday it was two meals.

Picking up my chopsticks, I thought of my older brother. I know now how my little sister died; it was all because of him. My sister was only five at the time. Her lovable and pitiful look is still before my eyes. Mother wept endlessly, but he begged her not to cry; probably because he had eaten our sister himself and this weeping made him somewhat sorry. If he could still feel sorry. . .

My sister was eaten by my older brother, but I don't know whether mother knew it or not.

I think mother must have known, but when she wept she did not say so outright, probably because she also thought it a proper thing to do. I remember when I was four or five, sitting in front of the family room to cool off, my older brother told me that if a man's parents were ill, he should cut off a piece of his flesh and boil it for them to eat;[13] then he would be considered a good man; and mother did not contradict him. If one piece could be eaten, naturally so could the whole body. And yet, just thinking of the weeping on that day still makes my heart sad; it is the strangest thing!

12

Can't bear to think about it.

It has just dawned on me today that all these years I have been living in a place where for four thousand years humans have been eaten. My older brother was in charge of the house when our sister died, and he may well have mixed her flesh in our food, secretly giving it to us to eat.

I may have unwittingly eaten several pieces of my sister's flesh, and now it is my turn. . . .

Although I did not know it in the beginning, now that I understand it, it is hard for me, a person who has been a part of four thousand years of man-eating history, to face real men!

13

Perhaps there are still children who haven't yet eaten men? Save the children. . . .

NOTES

1. The Seventh Year of the Republic—1917. In Chinese dynasties, the founding year of the dynasty is called the First Year of that specific dynasty and the other years are numbered accordingly. Although the Republic of China was not founded as a feudal empire, the traditional way of enumerating years persisted for a long time and is still used in many ways in the island of Taiwan, which is presently the only territory occupied by the Republic of China.

One more important note about this first paragraph: In the Chinese version, the author uses, only in the beginning paragraph, classical Chinese instead of vernacular Chinese. Two effects are created by such a preface. First, the preface aims to give the story a sense of credibility, although the practice of using a diary had already been frequent for over two decades in Chinese fiction by that time, especially among the New Novelists (1897–1916). Second, the preface noting the context of a diary written by a madman makes it easier for the readership of the time to accept the exclusively vernacular language in the rest of the story. The use of vernacular Chinese was a practice not yet common among the fiction writers, even though some other writers, such as Zhou Shoujuan and Li Boyuan, had already written stories and novels in the vernacular. In the English translation, I have used the same language throughout the story for fear of causing unnecessary confusion for Western readers.

2. "Tonight there is no moonlight at all"—In traditional Chinese culture, a moonless night evokes notions of uncertainty, fear, and ill fortune.

3. "Mr. Gu Jiu's old ledger books"—Gu Jiu, although used as a proper name in the story, is a Chinese phrase that means ancient and old. The "old" ledgers of Mr. Gu Jiu may imply the long history of Chinese culture and kicking the old ledgers may indicate a certain disdain in the author for such an ancient and stagnant traditional culture.

4. Old Fifth Chen—probably a hired hand of the narrator's family. He is called such a name possibly because he is the fifth child of the Chen family and also because he is probably no longer young.

5. ". . . he would mark them with several circles"—Obviously the narrator's older brother once taught the narrator essay writing. It is a Chinese tradition, in reading a student's writing or any writing, to mark important words, phrases, or sentences with circles either for emphasis or to point out anything extraordinary, not necessarily as a mistake. But the madman seems to remember those circles only as marks of his errors.

6. "Mr. He"—a surname in Chinese, pronounced the same as the first syllable in "hallucination."

7. "To be eaten at once!"—This is the instruction given by the doctor for the older brother to administer the intake of the medicine. "Eat" in Chinese can be used to mean both eating food or taking medicine, and therein lies the confusion on the part of the "insane" narrator.

8. "In the books called 'Herbs something'. . . was clearly written that men's flesh could be boiled to eat"—The book is *Compendium of Materia Medica*, written by Li Shizhen (1518–1593) during the Ming Dynasty (1368–1644). A pioneering book, it contains one of the most complete and accurate documentations of prescriptions in Chinese medicine (which uses a lot of herbs) and today it is still taught, studied, and used in many ways in traditional Chinese medicine. In the book, Li Shizhen mentions and then actually rebuts a Tang Dynasty (618–907)

prescription that uses human flesh to cure tuberculosis. He does not advocate the eating of human flesh.

9. "exchange sons to eat"—The story comes from the ancient history book *Zuo Zhuan* (or *Zuo's Writings on History*), reputed to have been written by Zuo Qiuming, who lived in the Spring and Autumn Period, or the Warring States Period (ca. 700–200 B.C.). The book records in detail certain events and people of the period from 700 B.C. to 400 B.C. According to the book, in a battle between the states of Chu and Song, the capital of Song was surrounded by Chu troops for so long that the people inside the city were rumored to be eating each other's children for survival.

10. "Yi Ya boiled his son for Jie and Zhou to eat"—In the Spring and Autumn Period (770–476 B.C.), Yi Ya, a man despised by all but good at cooking in the state of Qi, heard his king say that he had never eaten human flesh. So Yi Ya cooked his own son and presented the dish to the king. But the narrator is confused about history, because Jie and Zhou were earlier Chinese emperors from different dynasties and could not have met even each other, not to mention Yi Ya.

11. ". . . the creation of heaven and earth by Pan Gu"—Pan Gu, a legendary figure in Chinese mythology, was said to have created heaven and earth by slicing the turbid universe into two parts: the heaven and the earth.

12. ". . . from the time of Yi Ya's son to the time of Xu Xilin"—Xu Xilin (1873–1907) was a key member in the revolutionary organization "Guangfu Hui" (Association for Recovering China) against the Qing Empire. In July, 1907, when he was arrested in an attempt to assassinate the governor of Anhui Province, his heart was said to have been fried and eaten by the bodyguards of the governor.

13. ". . . he should cut off a piece of his flesh and boil it for them to eat"—In Chinese culture, there used to be an old teaching of twelve things a loyal son should do for his parents. One of them was to use his own flesh to cure his parents when necessary.

BIBLIOGRAPHY

Chang, Hao. *Liang Ch'i-ch'ao and Intellectual Transition in China 1890–1907.* Cambridge, MA: Harvard University Press, 1971.

Chen, Pingyuan. *History of Twentieth Century Chinese Fiction, Volume One 1897–1916.* Beijing: Beijing University Press, 1989.

Chow, Rey. "Mandarin Ducks and Butterflies: A Response to the 'Post Modern' Condition." *Culture Critique* 5 (1986–87): 69–93.

Chow, Tse-tung. *The May Fourth Movement: Intellectual Revolution in Modern China.* Cambridge, MA: Harvard University Press, 1960.

———. *Research Guide to the May Fourth Movement: Intellectual Revolution in Modern China 1915–1924.* Cambridge, MA: Harvard University Press, 1963.

Creel, H. G. *Chinese Thought from Confucius to Mao Tse-tung.* Chicago: University of Chicago Press, 1953.

Gasster, Michael. *Chinese Intellectuals and the Revolution of 1911.* New York: Knopf, 1972.

Gibbs, Donald A., and Yun-chen Li. *A Bibliography of Studies and Translations of Modern Chinese Literature, 1918–1942.* Cambridge, MA: Harvard University Press, 1975.

Hsia, C. T. *A History of Modern Chinese Fiction.* New Haven, CT: Yale University Press, 1971.

Lee, Leo Ou-fan, Ed. *Lu Xun and His Legacy.* Berkeley: University of California Press, 1985.

Li, Tien-yi. *Chinese Fiction: A Bibliography of Books and Articles in Chinese and English.* New Haven, CT: Far Eastern, 1968.

Lu, Xun. *The Complete Works of Lu Xun.* Beijing: People's Literature (Renmin Wenxue Chubanshe), 1981.

———. "Suggestions about the Left Wing Writers' Association." In *Selected Materials in Modern Chinese Literary Movement.* Ed. Shouli Cheng. Beijing: Beijing Publishing House (Beijing Chubanshe), 1985. 225–27.

Lyell, William A., Jr. *Lu Hsun's Vision of Reality.* Berkeley: University of California Press, 1976.

Schiffrin, Harold Z. *Sun Yat-sen and the Origins of the Chinese Revolution.* Berkeley: University of California Press, 1970.

Wang, Shiqing. *Lu Xun.* Beijing: Foreign Languages, 1984.

Weiss, Ruth F. *Lu Xun. A Chinese Writer for All Times.* Beijing: Foreign Languages, 1985.

Yang, Winston L.Y., and Nathan K. Mao, Eds. *Modern Chinese Fiction: A Guide to Its Study and Appreciation: Essays and Bibliographies.* Boston: Hall, 1981.

Yue, Daiyun. *Comparative Literature and Modern Chinese Literature.* Beijing: Peking University Press, 1987.

Zhao, Xiaqiu, and Zeng Qingrui. *A History of Modern Chinese Fiction.* Beijing: Chinese People's University Press, 1984.

CHAPTER 2

"New Year's Sacrifice"
(Zhu Fu)

Lu Xun (1881–1936)

Introduction to the Author

While much has been said in the previous chapter about Lu Xun, "New Year's Sacrifice" may necessitate certain background information about the author because of the unusual focus in this story. Memories of his childhood spent with a grandmother who was mistreated by other family members, and his first marriage to a woman he did not love may have played an important part in the creation of "New Year's Sacrifice," even though some of his critics in China often make little effort to link his family life to his works. This silence in China about his family life was especially evident in the era in which he was labeled "revolutionary writer" or "writer of the people." Even after much freedom was given to academic and literary critics in the 1980s, whenever there was any negative comment or even a question about Lu Xun's life and works, the authoritative and dominant critics, such as Tang Tao, who was one of Lu Xun's close friends, would denounce it as blasphemy.

One of the best-kept "secrets" in China can well be Lu Xun's first marriage, which has rarely been included in the discussion of his works and life. Many Chinese may still have the misconception that Lu Xun had in his entire life only one wife, namely, the late Xu Guangping, who, as a student activist in Beijing Women's Normal School, met Lu Xun, the famous writer of the time. Not many people know that prior to meeting and later marrying Xu Guangping, Lu Xun already had a wife, whom he married young in an arranged marriage. Although Lu Xun was neither happy about this arranged marriage nor did he love the woman, he never made any great effort to obtain a divorce or take any legal action to annul this bondage. As a matter of fact, his first wife was living with him in Beijing when he met Xu Guangping, his second wife. When he went to teach in Amoy University in 1926, later in Sun Yat-sen University in Canton in 1927, and then eventually settled down in Shanghai, he took with him Xu Guangping, whom he married only later. He would stay in Shanghai for the rest of his life, with the exception of two visits to Beijing. He left behind his first wife with his mother in Beijing. Both his mother and his first wife survived him, supported financially by his copyright money and his younger brother, who, for a long period, earned a comfortable living as a professor at Peking University. According to records and recollections of people close to Lu Xun, his first wife unfortunately seemed to have been caught in the middle of Lu Xun's struggle for real love and a better marriage. He treated her without much warmth, speaking little to her and frequently questioning her when she asked for spending money for the household. Yet, clearly Lu Xun could not have been blind to the miseries his first wife might have been experiencing in an empty marriage. This awareness of her situation could have been part of the reason why he never formally severed ties with her, for, as an old Chinese saying goes, a married woman is like water poured on the ground, no longer clean or marketable, if she is sent back home by her husband. Even in Lu Xun's time, abiding by the Confucian tradition, a woman was supposed to "follow a chicken if she marries it or a dog if she weds it." The lowly social status of women in China, as witnessed first-hand by Lu Xun in his family life, therefore could have been a major factor in the creation of the tragic "New Year's Sacrifice."

In his childhood, Lu Xun was close to his stepgrand-mother. She was the second wife of Lu Xun's grandfather, whose first wife (Lu Xun's biological grandmother) died young, leaving behind a daughter and a son, namely, Lu Xun's father. Since this second grandmother had no blood relationship with the rest of the family, the members showed little respect for her, even telling young Lu Xun that she was not his "real" grandmother. What made things worse was that this grandmother was able to give birth only to a daughter, not a son who could pass on the family name. More tragically, this daughter was married off and not long afterward died in childbirth. Hence this grandmother's status was soon diminished and she was forever isolated in the family. Although Lu Xun was close to her, her life in the family could not be said to be happy. When she died, Lu Xun came back to his hometown to bury her, and wrote a story, "The Isolate," much of which was based on her life. Therefore, it is highly possible that this second grandmother "had much to do with the formation of a strong feminist element in Lu [Xun]'s adult thought, for she was very close to him and was treated badly [by the other members of the family]" (Lyell, p. 20). The worst treatment, however, came not from other family members, but from her husband, Grandfather Zhou, who was a Royal Academy scholar (Hanlin). He would stay in Beijing for long periods, taking in concubines one after another. Once he even brought home a beautiful concubine to live with the family, which at the time was allowed by the law. With this new concubine and other women to please him, Grandfather Zhou would treat his wife with little respect and would even curse her at times. Many times, she was blamed when something went wrong in the family, such as the late marriage of Lu Xun's aunt and her accidental drowning later in a river during a storm.

The humiliating social status of women in Lu Xun's time was witnessed by Lu Xun at home at a tender age. Many documents, sources, and even Lu Xun's own works directly or indirectly confirm this fact, although much of the information about Lu Xun's early family life is found in the books and articles written after Lu Xun's death by his younger brother Zhou Shuren, who was not on good terms with Lu Xun all the time, especially later in their lives in Beijing.

Therefore, in light of his complicated and close contact with women in life, Lu Xun's charges of injustice to women in "New Year's Sacrifice" may be easier to comprehend. While his actions might seem weaker than his written words, in his awakening to women's miseries he was still decades ahead of the whole nation.

New Year's Sacrifice

[1924]

The end of a year in the Chinese calendar[1] seemed indeed to be more like a year's end than any other time. To say nothing of the villages and towns, even the sky displayed the look of the approach of the New Year. From the thick gray evening clouds came intermittent flashes, followed by a dull explosive sound. They were firecrackers bidding farewell to the Hearth God.[2] The ones that were fired nearby were even more violent. Before the deafening sound died down, the air was filled with the slight fragrance of the gunpowder. It was on such a night that I came back to my hometown, Luzhen. Although it was my hometown, there was already no home for me, and so I had to stay for the time being in the residence of Master Lu the Fourth.[3] He belonged to the same family as I, was one generation older, and I should call him "Fourth Uncle." He was a former Royal Academy licentiate in neo-Confucianism. He did not seem much changed from before, only that he was a little older, but still he had not grown a beard.[4] As soon as he saw me, he greeted me. After the greetings, he said that I "had put on weight."[5] After saying that I "had put on weight," he then vociferously attacked the revolutionaries. But I knew that he was not really using the topic to condemn me, because he was still attacking Kang Youwei.[6] The conversation, however, was never quite congenial, and so, not long afterward, I was left alone in the study.

I arose very late the next day and went out after lunch to see several relatives and friends; the third day was the same. They had all changed very little, were just slightly older, but every family was busy preparing for the New Year's sacrifice.

This was the great end-of-year ceremony in Luzhen, during which reverent and splendid welcome was extended to the God of Fortune and good luck for the coming year was prayed for. Chickens and geese were killed; pork was bought; and they were washed with care. The women's arms were red from soaking in the water; some of these women even wore braided silver bracelets on their arms. After the meats were cooked, chopsticks were stuck into them at random angles, and these would then be called the "sacrificial offerings." At dawn they were set out on display, while incense candles were lit to respectfully invite the God of Fortune to come to enjoy them. The worshipers were limited to men and, of course, after worshiping they would naturally continue setting off firecrackers as before. It was the same every year, the same in every family—as long as they could afford the offering and the firecrackers—and naturally this year was no exception. The sky became even darker and in the afternoon it even started to snow. The bigger snowflakes were as large as plum-blossom petals; they were twirling all over the sky, and they merged with the smoke and the bustling atmosphere to put Luzhen in a welter of confusion. By the time I returned to Fourth Uncle's study, the roof of the house was already white with snow, and the room was made brighter by the reflection of the snow, revealing very clearly the big red stone rubbing of the character "Longevity" on the wall. It was written by the Taoist saint, Chen Tuan. One of the pair of scrolls had fallen down and was lying loosely rolled up on the long table. The other, still in its place, stated: "Know things and understand reasons, heart in peace and spirit in harmony." In my boredom I went over to the table beneath the window to thumb through the books on it, but only found a pile of a set of the *Kang Xi Dictionary*, possibly incomplete, *An Annotated Selection of Recent Thoughts*, and *Commentary on the Four Books*.[7] No matter what, I decided firmly that I would leave the next day.

Besides, whenever I thought of my meeting with Sister Xianglin[8] the previous day, I could not stay here in peace. It was in the afternoon. After visiting a friend in the eastern part of the town, I walked out and then met Sister Xianglin right by the river, and seeing the fixed look in her eyes, I knew she was obviously walking toward me. Of all the people I had seen during this visit to Luzhen, nobody's change was greater than hers: Her hair, streaked with gray five years ago, was now completely white, making her appear not at all like a person of around forty. Her face was extremely sallow, with a shade of black in the yellow skin, and the sad look that was there before had all disappeared, as if her face was carved out of wood; only the eyeballs that turned once in a while still showed that she was a living thing. In one hand she had a wicker basket in which there was a broken bowl, empty; in the other, she was holding a bamboo pole that was taller than herself and split at the bottom end: she clearly had become a beggar completely.

I stopped, waiting for her to come and ask for money.

"So you are back?" she first asked, like that.

"Yes."

"That's just great. You are a scholar, and you have also traveled around and seen the world. I just happen to want to ask you about something. . . ." Her lackluster eyes suddenly brightened.

I never expected her to say such things, and stood there in surprise.

"It's . . . " She walked two paces closer, lowered her voice, and said with extreme secrecy in a whisper, "After a person dies, is there indeed a spirit?"

My flesh crawled, and seeing her eyes staring at me, I seemed to feel my back being punctured by thorns and I was more nervous than when I had to take an unprepared pop quiz at school as the teacher just happened to be standing right next to me. As for the existence of ghosts, I had never paid any attention to it myself; but at this moment, what was the proper way to answer her? In the very short moment of hesitation, I thought, the people here believed in spirits generally, but she instead has her doubts—or I should rather say her hopes: hoping that there were spirits, and hoping there weren't any at the same time. . . . Why should people add to the sufferings of desperate people? For her sake, it would be better to say there was a spirit.

"Maybe there is . . . I think," I then told her hesitantly.

"If that is so, there is also a hell then?"

"Uh, hell?" I was much taken aback and had to speak evasively. "Hell? —Logically speaking, there should be one, too. But not necessarily . . . Who cares anyway? . . ."

"Then, will all the dead members of a family meet one another again?"

"Oh, oh, do they meet or not? . . ." By this time I had realized what an utter fool I was. All my hesitation and maneuvering had been no match for her three questions. All at once I became cowardly and wanted to recant all that I had said earlier. "That is . . . actually, I'm not sure. . . . in fact, whether there are indeed spirits or not. I'm not sure either."

I took the opportunity when she did not keep up her questioning and walked away with hasty steps. After hurriedly escaping back to Fourth Uncle's house, I felt rather uncomfortable at heart. I thought to myself, my answer as such might pose some danger to her. She might have felt lonely herself when others were preparing the New Year's sacrifice, but could she have some other intentions? Maybe she had some premonitions? Should she have other intentions, and should something else happen, then my answer would indeed be partly responsible. . . . But afterward I laughed to myself, feeling that the incident did not have any significance in itself. But I insisted on careful scrutiny; no wonder educators would call such behavior neurotic. Besides, I had clearly said, "I am not sure," and had recanted my whole answer, so that, if anything happened, I would then have nothing to do with it.

"I'm not sure" is a most useful phrase. Bold, inexperienced youngsters often take it upon themselves to solve problems or choose doctors for other people, and if by any chance the results are no good, they usually become the ones to blame; but by concluding their advice with this expression of uncertainty, they achieve blissful immunity from reproach. At such a moment, I felt even more the necessity of such a phrase, which could not be left out even if I were talking to a woman beggar.

However, I still felt uneasy all the time, and after a night, I still now and then thought of it, as if feeling inside me some unfortunate omen; in the cloudy snowy day, in the boring study, this uneasiness became heightened. It would be better to leave and go to the city. Clear shark's fin soup at the Fuxing

Restaurant—a dollar got you a big bowl of it, low price but nice stuff. I wondered if the price had gone up or not. Though the friends I had gone there with had scattered like clouds, those shark fins must still be consumed, even if it was just me alone. . . . No matter what, I decided firmly that I would leave the next day.

Since I have often seen the coming of expected things that I had hoped would not happen as expected because they just might not happen as I had expected, I was quite afraid that this thing would be just the same. Sure enough, peculiar things started to happen. At dusk, I heard some people talking together in a room, as if discussing something. But in a short while, the voices stopped; only Fourth Uncle was talking loudly as he walked around:

"Not sooner, not later, but just at this moment; from this, you can see she is a bad lot!"

At first, I was startled, and then I felt rather uneasy, as if what he said had something to do with me. I looked outside the door, and no one was there. Not until their part-time helper came to brew tea before dinner did I finally have the chance to ask some questions.

"Just now, who was Fourth Uncle angry with?" I asked.

"With Sister Xianglin, of course," the part-time helper said curtly.

"Sister Xianglin? What about her?" I pressed.

"She's gone."

"Dead?" My heart suddenly tightened, and I almost jumped up, and my face probably also changed color. But since he never raised his head, he did not notice all this. I pulled myself together and kept on, asking:

"When did she die?"

"When did she die? Last night, or maybe today—I'm not sure."

"How did she die?"

"How did she die? Died of poverty, of course." He answered indifferently, and still without raising his head to look at me, he went out.

But my agitation was only short-lived. Then I felt that the thing that would come had come and gone, not dependent upon the consolation of my being "not sure" and his so-called "dying of poverty," and my heart gradually felt light; but at times, I still felt somewhat guilty. Dinner was set out, and Fourth Uncle solemnly kept me company. I still wanted to ask something about Sister Xianglin, but I knew that although he had read that "ghosts and spirits are the good tricks of the two forces of nature," he still had a great many taboos; when approaching the New Year's sacrifice, it was absolutely forbidden to mention such words as death and illness; in case of necessity, one should use a kind of euphemism instead. A shame it was that I did not know any, so after wanting to ask several times, I eventually gave up. From his stern face, I suddenly suspected that he was thinking I was a bad lot to have come neither sooner nor later, to disturb him at just such a moment, so I immediately told him that I would be leaving Luzhen the next day to go to the city, so as to let his heart feel at ease. He did not press me to stay. Thus, in that depressed mood, I finished the meal.

The winter days were short, and it was also snowy, so that darkness had already enveloped the whole town. People were all busy under the lights, but it was very quiet outside the window. Snowflakes fell on the thick blanket of accumulated snow; there seemed to be a rustling sound when one listened that made the stillness seem even greater. I sat alone under the oil lamp that was giving off a yellow light, thinking that this bored Sister Xianglin, who was like an old toy that people got tired of looking at and had thrown away in the dust pile, still had her body sticking out in the dust. The people who enjoyed living might be surprised why she still existed. Now she had finally been swept away cleanly by death. Whether there are spirits, I do not know; but in this present world, when a futile existence no longer lives, so that it is no longer seen by people tired of seeing it, for the person and the others, it is all pretty fair. I listened quietly to the snowflakes that seemed to be making a rustling sound, and contemplated, feeling gradually relaxed.

But the fragments of half Sister Xianglin's life that I had seen or heard about before seemed now to form a whole.

She was not from Luzhen. Early one winter, when my uncle's family wanted a different maid, Old Mrs. Wei, the go-between, brought her in. She wore a white string on her hair[9]; black skirt, blue jacket, pale blue vest; her age was probably twenty-six or twenty-seven, and her face was sallow, but her two cheeks were still rosy. Old Mrs. Wei called her Sister Xianglin, saying that she was a neighbor of her mother's family, and the head of her family had died, so she had come out to work. Fourth Uncle frowned a little, and Fourth Aunt knew what he meant, knowing that he disliked her being a widow. But seeing that her look was decent, her hands and feet were all strong and big, her eyes were always downcast, and, not speaking a word, she seemed very much like a hardworking and obedient person. Fourth Aunt then ignored Fourth Uncle's frown and kept her. During the trial period, she worked all day long, as if she would be bored if she did not do anything. She was also strong, almost as strong as a man, so on the third day she was hired for 500 dollars a month.[10]

Everybody called her Sister Xianglin; no one asked her about her family name, but the middle-woman was from the Village of the Weis and she was said to be her neighbor, so that her family name was probably Wei. She did not like to talk and answered only when others asked her questions, and even that was not much. Only after a dozen days did people gradually learn that she still had a strict mother-in-law at home and a young brother-in-law, over ten years old, who could already cut wood for fuel. It was in the spring that she lost her husband, who also made a living cutting wood to sell as fuel, and was ten years younger than she: That was all that people knew.

Time passed quickly. She went on working as hard as before, was not picky about what she ate, and did not spare her strength. Everyone said that Fourth Lord's[11] family had hired the right maid, and she was indeed more hardworking than hardworking men. By the end of the year, sweeping, scrubbing the floor, killing chickens and ducks, and cooking New Year's sacrifice all night long were completely undertaken by her, and the family did not even add a part-timer. But she was satisfied; smiles were gradually creeping up the corners of her mouth, and her face also became whiter and fuller.

Just after the New Year, when she came back from washing the rice at the river, her face suddenly lost its color, and she said that she saw from afar a man pacing on the other bank, looking very much like an uncle from her husband's family who might have come just to look for her. Fourth Aunt was very startled and bewildered, asking her for the details, but she would not tell. As soon as Fourth Uncle knew about it, he frowned a little, saying:

"This is not good. I am afraid she is a runaway."

She was indeed a runaway, and not long afterwards, this guess proved to be true.

About a dozen days after this, everyone had already forgotten that earlier matter, but Old Mrs. Wei suddenly brought in a woman over thirty, saying that she was the mother-in-law of Sister Xianglin. Though the woman had the look of someone from the mountains, she was smooth in her dealings and good at talking; after the greetings, she then apologized, saying she made this special trip to ask her daughter-in-law to go back, because things got busy after the start of the spring season; but at home there were only people too old or too young, so they were short of hands.

"If it's her mother-in-law who wants her back, what else is there to say?" Fourth Uncle said.

So the pay was calculated, all together $1,750, all of which she had deposited at her boss's home and had not used a cent. It was all turned over to her mother-in-law. That woman also took away Sister Xianglin's clothes, thanked them, and left. By this time it was already noon.

"Oh, oh, where is the rice? Didn't Sister Xianglin go to wash the rice? . . ." Fourth Aunt cried out in her surprise only after a long while. Maybe she was a little hungry and remembered her lunch.

So everyone went off in different directions to look for the rice-washing basket. Fourth Aunt first went to the kitchen, then to the living room, and then to the bedroom, but there was not even a shadow of the basket. Fourth Uncle stepped outside the door and did not see it either. Not until he got to the river did he see it sitting squarely on the bank, and beside it there was a stock of vegetables.

The people who saw it reported that in the morning a boat with a white cabin was anchored in the river. The cabin was all covered and it was not known what people were in it, but no one paid attention to it before it happened. When Sister Xianglin came out to wash the rice, just as she knelt down, two men jumped out of the boat, looking like the people from the mountains. One held her and the other helped, and she was dragged into the boat. Sister Xianglin even cried out several times, and after that there was no more noise; maybe her mouth was stuffed with something. Then two women walked up; one was unknown, and one was none other than Old Mrs. Wei. When people looked into the boat, it was not quite visible inside; she seemed to have been roped and was lying on the floor of the boat.

"Outrageous! But . . ." said Fourth Uncle.

That day Fourth Aunt cooked the lunch herself; their son Ah Niu fed the stove.

After lunch, Old Mrs. Wei came again.

"Outrageous!" said Fourth Uncle.

"What does this mean? The nerve of you to come back to see us." Fourth Aunt was washing the dishes while talking in anger. "You recommended her yourself, and then you abducted her with the others, causing such an uproar. What will people think after seeing that? Are you playing a trick on our family?"

"Oh, well, well, I was truly taken in. This time, I have made this special trip to explain it. She came to ask me to recommend her to a place; how would I have expected that she was hiding it from her mother-in-law? I am sorry, Fourth Lord and Fourth Mistress. It is because I am confused in old age and careless that I have let my old patrons down. Luckily, your household has always been bighearted and kind to the lowly people. This time I will surely recommend a good one to make it up. . . ."

"But . . ." said Fourth Uncle.

Thus the matter about Sister Xianglin ended, and soon it was forgotten.

Only Fourth Aunt would mention Sister Xianglin because the maids they hired later either were lazy or ate too much, or were both lazy and ate too much, and were never satisfactory. At such moments, she would usually say to herself, "I wonder how she is now." What she meant was she hoped that Sister Xianglin would come back. But by the first month of the following New Year, she also gave up hope.

When the first month was almost over, Old Mrs. Wei came to wish them a happy New Year. She was already pretty drunk, saying that she came late because she went back to her own family in the Village of the Weis and stayed there for a few days. As they talked, they naturally brought up Sister Xianglin.

"Her?" Old Mrs. Wei said gleefully, "Now she is lucky. When her mother-in-law came to grab her home, she had already been promised to the Sixth He of the Village of the Hes. So not long after she returned home, she was put in a sedan chair to be carried over there."

"Oh, my, such a mother-in-law! . . ." Fourth Aunt said in surprise.

"Oh, yes, my lady! You are really speaking like the lady of a rich family. What's the big deal about that to us people in the mountains and lowly people? She has a young brother-in-law, who also has to marry. If they don't marry her off, where would the money come from to buy gifts for the bride? Her mother-in-law is a clever and capable woman and was good at her calculations, and that is why she married her off into the mountains. If she was married to a man in the same village, there would not be many gifts. And just because there are few women willing to be married to a man deep into the mountains she got ahold of 80,000 dollars. Now the wife of the second son has been taken in, and the gifts cost only 50,000 dollars. Minus the costs of the wedding, there was more than 10,000 dollars left over. Ha, you see, what a good plan it was. . ."

"Was Sister Xianglin willing? . . ."

"How can one be either willing or not? Anyone would make a fuss, but as long as a girl is roped, put in a fancy sedan chair, carried over to the man's house, forced to put on a flowery cap and make a series of wedding bows, and locked in the room, then it is over. But Sister Xianglin was really different. I heard that she made a really big fuss. Everyone was saying that she was different from others possibly because she had worked for an educated family. My lady, we have seen a lot: When widows marry, there are those who cry and yell; there are those who try to commit suicide; there are those who cannot be made to bow after being carried over to the man's house, and there are those who even smash wedding candles. Sister Xianglin was extraordinary. They say that all the way she was wailing and cursing. When they carried her to the Village of the Hes, she had lost her voice completely. When she was dragged out of the sedan chair, with two men and her younger brother-in-law holding onto her, they still could not make her bow. Just when they got careless and loosened their grip, oh, well, amituofuo,[12] she knocked her head on the corner of the shrine table and made a big hole in her head. Bright red blood was flowing out and it would not stop after it was wrapped with two bags of shrine ashes[13] and two pieces of red cloth. She was still cursing when they locked her and her man in the bridal chamber; oh, well, well, it was really. . ." She shook her head, lowered her eyes, and said no more.

"What happened later?" Fourth Aunt was still asking.

"I heard that she did not even get up the next day." She raised her eyes to speak.

"And later?"

"Later? She got up. By the end of the year, she gave birth to a baby, a boy, and he is two years old in the new year. During the last few days when I was living in my parents' house, some people went to the Village of the Hes. They came back to tell us that they saw both the mother and the child; the mother was plump, and the son was also plump; there was no mother-in-law to control her; the man was quite strong and was good at his work; the house was their own. Ah, she had really become lucky."

From then on, Fourth Aunt did not mention Sister Xianglin.

But in the fall of one year, about two New Years after the good news about Sister Xianglin, she was again standing in Fourth Uncle's living room. On the table was set a round basket in the shape of a water chestnut, and under the eaves there was a small bedding package. On her hair she was still wearing a mourning string; she wore a black skirt, blue jacket, and pale blue vest. Her face was sallow, but now the two cheeks had lost their pink color; her eyes were downcast. In the corners of her eyes there were still signs of tears, and the shine in her eyes was no longer as spirited as before. And again she was led in by Old Mrs. Wei, who showed a look of sympathy, saying to Fourth Aunt long-windedly:

". . . It was indeed what is called 'in nature there are unexpected winds and clouds.' Her man was a strong man, but who would know that at such a young age he would die because of typhoid fever? Actually he almost recovered from it, but he ate a cold meal, and the illness kicked in again. Luckily she still had her son; she was good at doing things, and was able to cut firewood, pick tea, and raise silkworms; she could have kept at it, but who would know that the child would be carried away by a wolf with its teeth? Spring was at its end, but wolves still showed up in the village; who had expected that?[14] Now she is left alone. Her uncle-in-law came to claim the house and drove her away. She has nowhere to go and has come to ask a favor from the old master. The good thing is that she does not have anything to worry about. My lady's house just happens to be replacing your maid, so I have brought her here. I was thinking, familiar place familiar routines, it is much better than a green hand. . . ."

"I was really stupid, really," Sister Xianglin said; she raised her lackluster eyes and continued. "I only knew that when it snowed the animals in the mountains didn't have things to eat and might come to the village; I didn't know that there would be animals in the spring, too. I opened the door early in the morning as soon as I got up, fetched a little basket to put pea pods in, and asked our Ah Mao to sit on the threshold to shell the pea pods. He was very obedient and obeyed every word I said, so he went. I then split some wood behind the house, washed the rice; when the rice was put in the wok, I wanted to steam the peas. I called for Ah Mao; no answer. I went out and saw that peas were scattered all over the ground, but our Ah Mao was not there anymore. He would not go to other people's houses to play; I went to every house and asked, and indeed he wasn't around. I got worried and asked people to look for him. They looked here and there until in the afternoon they got to look in the valley and saw that a little shoe of his was hanging on a thorny brush. Everyone said, 'Oh, no, he must have been snatched away by a wolf.' They went farther; he was indeed lying in the straw den, and his insides had all been eaten, but his little hand was still tightly clutching that little basket. . . ." Following this speech, she started to sniff and sob and could not utter a complete sentence.

At first Fourth Aunt was hesitating, but after she heard what Sister Xianglin said, her eyes reddened a little. She thought a little, then told her to put the basket and the bedding in the maid's room. Old Mrs. Wei sighed as if she had put down a heavy load off her shoulders; Sister Xianglin was in higher spirits than when she first showed up, and without directions set down her bedding in the old familiar way. From then on, she was working as a maid in Luzhen again.

And everyone still called her Sister Xianglin.

But this time, her situation underwent tremendous changes. After she had worked for two or three days, her masters felt that her hands and feet were not as flexible as before, and her memory was much worse; her corpse-like face was without the hint of a smile all day; as evident in the way she talked, Fourth Aunt was already somewhat dissatisfied. When she first came back, though Fourth Uncle frowned, he was not quite against it because it was hard to hire a maid; he only told Fourth Aunt secretly that, though these kinds of people might seem very pitiful, they would actually corrupt the customs; it was all right to use her help, but, when it came to sacrifices for the ancestors, she should not touch them. All those meals should be cooked by the family; otherwise they would not be clean and the ancestors would not eat them.

The most important thing in the household of Fourth Uncle was to offer sacrifices to the ancestors, and originally the busiest time for Sister Xianglin was also to offer sacrifices to the ancestors, but this time she became idle. The table was set in the middle of the family room, the table cloth tied, and she still remembered to set out wine cups and chopsticks as before.

"Sister Xianglin, you leave them there! Let me set them," Fourth Aunt said in a hurry.

She took her hands back in embarrassment and went to get the candleholders.

"Sister Xianglin, you set it down! Let me get it," Fourth Aunt again said in a hurry.

She walked around in circles several times, and eventually, having nothing to do, she had to walk away puzzled. The only thing she could do on this day was to feed the stove.

The people in the town still called her Sister Xianglin, but the tone was different from before; they still talked to her, but their smiles were cold. She did not notice those things, but with her eyes staring straight, she only talked with them about the story that she could not forget day or night:

"I was really stupid, really," she said. "I only knew that when it snowed the animals in the mountains didn't have things to eat and might come to the village; I didn't know that there would be animals in the spring, too. I opened the door early in the morning as soon as I got up, fetched a little basket to put pea pods in, and asked our Ah Mao to sit on the threshold to shell the pea pods. He was very obedient and obeyed every word I said; so he went. I then split some wood in the back of the house, washed the rice; when the rice was put in the wok, I wanted to steam the peas. I called for Ah Mao, no answer; I went out and saw that peas were scattered all over the floor, but our Ah Mao was not there anymore. I went to every house and asked, and indeed he wasn't around. I worried and asked people to look for him, until in the afternoon, several people got to the valley to look and saw a little shoe of his was hanging on a thorny brush. Everyone said, 'Damn it, he might have been snatched by a wolf.' They went further; indeed, he was lying in the straw den, and his insides had all been eaten, but it's pitiful that his hand was still tightly clutching that little basket. . . ." She then would shed tears and her voice would become a sob.

This story turned out to be rather effective. The men, listening to her to this point, would stop smiling and walk away without a smile; the women seemed not only to have forgiven her, but also to have changed the scornful look on their faces, and would shed many tears with her. Some old women who had not heard her tell the story on the street would come looking for her to listen to this sad story of hers. When she spoke till she sobbed, they would together shed the tears that had stayed at the corners of their eyes, sigh for a while, and go away satisfied, busily talking about it.

She would then repeatedly tell people her sad story, often attracting three to five people to listen to her. But soon everyone was thoroughly familiar with it after listening to her, and so even the kindest old ladies who chanted Buddhist sutras did not show the sign of a single tear in their eyes. Later on the whole town could almost recite her words and was irritated to the extent of having headaches from hearing them.

"I was really stupid, really," she would start saying.

"Yes, you just knew that when it snowed the animals didn't have things to eat deep in the mountains and might come to the village only then." They interrupted her speech and walked away.

She stood there with her mouth open, staring straight at them. Then she would walk away, as if she felt put out herself. But she still wanted to start a story about the other things, like a little basket, the peas, and other people's children. When she saw a two- or three-year-old child, she would say:

"Oh, if our Ah Mao was still alive, he would be this tall, too. . . ."

Children would be startled when they saw the look in her eyes and grab their mothers' hems and urge her to leave. So she would be by herself again, and she would walk away disconsolately. Later on people all got to know her habit, and whenever there was a child present, they would ask her with a fake smile, saying:

"Sister Xianglin, if your Ah Mao were still alive, would he be this tall?"

She might not have known that her sadness had been chewed and tasted in people's mouths for many days and now it had already become dregs to be disliked and spat out; but from the smiles of the people, she seemed to have felt the coldness and sharpness, and there was no need for her to open her mouth again. She only glanced quickly at them and did not answer a word.

Luzhen would always celebrate the New Year, and people already had started to get busy after the twentieth of the last month of the old year. This time Fourth Uncle's family had to hire a male part-timer, but they were still too busy, so they asked Auntie Liu to help out by killing chickens and geese; but Auntie

Liu, a woman who believed in Buddhism, was a vegetarian, so she would not kill living things and only washed containers. Apart from feeding the fuel in the stove, Sister Xianglin had nothing else to do and had to sit there idly, watching Auntie Liu wash the containers. Light snow was falling down flake by flake.

"Oh, well, I was really stupid." Sister Xianglin looked up at the sky and sighed, speaking to herself.

"Sister Xianglin, there you go again." Auntie Liu looked at her face impatiently.

"Oh, oh," she responded unclearly.

"Let me ask you: How did you give in eventually?"

"Me? . . ."

"You. I was thinking: It was, after all, because you became willing; otherwise . . ."

"Ah, ah, you don't know how strong he was."

"I don't believe you. I don't believe that, strong as you are, you were not able to really resist him. You must have become willing later, and now you say instead that he was strong."

"Ah, ah, you . . . you try it yourself and see." She smiled.

The wrinkled face of Auntie Liu also smiled, making her face shrink and look like a walnut; her small dry eyes took a look at the corner of Sister Xianglin's forehead, and then stared at her eyes. Sister Xianglin seemed to be very uncomfortable and stopped smiling right away; she rolled her eyes around to watch the snowflakes.

"Sister Xianglin, you really had a bad bargain," Auntie Liu said mysteriously. "It would have been all right if you had resisted more, or simply knocked yourself dead. Now, you lived with your second man for no more than two years, but in return you have got yourself a great sin. Just think about it, when you go to the nether world, the ghosts of the two men will fight over you; which man is it good to give yourself up to? The Lord of Death will have to saw you into two, and divide you between them. I think this is really. . ."

Her face then showed a look of terror, because this had been something unknown to her in the mountain villages.

"I think you'd better ward it off early. Go to the temple of the village god and buy a threshold, which will be used as your surrogate to be trampled upon by thousands of people and stepped over by tens of thousands of people to make up for the sin of this life and avoid suffering after death."

Sister Xianglin did not give any response at the time, but she was probably quite depressed; when she got up the next morning, her two eyes had large dark shadows around them. After breakfast, she then went to the temple of the village god at the western end of the village, begging to give a donation for a threshold. The person in charge in the temple at first would not agree, no matter what; not until she was so worried that she shed tears did they agree reluctantly. The price was 12,000 dollars.

She was no longer talking to people because the story about Ah Mao had already been discarded by people who told it around; but since her talk with Auntie Liu, which seemed to have been spread around, many people found a new interest, and came to tease her to get her to talk. As for the topic, it naturally changed to a new one, which focused on the wound on her forehead.

"Sister Xianglin, let me ask you: Why did you become willing at that time?" one person would say.

"Oh, a shame that the knock was for nothing." Another person looked at her wound, echoing the other.

She knew well from their smiles and tones that they were making fun of her, so she would open her eyes wide, not saying a word, or later on even turning her head. With her lips tightly closed, bearing the wound that was regarded by others as a mark of disgrace, she walked on the streets silently, sweeping the floors, washing vegetables, and washing rice. Almost a year later, she took from the hands of Fourth Aunt all the wages she had saved from the beginning, which she exchanged into twelve silver Mexican dollars, and took her leave to go to the western end of the village. But in the time it takes to have a meal, she came back, her mood quite happy and her eyes uncommonly bright; she told Fourth Aunt that she had donated a threshold in the temple of the village god.

By the time of ancestral sacrifice at the Winter Solstice,[15] she was working even harder; seeing that Fourth Aunt had arranged the sacrifices and was lifting the table to move it to the middle of the living room with Ah Niu, she went with confidence to get the wine cups and chopsticks.

"You put them down, Sister Xianglin!" Fourth Aunt said hurriedly in a loud voice.

She took her hands back as if she had been scorched and her face turned dark gray at the same time, not daring to get the candleholders any more, only standing there dispirited. Not until Fourth Uncle lit the incense and told her to leave did she walk away. This time her changes were very great; the second day, not only were her eyes sunken, but her spirit was no good. She was also afraid of things, not only fearing dark nights, but also feeling alarmed about people, even if they were her own masters, just like a little mouse walking around out of its hole in daylight; otherwise, she would be sitting there in a daze, just like a wooden puppet. In less than half a year, her hair also became streaked with gray and her memory became especially bad, to the extent of often forgetting to wash the rice.

"How come Sister Xianglin is like this? We would have been better off if we had not kept her in the beginning." Fourth Aunt would sometimes say this right in her face, as if warning her.

But she still behaved the same way and was without the hope of recovering her wits again. They then wanted to get rid of her and to ask her to go back to Old Mrs. Wei. When I was still in Luzhen, they were just talking about this. Judging from the situation now, I saw clearly that it was finally carried out. But did she turn into a beggar right after she left Fourth Uncle's family or did she first go to Old Mrs. Wei and then turn into a beggar? That I do not know.

I was startled awake by nearby and therefore especially loud firecrackers and saw a flicker of yellow light; then I again heard the snapping sounds of firecrackers and knew that Fourth Uncle's family was offering their New Year's sacrifices; I knew that it was almost dawn. Being half awake, I heard firecrackers snapping endlessly in the distance, as if they had been combined into a thick cloud of explosions mixed with whirling snowflakes, embracing the whole town. In this embrace of numerous explosions, I also felt lazy and comfortable, and the doubts I had from daytime to early evening were cleanly swept away by the air of New Year's sacrifice; I felt only that the saints of both heaven and earth had enjoyed the sacrifices and the fragrant smoke and were stumbling in the air in intoxication, preparing to grant the people in Luzhen endless happiness.

NOTES

1. the Chinese calendar—The Chinese calendar is a lunar calendar and is thus different from the Western solar calendar. The Chinese New Year, or the Spring Festival, does not have a fixed date in the Western calendar, but is usually celebrated in what would be January or February in the Western calendar. Although the Western calendar has long been adopted for all practical functions, traditional holidays in China are still arranged and observed according to the Chinese lunar calendar.

2. ". . . firecrackers bidding farewell to the Hearth God"—This is part of the tradition in celebrating the Chinese New Year, in which the Hearth God supposedly goes to heaven to report on earthly conditions. The farewell is meant to urge the Hearth God to say kind things to Buddha about the earthlings. This activity is conducted on December 24 in the Chinese calender.

3. Master Lu the Fourth—This is probably the way the people in the town address him because of his learning and status, although he is the narrator's uncle.

4. ". . . but still he had not grown a beard"—Growing a beard, in traditional Chinese culture, is a sign of maturity and old age.

5. "After the greetings, he said that I 'had put on weight.'"— Saying one has put on weight in Chinese culture was not and may still not be an insult, but rather a compliment on the person's ability to stay fit and healthy, because being thin has been more or less regarded as a sign of malnutrition.

6. "But I knew that he was not really using the topic to condemn me: because he was still attacking Kang Youwei"—Kang Youwei was an old-fashioned reformist who failed to carry out a reform with the last Qing emperor. By the time this story took place, Kang Youwei was already regarded as a conservative in the big cities. The attack by the narrator's uncle on Kang Youwei makes him a more conservative and old-fashioned person than Kang Youwei.

7. "... but only found a pile of possibly incomplete set of the *Kang Xi Dictionary, An Annotated Selection of Recent Thoughts,* and *Commentary on the Four Books"*—Most of these (except *Kang Xi Dictionary*) are traditional books representing the Confucianist tradition of learning, which Lu Xun regarded as decadent and outdated.

8. Sister Xianglin—The Chinese word used for "sister" in this context actually means "sister-in-law." In traditional Chinese culture, when a woman was married, her husband's first name was added to the words *sister-in-law* to create for her a name that was used by people outside her immediate family. She was very seldom referred to by her maiden name.

9. "She wore a white string on her hair"—Chinese women in certain areas used to wear a white string on their hair to mourn a recent death in the immediate family, especially the death of a husband.

10. "... she was hired for 500 dollars a month"—I find no better word for the Chinese currency used in that period, but one should note that 500 dollars was not much at all.

11. Fourth Lord—The narrator's uncle, so called by people because of his status in his town.

12. "amituofuo"—This is an expression that is similar to "Oh my God" or "God bless." It is an expression related to Buddhist prayers and I find no better way to translate it than to transcribe it phonetically.

13. "it was wrapped with two bags of shrine ashes"—Bags of shrine ashes were often used to stop bleeding.

14. "Spring was at its end, and wolves show up in the village; who had expected that?"—Wolves are expected to show up in villages in winter or cold weather to look for food, but not in spring when there are plenty of small animals for wolves to hunt.

15. Winter Solstice—In the Chinese calendar, a year is divided into twenty-four solar segments, of which Winter Solstice is the twenty-second.

BIBLIOGRAPHY

Fu, Hu, and Zhengru Xiong. "Lu Xun's Influence on Tang Tao." *Chinese Literature* 12 (1981): 110–23.

Hsia, C. T. *A History of Modern Chinese Fiction*. New Haven, CT: Yale University Press, 1971.

Lu, Xun. *The Complete Works of Lu Xun*. Beijing: People's Literature (Renmin Wenxue Chubanshe), 1981.

Lyell, William A., Jr. *Lu Hsun's Vision of Reality*. Berkeley: University of California Press, 1976.

Zhao, Xiaqiu, and Qingrui Zeng. *A History of Modern Chinese Fiction*. Beijing: Chinese People's University Press, 1984.

CHAPTER 3

"Kong Yi Ji"

Lu Xun (1881–1936)

Introduction to the Author

Here the focus will be on Lu Xun's interaction with the Chinese intellectuals of his time and his opinions of the two kinds of radically different Chinese intellectuals at the turn of the century.

The introduction of Western civilization into China thrived at the dawn of the twentieth century due, in part, to trade with the West by means of gunboat diplomacy. As the century began, more urgently than ever, China was facing the question of survival and had to find a way to gain military strength for its self-defense. The obvious way out, to many educated Chinese, was to learn from the West. In the nineteenth century, when the West came to Asia seeking trade and possible dominance, the same challenge was facing both China and Japan. But while the Meiji Restoration (1852–1912) in Japan launched an era of Westernization, started the movement toward industrialization, and established a comparatively democratic rule with a reorganized political structure and a modern constitution, a similar movement in China at the end of the nineteenth century, called Wuxu Bianfa (Wuxu Reform), failed miserably and tragically as several leaders of the reform were beheaded. Yet after many humiliating defeats in the battles against foreign invaders, the corrupt and weak Qing Empire decided on its own initiative or was coerced to send some bright young students to different, more advanced countries to acquire practical Western knowledge, mostly in science and technology, so that they could come back to strengthen their country. These efforts ironically produced many of the enlightened intellectuals who would be vital in the Nationalist movement that brought down the Qing Empire in 1911 and established the Republic of China. But at the beginning of the century, when only a few Chinese were sent abroad to study and the Western influence was largely limited to the coastal or port cities of Shanghai, Guangzhou, and Wuhan, such intellectuals were few and far between. Most of the intellectuals were still educated in the traditional way with one goal in mind: to pass the official examinations at different levels and gain a prominent and powerful position in the government.

Lu Xun's own education started out in the traditional way at a private school established by and for the clan, where he learned mostly classical Chinese. Judging from many of his reminiscences of that time, we know that the teaching in the private school was outdated, and that there was no strict discipline in class. There was just one teacher in the one-room school, and the teacher would teach students reading, writing, and calligraphy, but not much else. The texts were classical Chinese works that had been passed down from generation to generation and had sometimes been heavily annotated by prominent scholars. Although there were fun moments behind the teacher's back at school, Lu Xun did not take to the old-fashioned learning, but he had no other choice. It was not until 1898, when he was about eighteen, that he left for Nanjing to study at Jiangnan Naval Academy. Later, however, he would transfer to the School of Mines and Railroads in Nanjing, which was run by the Jiangnan Army Academy. It should be noted here that the old-fashioned essay-writing examinations designed by the government to select administrative officials were not eliminated until 1906, and that Lu Xun could have taken these exams at different levels to advance in the government. Instead, he took a path less traveled but definitely more exciting and promising, the opportunity to go overseas and study medicine in Japan.

After he graduated from the School of Mining and Railroads in 1901, he went to Japan in 1902. As a government-sponsored student, he would stay in Japan for many years before he finally came back home in 1909, although he never completed a degree. Thus, in Lu Xun, there existed both the traditional Chinese learning and the new Western wisdom. He loathed the traditional learning but called for the spread of Western knowledge in China. Seeing the powers of the West, Lu Xun not only called on people to learn from the West, but he and his brother actually set out to contribute to such learning. Before he published his own stories, he and his brother translated and introduced many Western stories for Chinese readers. From what he had learned from and about the West, Lu Xun came to see the traditional Chinese intellectuals as a dying breed who would never be able to compete against the more advanced scholars of the West. The kind of narrow and superficial knowledge that traditional Chinese intellectuals acquired for governmental duties would be easily overwhelmed by the powerful and advanced Western learning. It was therefore inevitable that Lu Xun came to regard the traditional Chinese scholars as powerless, useless, pathetic, and doomed to disappear unless they caught up with the rest of the world. In "Kong Yi Ji," we are given such a perception of the old-fashioned Chinese intellectuals in shocking detail.

Kong Yi Ji

[1919]

The layout of the taverns in the town of Luzhen is different from all other places: All of them have an angular-shaped counter facing the street. In the counter, hot water is kept ready to warm wine at all times. The laborers, after work around noon or dusk, spend four copper pennies to buy a bowl of wine—this was the price more than twenty years ago; now the price for a bowl has gone up to almost ten pennies—then they stand outside the counter and drink their wine as they rest. If a laborer spends one more penny, he then may buy a small plate of salted bamboo shoots or boiled aniseed-seasoned beans to go with the wine. A meat dish can be purchased if one puts out over ten pennies. But these customers are mostly workers wearing short coats, and most probably are not so extravagant. Only those who wear long gowns[1] stroll into the adjacent room in the tavern, ordering their wine and their dishes. They sit down and drink slowly.

When I was twelve, I started to work as a waiter in Prosperity Tavern at the end of the town. The owner said I looked too stupid, and he was afraid I could not wait on the long-gown customers; therefore I would work at the outer counter. The short-coat customers at the outside counter were easy to deal with, but oftentimes they could also go on and on with their confusing yet persistent talk. They often demanded to watch closely the yellow wine being scooped out of the tub, to examine whether there was water added to the bottom of the wine kettle, and to watch the wine kettle being placed in the hot water. Then they would feel relieved. Under such strict scrutiny, adding water to the wine became very difficult. So after I worked there for several days, the owner said I was not suited for that job. To fire me was yet not appropriate due to, luckily, the importance of the person who recommended me. My job was then changed solely to the boring work of wine-warming.

From then on, I would stand all day behind the counter, taking care of my work. Although I made no blunder on my job, I always felt it was somewhat monotonous and boring. The owner always put on a fierce-looking face, and the customers were not polite either when they talked, making it hard for me to be happy. Only when Kong Yi Ji came to the tavern would I laugh a few times. So I still remember him to this day.

Kong Yi Ji was the only long-gown customer who would stand by the counter to drink his wine. He was very tall. His face was pale, and in between the wrinkles on his face there were often some scars. His messy beard was gray streaked with white. Although he had on a long gown, it was both dirty and torn, as if for ten years it had been neither mended nor washed. When he talked to people, he would use some archaic and learned words all the time, making his speech incomprehensible to people half of the time. Since his family name was Kong, some people had given him the nickname "Kong Yi Ji," because they saw such confusing characters as "Shang Da Ren Kong Yi Ji" on the opening page in the copybook for schoolboys.[2] As soon as Kong Yi Ji got to the tavern, all the drinkers would look at him and laugh. Someone would yell out: "Kong Yi Ji, your face's got some new scars again!" He would not reply and spoke to the waiter inside the counter: "Warm two bowls of wine, and give me a plate of aniseed-seasoned beans." Then he would lay down nine copper pennies. One of the drinkers would again purposely say in a loud voice: "You must have stolen other people's belongings again!" Kong Yi Ji opened his eyes wide and said: "How can you blemish my innocence without any evidence? . . ." "What innocence? The day before yesterday I saw with my own eyes the He clansmen hang you up and whip you. You stole their books." Kong Yi Ji then became red-faced, the veins on his forehead bulging, and argued: "Taking books cannot be regarded as . . . stealing books! . . . I am a learned man. Can taking books be regarded as stealing?"[3] Then he would follow with unintelligible speech, such as "whereas poor a gentleman man can be . . ." or some archaic words, causing everyone to roar with laughter all together. In and out of the tavern, the air would be filled with merriment.

Behind Kong Yi Ji's back, I heard from the people's gossip that he did indeed go to school. But in the end he was not able to pass the official examination to earn a government position.[4] Nor was he able to make a good living. So he became poorer and poorer, almost to the point of begging. Fortunately, he was good at calligraphy. He then would copy books for some people to earn a few meals. It was a shame, however, that he had bad habits: bone laziness and heavy drinking. He would sit down to copy books in someone's house for a few days; then he would disappear altogether along with their books, paper, pens, and ink. After he did that several times, no one would ever again ask him to copy books for them. At his wits' end, Kong Yi Ji inevitably went into stealing now and then. But when he was at our tavern, he behaved better than all the others, never leaving a debt unpaid. Although sometimes he did not have cash and the amount was written on the blackboard, within a month he would pay it back. His name, Kong Yi Ji, was then erased from the board.

After Kong Yi Ji drank half a bowl of the wine, his face gradually returned to its normal pale color. People around him then asked him again: "Kong Yi Ji, do you really read the characters?" Kong Yi Ji would look at the person asking the question, putting on an air of contempt without answering. They would then continue, "How come then you were never even half qualified in the official examination?" Immediately, Kong Yi Ji appeared dejected and uneasy, his face covered with a layer of grayness, his mouth muttering some words. This time the words were all archaic; none were intelligible. At this moment, all the men would start to laugh together. In and out of the tavern, the air would be filled with merriment.

At times like this, I could laugh with the others and the owner would never scold me. The owner himself, when seeing Kong Yi Ji, would always ask him those questions to make people laugh. Kong Yi Ji knew that he could not talk with those people, so he would turn to talk to children. One time he said to me, "Did you go to school?" I nodded my head slightly. He said, "Went to school . . . let me give you a quiz. The character aniseed as in aniseed-seasoned beans, how do you write it?" I thought: Being almost a beggar, are you fit to quiz me? I turned my face, not answering him. Kong Yi Ji waited for a long time, then said earnestly, "Can't write it? . . . Let me teach you; remember it! You should remember such characters. When you become an owner, they will be needed in bookkeeping." I thought to myself that my status was a far cry from that of an owner. Besides, our owner never counted aniseed-seasoned beans as an item in bookkeeping. I felt amused yet impatient, lazily answering him, "Who asked you to teach me? Isn't it 'grass' on top and 'return' at the bottom?"[5] Kong Yi Ji seemed to be extremely happy, knocking on the counter with two long fingernails, and he nodded his head while saying, "Yes, yes! . . . 'Return' can be written in four different ways. Do you know?" I got more fed up and walked away with pouted lips. Kong Yi Ji had just dipped his fingernail in his wine and wanted to write the characters on the counter. Seeing that I was not at all enthusiastic, he gave a sigh and seemed to think it was an extreme pity.

There were several times when the children in the neighborhood heard the laughter and, rushing over to join the fun, they circled Kong Yi Ji. He then gave them aniseed-seasoned beans to eat, a bean for each kid. The children ate their beans and still would not leave, their eyes looking at his plate. Kong Yi Ji got into a panic, stretched his five fingers to cover up the plate, and bent down to say, "Not much left, I don't have much left anymore." Straightening himself to take a look at the beans, he shook his head, saying, "Not many, not many! Are there many? Not many." Then the bunch of kids would disperse laughing.

Kong Yi Ji thus made people happy, but without him, everyone could still go on with their living.

One day, maybe two or three days before the Mid-Autumn Festival, the owner was slowly making up the accounts when he took down the blackboard, suddenly saying, "Kong Yi Ji has not been here for a long time. He still owes me nineteen cents." I then also realized he indeed hadn't been around for a very long time. A customer said, "How could he come? . . . His legs were broken during a beating." The owner said, "Oh!" "He was still stealing. This time, he was out of his mind and went to steal in the house of Ding, the provincial scholar.[6] How dare one steal the things in his house?" "What happened later?" "What happened? First he had to write a confession. Then the beating started. It went on for over half the night, and then his legs were broken." "And later?" "Later his legs were broken." "What happened after his legs were broken?" "What happened? . . . Who knows? Maybe he died." The owner did not ask anymore, but was still slowly making up his accounts.

After the Mid-Autumn Festival, the autumn wind got colder day after day. It was slowly getting on toward early winter. Although all day I leaned close to the fire, I still had to put on my padded coat. One day in the afternoon, there was not a single customer; I sat there with my eyes closed. Suddenly I heard a voice, "Warm me a bowl of wine." Though the voice was extremely low, it sounded familiar. When I looked, I saw no one. I stood up to look outside, and Kong Yi Ji was sitting under the counter facing the doorstep. His face was dark and skinny, hardly a face anymore. He wore a torn jacket, his legs folded upon a rush sack, which was hung on his shoulders with straw strings. When he saw me, he again said, "Warm me a bowl of wine." The owner also looked out and said, "Kong Yi Ji? You still owe me nineteen cents!" Kong Yi Ji looked up with a depressed expression to answer: "This . . . let me pay you back that next time. This time will be cash. The wine must be good." Just as usual, the owner said to him, laughing, "Kong Yi Ji, you must have stolen again!" This time, however, he did not explain in earnest, and only said, "Don't tease me!" "Tease you? If you didn't steal, how would your legs be beaten and broken?" Kong Yi Ji said in a low voice, "I fell and broke them, fell, fell. . . ." His eyes seemed to beg the owner not to mention it again. By then several people had gathered around, and they all laughed with the owner. I warmed the wine, carried it out, and put it on the doorstep. He groped in the torn jacket pocket and produced four copper pennies. When he put the four copper pennies in my hand, I saw that his hands were covered with mud. I realized that he had walked all the way to the tavern on his hands. Not taking long, he drank his wine, and amidst the talking and laughing of other people, he used those hands to slowly walk away.[7]

From that time on, we did not see him again for a long time. At the end of the lunar year, the owner took down the blackboard and said, "Kong Yi Ji still owes me nineteen cents!" At the time of the Dragon Boat Festival, the owner again said, "Kong Yi Ji still owes me nineteen cents!" But he would not mention it again by the Mid-Autumn Festival. We did not see Kong Yi Ji again even at the end of the year.

Nor have I ever seen him since—probably Kong Yi Ji has indeed died.

NOTES

1. Long gowns were almost a sure indication of one's social status in traditional Chinese culture, especially before a new culture was introduced in 1949 by the Chinese Communist Party. The long gown was mostly worn by men of letters, successful business people, big landlords, and important government officials. The working class would very seldom wear a long gown either because they abode by the tradition or because they could not afford one.

2. "Sang Da Ren Kong Yi Ji—Those who were fortunate to go to school in those days would start their Chinese lessons by practicing calligraphy on sheets of paper with characters already sketched out by dotted lines. Some of the beginning characters were "Sang Da Ren Kong Yi Ji," six characters alluding to Confucius as a saint but really making not much sense. But when the character Kong Yi Ji is linked to the traditional learning in China and also to Confucianism, the story seems to be making good use of such an allusion to subtly comment on the defunct traditional education system in China.

3. ". . . can taking books be regarded as stealing?"—At this point in the Chinese text, there is a subtle play of two words, both of which mean "to steal," but they have slightly different connotations or implications. "Qie" is the more euphemistic and diplomatic word, which I translate into "take," whereas "tou" is the most commonly used word and is much more direct, which I translate into "steal." Kong Yi Ji's effort at differentiating them seems, to the uneducated, quite futile.

4. ". . . he was not able to pass the official examinations to earn a government position"—Starting from the Sui Dynasty (581–618), official examinations were held at different levels to test the knowledge of learned men. When the examinees passed certain examinations, they were awarded government positions at the appropriate levels. Because of this narrow goal for the educated Chinese, the development of science and technology was neglected and was often regarded as trivial in Chinese culture. In 1906, that system was abolished by the Qing Empire to make way for a new and modern educational system, thus leaving tens of thousands of traditionally educated men at a loss.

5. ". . . Isn't it 'grass' on top and 'return' at the bottom?"—The narrator is talking about the structure of the Chinese character in discussion here. In Chinese, characters are often made up of other characters or parts of those characters, which are often used to indicate certain semantic connections or phonetic similarities. In the first character of "aniseed," the "grass" on top implies that the beans come off a plant, and the "return" at the bottom reminds one of the sound because "return" is pronounced the same as the first character of "aniseed" in Chinese.

6. ". . . he was out of his mind and went to steal in the house of Ding, the provincial scholar"—Obviously, this Ding family is a powerful family that is rich enough to have hired hands beat up an intruder without any regard for due process of the law. Such beatings were not uncommon in those lawless days, especially when someone was rich and powerful and the intruder was just a nobody.

7. "... he used those hands to slowly walk away"—not in the fashion of a handstand, but rather like scooting along.

BIBLIOGRAPHY

Note: Please see the chapter 1 bibliography for more sources on Lu Xun.

Chow, Tse-tsung. *The May Fourth Movement: Intellectual Revolution in Modern China*. Cambridge, MA: Harvard University Press, 1960.

———. *Research Guide to the May Fourth Movement: Intellectual Revolution in Modern China 1915–1924*. Cambridge, MA: Harvard University Press, 1963.

Hsia, C. T. *A History of Modern Chinese Fiction*. New Haven, CT: Yale University Press, 1971.

Lu, Xun. *The Complete Works of Lu Xun*. Beijing: People's Literature (Renmin Wenxue Chubanshe), 1981.

Lyell, William A., Jr. *Lu Hsun's Vision of Reality*. Berkeley: University of California Press, 1976.

Yue, Daiyun. *Comparative Literature and Modern Chinese Literature*. Beijing: Beijing University Press, 1987.

Zhao, Xiaqiu, and Zeng Qingrui. *A History of Modern Chinese Fiction*. Beijing: Chinese People's University Press, 1984.

CHAPTER 4

"Spring Peach"
(Chun Tao)

Xu Dishan (1893–1941)

Introduction to the Author

Among the writers who dominated the Chinese literary scene in
the years of freedom in the 1930s and 1940s, Xu Dishan was a
bona fide scholar whose education was solid and academic work
remarkable. He was nonetheless deeply sympathetic about the
sufferings of the people on the lowest rung of the social ladder,
and such sympathies are clearly evident in most of his stories.
Many of his stories are tragic, often ending in deaths or
destruction. But in "Spring Peach," a story about a strong
woman surviving in desperate times, the ending is a happy one,
or at least happy by Xu Dishan's standards. No matter how his
stories end, they all share close ties with the social issues and
problems of the author's time, a traumatic period for the whole
nation.

Xu Dishan was born in 1893 as Zhan Lei in Taiwan, and
his formal name was Dishan, which later became part of his pen
name. His parents were originally from Fujian Province on the
east coast of China, so that after Taiwan was occupied by Japan
by the end of the nineteenth century, his family made the
patriotic move from Taiwan to the mainland.

In 1917, at age twenty-four, he entered Yanjing University, one of the most prestigious universities in China. After graduation, he taught at the same university as a lecturer. His literary career started to flourish when he became a founding member of a literary study society that included such important members as Mao Dun, Zheng Zhenduo, and Ye Shentao, all prominent writers at the time. In 1922, he received his bachelor's degree in theology from the College of Religion at Peking University and went on to Columbia University to study religion. In 1924, he studied religion and Indian philosophy at Oxford University, and on his way home to China in 1925, he stayed in India for some time to study Buddhism and the original language of the Buddhist scriptures. Eventually he returned to China in 1926 to teach courses in Indian philosophy, religion, and anthropology at Yanjing University and Qinghua University.

He published his first story in 1921, three years after Lu Xun published "The Diary of a Madman." Following that, he published numerous stories and soon became one of the foremost figures in the New Literature Movement launched by Hu Shi and Cheng Duxiu in 1916. His first collection of short stories was published in 1925. Two of his works best known to his countrymen today are probably the essay "Peanuts" and the short story in our collection, "Spring Peach." The topics in his works before the Anti-Japanese War largely involve romantic and family matters and his works during that period were somber treatments of the social conditions of China. When the Anti-Japanese War broke out, he wrote more realistically and more passionately. He praised the Chinese people's bravery and efforts against the aggressive Japanese, exposed the poorly planned and executed military actions of the Nationalist Army, and revealed the social problems caused by the Nationalist Government. Often he wrote about the common people and their brave efforts to fight the aggressors and survive the national tragedy on their own. In 1941, hoping for a Chinese victory, he died in Hong Kong, years before the Japanese surrender.

Yet in many books on modern Chinese literature his works are often ignored, and his name is sometimes not even mentioned. Clearly he was not leftist enough in his works to be favored by the Communist government publications. Still, in certain books that are more even-handed and less biased, his works are lauded for both their idealistic themes and their realistic narratives. A relatively fair treatment of Xu Dishan is given in *A History of Modern Chinese Fiction* by Xiaqiu Zhao and Qingrui Zeng, professors at Chinese People's University in Beijing. The discussion in this book of Xu Dishan's works is relatively comprehensive and even-handed because the critics situate his works in their appropriate historical and cultural background.

Spring Peach

[1934]

Summer was unusually hot that year. Although the street lamps were already lit, the man selling sweet-and-sour plum juice at the lane's entrance was still clicking two small brass bowls rhythmically, as would a female ballad singer. A woman walked past him with a large basket of scrap paper on her back. Though unable to see her face clearly under the torn straw hat, one could catch a glimpse of her mouthful of snow-white teeth when she greeted him. The load on her back was so heavy that she could not hold her back straight. She walked solemnly placing one foot in front of the other, like a camel, until she entered the gate of her home.

Beyond the gate was a small courtyard. The woman lived in two side rooms that had not collapsed like the rest of the rooms in the compound. Most of the yard was covered with rubble. Before her door were an arbor of cucumbers and a few stalks of corn. Beneath the window there were a dozen or so tuberoses. A few rotted wooden beams lay under the arbor of cucumbers; this was perhaps the most elegant place to sit in her home. As soon as she got to the door, a man came out of the house and promptly helped her lower the heavy load.

"Wife, you are back late today."

The woman looked at him, as if surprised by his words. "What do you mean? Have you been wishing for a wife so much that you have gone insane? Don't call me wife, I tell you." Saying this, she entered the room, took off her battered straw hat, and hung it behind the door. She took a bamboo scoop from the side of the water vat, scooped water from it several times in succession, and drank so rapidly she couldn't catch her breath. She opened her mouth to gasp for a moment, then walked out to the arbor, pulled the big basket to one side, and sat down on a rotted wooden beam by herself.

The man's name was Liu Xianggao. The woman was about the same age as he, around thirty. Her maiden name was also Liu. Except for Xianggao, no one knew her given name was Chuntao.[1] The neighbors referred to her as Sister Liu, the scrap paper collector, because her occupation was poking through garbage piles on street corners and lanes' ends to earn a living, calling sometimes along the streets, "Scrap paper for matches!" From morning till night, beneath the blazing sun or in the cold wind, she was eating her full share of dust. But she had always loved cleanliness. Be it winter or summer, each day when she returned home she would clean her body and wash her face. It was Xianggao who, without any exception, would prepare the water for her.

Xianggao was a graduate of a rural elementary school. Four years previously, soldiers were marauding through his native region, and his whole family was forced to flee and scatter. On the road he met Chuntao, another refugee. After walking together for several hundred miles, they then separated.

She came with some people to Beijing. When a foreign woman in Zongbu Lane[2] wanted to hire a naive country girl as a maid, she was recommended for the job. Seeing that she was delicate and pretty, her mistress was very fond of her. She saw that her masters always ate beef, put butter on bread, and even added milk in their tea; because of all this, they smelled in passing,[3] and so she could not get used to it. One day the master asked her to take their child to the Sanbeizi Park. Then she realized that the smell of her masters was like that which came out of the tiger and wolf cages in the park. She felt even more miserable and quit before two months were up. In ordinary people's homes, country people could not get used to being servants, and they could not stand being scolded. Not long after they started, they would quit. At wits' end, she chose the profession of trading matches with people for scrap paper and thus could make a scanty living every day.

Xianggao's story, after he had parted with Chuntao, was quite simple. He went to Zhuozhou County[4] to look, without any success, for his family. A couple of distant family friends, hearing that he had come as a refugee, were not very willing to ask him to live with them. He had to drift back to Beijing. Due to the introduction of someone, he got to know Old Wu, who sold sweet-and-sour plum juice on the street corner. Old Wu let him stay in the run-down courtyard where he now lived, on the understanding that if anybody wanted to rent it, he would have to look for another place to live. Xianggao had no job; he only helped Old Wu keep his accounts a little and sell some sweet-and-sour plum juice. He lived there free, worked for nothing, and earned only two meals a day. Chuntao's business gradually improved, but at the place where she was originally staying, people would not allow her to store her merchandise. She then went looking for a place along the wall by Desheng Gate.[5] When she knocked on a gate, it turned out to be Xianggao, whom she knew. Without going through a lot of formalities, she rented the rooms from Old Wu and kept Xianggao on as her helper. All that was three years ago. Xianggao could read a little; among the paper that Chuntao collected and traded in, he could pick out a few relatively valuable pieces, such as paintings, or letters and scrolls written by some general or some chief. The two cooperated and business much improved. Occasionally, Xianggao tried to teach Chuntao to read a few characters, but without much success. He could not read very well himself and therefore had even greater difficulties in explaining the words to others.

In these years when they lived together, their life, if not comparable to the romance of a couple of mandarin ducks,[6] was as cheerful as a pair of little sparrows.

But back to the present story. When Chuntao went inside the house, Xianggao was already following her with a bucket of water. He said with a happy tone: "Wife, wash up quickly. I'm starved waiting for you. Let's eat something good tonight, griddle cakes with onions. Do you want to or not? If you want to, I'll go out and buy the onion sauce."

"Wife, wife, don't call me that, all right?" Chuntao said impatiently.

"Just answer me once, and I'll buy you a good straw hat in Tianqiao Market.[7] Haven't you been saying you needed to change your hat?" Xianggao pleaded.

"I don't like to hear it."

Seeing that the woman was a little annoyed, he changed the subject. "What do you want to eat? Tell me."

"Whatever you'd like to eat, I'll make it for you. Go buy it."

Xianggao returned with some onions and a bowl of sesame seed sauce, and placed them on the table in the outer room. Chuntao came out after her bath, holding in her hand a red card.

"Here again is some big lord's marriage certificate. Don't give it again to Old Li in the small market[8] this time. Have someone take it to the Beijing Hotel. We'll get more for it there."

"That's ours. Otherwise, how could you have become my wife? I have been teaching you to read for one or two years and you still can't recognize your own name!"

"Who can read so many words? Don't wife me; I don't like to hear it. Who wrote this?"

"I filled it out. This morning a policeman came around to check up on the residents, saying that the martial law has been more strict the last two days. Every family has to report exactly how many people there are in the family. Old Wu told me to claim us as husband and wife, so that it would save trouble. The policeman, too, said it wasn't appropriate if he wrote down that a man and a woman were living together. So I filled out the blank marriage certificate we couldn't sell last time. I wrote that we had our wedding in 1919."

"What? 1919? Did I even know you in 1919? Don't cause trouble. We never bowed to Heaven and Earth together, never drank from each other's wine cups, so we don't count as a couple."

Although she was a bit hesitant, Chuntao spoke her mind calmly. She had changed to blue cloth trousers. She was wearing a white blouse; though without makeup, her face had a natural, tender beauty. Had she been willing to marry, the local matchmakers could easily have passed her off as a young widow of twenty-three or twenty-four, still worth at least a hundred dollars or eighty.[9]

Smiling, she rubbed the card into a long roll and said: "Don't mess with it. What marriage certificate? Let's make our griddle cakes and eat." She lifted the stove lid and put the roll of paper into the flames. Then she walked to the table and began to mix flour with water.

Xianggao said: "You can burn it if you like. In any case the policeman has already registered us as husband and wife. If the government checks up on us, couldn't I say we lost it when we were refugees on the road? From today on, I'm going to call you wife. Old Wu recognizes our marriage; so does the policeman. Even if you aren't willing, I'm going to call you wife. Oh Wife! Oh Wife! Tomorrow I'm going to buy you a hat, but a ring I cannot afford."

"If you call me that again, I'm going to get angry."

"It looks like you are still thinking of that Li Mao." Xianggao was not as high-spirited as he had been a moment before. He was saying that to himself, not really meaning it to be heard by Chuntao, but Chuntao heard him.

"I'm thinking of him? We were husband and wife for one night, then separated for nearly five years, hearing nothing from each other all this time. Isn't it useless to think of him?" Chuntao said. She had told Xianggao what had happened on her wedding day. When the flowery sedan-chair brought her to the groom's home, before the guests even had a chance to take their seats at the wedding feast, people from two neighboring villages came rushing in to announce that an army of many soldiers had arrived. They were grabbing people everywhere to dig trenches. Everybody ran away in fear; the new couple also hastily bundled up their belongings and fled toward the west with the crowd. They walked together for a day and a night. On the second night, they suddenly heard people ahead of them shouting, "The bandits are coming. Hide quickly!" At that moment, everyone was concerned only with hiding themselves and could not care about others. When daylight dawned, more than ten people had disappeared, among whom was even Chuntao's husband Li

Mao. Continuing her speech of a moment ago, she said: "I think he must have gone with the bandits. Maybe he was killed long ago. That's it; let's not mention him again."

She finished baking griddle cakes and put them on the table. Xianggao scooped a bowl of cucumber soup from the crockery pot. They spoke no more, and ate the meal. When the meal was over, they sat as usual beneath the arbor and chatted. Stars twinkled among the leaves of the cucumber vines. A cool breeze sent fireflies up to the arbor, as if stars had come down. The night-blooming tuberoses were slowly sending out their perfume, stifling the foul smell around them.

"What fragrant tuberoses!" Xianggao plucked one of the flowers and put it in Chuntao's hair.

"Don't ruin my tuberoses. Wearing flowers in my hair at night—I'm no prostitute." She took the flower out, smelled it, and then laid it on the decayed beam beside her.

"Why did you come home late today?" Xianggao asked.

"Ha! Today I made a good business deal. As I was coming home this afternoon, passing the Houmen Arch,[10] I saw a street cleaner pushing a big cart full of scrap paper. I asked him where he got it. He said it was scrap paper thrown out from the Shenwu Gate.[11] I saw that it was a big pile of red and yellow paper.[12] I asked him whether he'd sell it to me. He said, if you want it, you can take it for a discount. Look!" Chuntao pointed at the big basket beneath the window. "I spent only a dollar for that big basket! I don't know if we'll lose money. We'll go through it tomorrow."

"You can't go wrong on things from the Palace. I'm only afraid of the stuff from schools and foreign business firms. Their paper is heavy and it smells bad. You are never sure if it's worth anything."

"In the last few years the shops have all got the habit of using foreign newspapers to wrap things.[13] I don't know where all the people came from who read foreign newspapers. When we pick them up, they are really heavy, but we don't get much money selling them."

"More and more people are reading foreign books. Everybody wants to read foreign newspapers so that they can have a job in a foreign business."

"They work at foreign jobs; we collect foreign newspapers."

"I'm afraid everything will have the word *foreign* added to it from now on. Rickshaw pullers will have to pull foreign rickshaws and mule-users will have to drive foreign mules. Maybe foreign camels will also come around." Xianggao caused Chuntao to laugh out loud.

"Don't you blame other people. If you had money, you'd probably want to study foreign books, too, and get yourself a foreign wife."

"The old lord of heaven knows, I'll never get rich. Even if I did, I wouldn't want a foreign wife. If I had money, I'd go back to the country, buy several acres of land, and we two could farm it together."

Ever since Chuntao had fled from her home and lost her husband, she had no pleasant feelings whenever she heard the word countryside. She said: "Do you still want to go back? I'm afraid that before you buy your land, both you and your money would be gone. Even if I were starving here, I wouldn't go back."

"I mean to go back to our Jinxian County."

"These years the countryside is the same wherever you go. If it's not marauding soldiers then it's bandits on a raid. If it's not the bandits, it's the Japanese. Who dares to go back? Just stay here and collect your scrap paper. All we need now is another person to help us. If we had another person to sort through the picking at home, you could set up a stall during the day. We'd avoid selling the goods through the middleman and losing some profits."

"I'd be all right after learning this trade for another three years. If we lose some money, it's not other people's fault; I can blame only my lack of good judgment. I've learned plenty the last few months. With stamps, which ones are worth money, which ones aren't, I pretty much know how to judge. The letters and handwritings of famous people, which would make a profit and which wouldn't, I'm also getting the hang of it. A few days ago I found a page written by Kang Youwei from that heap of paper. How much would you say I sold it for today?" Xianggao happily held up a thumb and an index finger to indicate a figure. "Eighty cents!"

"You see! If we could pick eighty cents out of our heap of scrap paper every day, that would be really good. Would you still need to go back to the countryside? Wouldn't that just be looking for trouble?" Chuntao's cheerful tones were like the chirping of an oriole in late spring. She continued: "I guarantee you'll find good stuff in today's heap. I hear there'll be more coming out of the Palace tomorrow. That street cleaner told me to wait for him at the Houmen Arch first thing in the morning. The last couple of days, things in the palace are being crated in a hurry and sent south, but nobody wants much of the scrap paper in the warehouse. I saw a lot outside the Donghua Gate,[14] too. One sack after another was thrown out. Tomorrow you should also go out and ask about it there."

After they talked much, the night watchman was already sounding the signal of approaching midnight. Chuntao stretched and stood up, saying: "I'm tired today. Let's rest."

Xianggao followed her into the house. There was a brick oven-bed[15] against the window, wide enough to sleep two or three people. In the tiny light of an oil lamp, dimly visible were a humorous painting of Eight Fairies[16] playing mah-jongg on one wall, and the "Still This Is Better"[17] tobacco company advertisement poster on the other. When Chuntao took off her battered straw hat, even if she did not go to the Rui Fu Xiang[18] shop or any other Shanghai fashion store, and if she could just go to Tianqiao, find a second-hand Chinese dress, put it on, and sit on any lawn, she would be a match for the modern girl in the "Still This Is Better" poster. Therefore, Xianggao often told Chuntao that it was her own little picture pasted on the wall.

She climbed onto the brick bed, totally undressed, then pulled a thin cover over her, and lay down on one side of the bed. Xianggao, as usual, massaged her back and legs. Every day her tiredness was thus gradually soothed with a faint smile on her face under the flickering light of the little oil lamp. Already half asleep, she murmured, "Xianggao, you come to bed, too. Don't burn the midnight oil. You still have to get up early tomorrow."

The woman slowly began to snore faintly. Xianggao then put out the lamp.

At dawn, like ravens searching for food, the man and the woman flew quickly out of their nest and went on with his and her own business.

Just as the noon cannon sounded, the drums and cymbals on the fairgrounds of the Ten Monastery Lake[19] were already sounding into the heavens. Chuntao came through the Houmen Arch bearing a basket of paper on her back and headed west toward the Buya Bridge. At the entrance of a temporary market, she heard someone calling her, "Chuntao, Chuntao!"

Her given name was barely used even once a year by Xianggao. In the four or five years since she left the countryside, no one else had ever called her that.

"Chuntao, Chuntao, don't you recognize me?"

She naturally turned to look and saw a beggar sitting by the roadside. The piteous cry had come out of a mouth covered by a beard. He was unable to stand because he had no legs. He wore a tattered gray uniform, the iron buttons on the uniform already rusting. His shoulders showed through the cracks in the epaulets and a nondescript army cap perched askew on his head. The insignia was already gone from the cap.

Chuntao stared at him, not uttering a single sound.

"Chuntao, I'm Li Mao!"

She took two steps forward. The man's tears were already running down with dust into his tangled beard. Her heart beat wildly. For a while she was unable to speak. Eventually, she said, "Brother Mao,[20] are you a beggar here? How did you lose your legs?"

"Oh, it's a long story. When did you start living here? What are you selling?'

"Selling nothing; I collect scrap paper. . . . Let's go home first."

Chuntao called a rickshaw, helped Li Mao in, put her basket also on the vehicle, and pushed it herself at the back. They arrived directly at the foot of the city wall by Deshun Gate, and the rickshaw man helped her to remove Li Mao down from the rickshaw. When they entered the lane's entrance, Old Wu clanged his little brass bowls as he asked, "Sister Liu, you are home early today. Business must be good!"

"A relative has come from the country," she answered in formality.

Li Mao was like a small bear, his two hands on the ground helping his two broken legs to crawl. Chuntao took the key out of her pocket, opened the gate, and led Li Mao in. She brought out a set of Xianggao's clothing. As Xianggao did for her every day, she drew two buckets of water from the well and poured it in a little bathing tub for the man to bathe. After he finished, she filled another basin with water for him to wash his face. Then she helped him to sit on the oven-bed. She also took a bath herself in the outer room.

"Chuntao, your place is kept very clean. Do you live alone?"

"There is also my partner," Chuntao answered without any hesitation.

"Are you in business?"

"Didn't I tell you it's collecting scrap paper?"

"Collecting scrap paper? How much can you make in a day doing that?"

"Don't ask about me first. You go ahead and tell me about yourself."

Chuntao poured out the bath water, came into the room combing her hair, and sat down opposite Li Mao.

Li Mao began to tell his story.

"Chuntao, oh, I can't begin to tell. I'll just give you a general idea.

"After the bandits roped me away that night, I hated them because I had lost you. I grabbed one of their rifles, killed two of them, and ran for my life. I fled to Shenyang[21] just when they were recruiting for the Border Patrol Army, and I joined up. During the three years in the army camp, I kept trying to get news from home. People all said our village had been razed to rubble. I don't know to whose hands the title deed for our land has fallen. When we ran out of the village, we just forgot to take that with us. And so I never asked for a leave to go back home for a look. I was afraid if I asked for leave, I'd even lose the soldier's pay of a few dollars every month.

"I settled down to being a soldier, looking forward to the pay every month. As for becoming an officer, at first I didn't dare to hope for that. It was just destined in my luck to run into trouble: Early last year, the colonel of our regiment issued an order saying that any man who could hit the bull's eye nine shots out of ten would get double pay every month and would also be promoted. In the whole regiment, no one ever hit the bull's eye four times in ten, and even those shots weren't right in the middle on the red dot. But I hit the red dot one time after another. I not only fired nine shots, but also wanted to fire the last one. I wanted to show off my skill. I turned my back to the target, bent down, and fired the tenth shot from between my legs. It hit the bull's eye right in the center. At the time, I was so very happy. The colonel asked that I be brought up to him. I thought I was sure to hear some praises. Unexpectedly that pig became very angry, swearing that I must have been a bandit, and wanted to shoot me. He said if I hadn't been a bandit, I wouldn't have been such a sharpshooter. My sergeant and my lieutenant both pleaded for me, guaranteeing that I wasn't a bad guy. After a lot of trouble, I was not shot, but I lost my private's rank; I wasn't even a private second class. The colonel said an officer was bound to hurt the feelings of his men sometimes. If he went to supervise the battle in the front, and if there was a crack shot like me in the ranks, and if I shot him in the back, though it would be death in the front, it wouldn't be as worthy as being killed by one's enemies. Others had nothing to say but urged me to quit the army and find some other trade.

"Not long after I was fired, the Japanese invaded Shenyang. I heard that dog of a colonel led all his troops over in surrender. When I heard it, I was so mad that I tried everything to find that lackey. I joined the Volunteer Army[22] and fought around Haicheng[23] for a few months. We gave ground slowly, retreating to the south of the Great Wall. Two months ago we were northeast of Pinggu[24] and I was on patrol duty. I ran into the enemy and was hit in both legs. I was still able to walk then and took cover behind a boulder and killed several of them. When I finally could not hold out any longer, I threw my rifle away and crawled into the paths in the fields. I waited for one day, two days, and still there was no sign of the people from the Red Cross or the people bearing the red swastika. My wounds were swelling worse and worse. I couldn't move, and, with nothing to eat or drink, I just lay there waiting to die. Luckily, a big cart came by. The man on the cart helped me into the cart and took me to a military medical tent. They wouldn't check my legs; they only put me on a truck to be sent to a rear hospital. But it was already the third day. The doctor unbundled my legs, and said they were all rotten and had to be amputated. I was in the hospital for more than a month. I recovered indeed, but without two legs. I thought I didn't have a single relative here and I couldn't go home; even if I could, how can I farm the land without any legs? I begged the hospital to keep me and give me something to do. The doctor said the hospital cures people but doesn't keep them and it's not its duty to find work for them either. This city has no soldiers' sanitarium either. I was forced to come out to beg on the streets. Today is just the third day. These couple of days I've been thinking constantly that if I went on living like this, I wouldn't be able to stand it and would surely hang myself."

Chuntao listened intently, her eyes already becoming moist at some point. Still she was silent. Li Mao paused to wipe the sweat from his forehead, taking a break.

"Chuntao, how have you been these years? Though this little place isn't as spacious as in our countryside, it looks as if you aren't suffering."

"Who's not suffering? Even if one is suffering, one still has to try to live. Even in the hall for the King of Hell, wouldn't one see any smiles? These few years, I've been trading matches for scrap paper for a living. There is also a person by the name of Liu who is my partner. The two of us share everything, you might say. We barely get by."

"You and the man named Liu live in this room together?'

"Yes, we sleep together on this oven-bed," Chuntao replied without the least hesitation, as if she had definite views on the subject for a long time.

"Then, are you married to him?"

"No, we just live together."

"Then, are you still my wife?"

"No, I'm not anybody's wife."

Li Mao's sense of his right as a husband was provoked, but he couldn't think of anything to say. His eyes were fixed on the ground, not that he wanted to look at anything, of course, but that he was a little afraid to look at his wife. Eventually, he muttered, "In that case, people would laugh at me for being a cuckold."

"Cuckold?" The woman's face hardened a bit at what he said, but her attitude was still peaceful. "Only people with money and power are afraid of being cuckolds. A man like you, who would recognize you? You live without fame and die without anyone to carry your name. How would it matter if you are a cuckold or not? Now I'm just myself, doing my own things, and would never taint you."

"But we are, after all, still a couple. As the old saying goes, one night of marriage, a hundred days of bliss . . ."

"I don't know anything about any hundred days of bliss." Chuntao interrupted Li Mao's speech. "If we talk about a hundred days of bliss, more than a dozen hundred days of bliss have passed since then. In the past four to five years, we didn't know each other's whereabouts. I suppose you never dreamed either that you'd meet me here. I was here alone. I had to live. I needed someone to help me. After living together with him all these years, as for love and affection, I naturally have very little for you. Today I brought you home because of my father's friendship with your father, and also because we come from the same village. If you claim I'm your wife, I'll deny it. Even if you take the case to court, I'm not so sure you would win."

Li Mao fumbled at the pouch in his belt[25] as if he was going to get something out of it. But then his hands suddenly stopped. Staring at Chuntao, he finally dropped his hands and propped them on the mat covering of the brick bed.

Li Mao said nothing. Chuntao wept. The shadows cast by the sun on the floor silently lengthened three to four inches during all this.

"All right, Chuntao, you call the shots. Look, I'm already crippled. Even if you are willing to be with me, I won't be able to support you." Li Mao eventually made a sensible remark.

"I can't get rid of you because you are handicapped. But I'm not willing to give him up either. Why don't we all just live here, and no one think about who's supporting whom, all right?" Chuntao, too, spoke the words that were in her heart.

Li Mao's stomach rumbled faintly.

"Oh, here we have been talking all this time and I haven't even asked you what you'd like to eat. You must be terribly hungry."

"Just anything. I'll eat anything that is available. I haven't eaten since last night. I had only some water."

"I'll go buy something." As Chuntao stepped out of the house, Xianggao entered the courtyard gaily. They bumped right into each other under the arbor. "What are you happy about? Why are you home this early?"

"I made a bunch of good deals today! In the load you carried home yesterday in the basket, when I opened it to look this morning, I found a packet of some Ming Dynasty petitions sent to the Emperor of China by the King of Korea. One is worth at least fifty dollars. We have ten of them in our hands! I just took a few down to the exchange to see what the buyers would offer and then I'll distribute these later. In the load there were also two sheets of paper bearing the stamps of the Emperor's Office. The experts say they belong to the Song Dynasty and their initial offer is already sixty dollars. But I didn't dare to sell; I'm afraid of selling it too cheap. I have brought them back for you as eye-openers. Look . . ." As he spoke, he untied the old blue cloth sack and took out the petitions and some old paper. "This is the seal from the Emperor's Office." He pointed at the stamped imprint on the paper.

"Without that mark, I really couldn't see anything good about this paper. Fine foreign paper is even whiter than this. How come the palace official lords are as blind as I am?" Though she was looking at it, Chuntao did not understand how it was worth money.

"Blind? If they weren't a little blind, how could people like us earn a couple of dollars now and then?" Xianggao took the paper and put it back together with the petitions in the bundle. Smiling, he said to Chuntao, "I say, wife . . ."

Chuntao gave him a look. "I told you not to call me wife."

Xianggao ignored her and said: "You happen to come home early, too. Business must be not bad."

"This morning I bought another basketful like yesterday's."

"Didn't you say there was a lot more?"

"They sent it all to the Morning Market and sold them to the countryside for peanut bags!"

"It doesn't matter. We've had a very good start today anyway. It's the first time we've done a business of more than thirty dollars. Say, it is rare we're both home together in the afternoon. Later let's go take a walk by the Ten Monastery Lake to cool off, all right?"

He went into the house and put his bundle on the table. Chuntao followed him in. She said, "We can't. We have a visitor today." Raising the door curtain of the inner room, she nodded to Xianggao. "Go on in."

He walked in, Chuntao following him. "This is my former husband, " she said, and then introduced Li Mao to Xianggao. "This is my helper."

The eyes of the two men met. If the pupils of both men's eyes had been equally apart, the lines of vision would have been linked in a parallel. Neither man spoke. Even the two flies resting on the windowsill were silent. Thus the shadows cast by the sun again moved one or two inches in silence.

"Your last name, please?" Xianggao had to ask for the sake of formality, though obviously he knew it.

They began to chat.

"I must go buy a little food," said Chuntao then to Xianggao. "I suppose you haven't eaten either. Will griddle cakes be all right?"

"I've eaten. You stay home. I'll go buy them."

Chuntao pulled Xianggao and sat him on the brick bed, saying, "You stay home to chat with the guest." Smiling at them, she went out.

Now there were only two men in the room. In a situation like this, they could either like one another as if they had been old friends or they would have to fight with each other to death. Fortunately, they chose to go with the former. But we should not think that since Li Mao had lost his legs he could not fight. We must remember that Xianggao had been wielding only a pen the past three to five years. Li Mao could easily have crushed him to death with his weight. If he had a gun, it would have been even easier. One crook of the trigger and Xianggao would have crossed the Bridge to the Nether World.

Li Mao told Xianggao that Chuntao's father was a landowner in the countryside, one who had about ten acres of land. His own father worked for her family and drove the donkey cart. Because Li Mao was a crack shot, Chuntao's father was afraid that he would go off to become a soldier, and therefore married his daughter to him, the purpose being that he would protect the people in the village. All these things, Chuntao had never told Xianggao before. Li Mao then told him of the conversation he had just had with Chuntao, and the talk gradually came around to the question that had immediate concern to both of them.

"Now that you, husband and wife, are reunited, I should leave," said Xianggao reluctantly.

"No. I've been away from her for so long, and, since I'm also a cripple now, I'm not able to support her. It wouldn't be any use. You've lived together all these years. Why break up? I could go to a home for the disabled. I hear there's one here. I can get in if I have some connections."

This surprised Xianggao greatly. He thought, although Li Mao had been a rough soldier, unexpectedly he had such chivalry. Yet even though his heart agreed with Li Mao, his mouth had to refuse. This is the courteous hypocrisy that is well known to all those who have read some books.

"There is no such thing," replied Xianggao. "I'm not willing to be condemned as a wife-stealer. And, thinking about it from your point of view, you wouldn't let your wife live with another man, either."

"I'll write a paper to disown her as a wife, or I'll write you a bill of sale. Either way will do," Li Mao said sincerely with a smile.

"Disown her? She hasn't done anything wrong; you can't disown her. I don't want her to lose face. Buy her? Where do I get the money to buy her? Whatever money I have is hers."

"I don't want money."

"Then, what do you want?"

"I don't want anything."

"Then why write a bill of sale?"

"Because if we just agree verbally you won't have any proof. It wouldn't be good if I have regrets later. We must first take care of our self interests, and then we can be gentlemen later."

Just then, Chuntao returned with the sesame seed griddle cakes she had bought. Seeing the two men talking together so agreeably, she was very happy in her heart.

"Lately I've been thinking a lot about finding another person to help us. It happens that Brother Mao has showed up. He can't walk, is just right to manage the house and sort through the paper. You can be out there selling things. I'll still do the collecting. The three of us will open a company." Chuntao had her own ideas.

Li Mao did not stand on ceremony but picked up a sesame seed griddle cake and put it in his mouth, as if he had just come back from the world of the starving ghosts. He had no time to talk.

"Two men and a woman form a company? And you put up the capital?" Xianggao asked needlessly.

"Are you unwilling?"

"No, no, no. I didn't mean anything." Xianggao was thinking about something, but he couldn't bring himself to say it.

"What can I do? When I sit at home all day, what can I get done?" Li Mao was also a bit afraid to consent. He understood Xianggao's hint.

"You both just take it easy. I have some ideas."

Hearing this, Xianggao moistened his lips with his tongue and swallowed once. Li Mao was still eating, but his eyes were fixed on Chuntao. He was waiting to hear her ideas.

Collecting scrap paper was probably an occupation the woman was devoted to. She had already in her mind assigned Li Mao to pick the old stamps and cigarette-pack wraps out of the paper at home. That could be done as long as one could see and had hands. She calculated that if Li Mao could find a hundred and several dozen odd cigarette pack wraps every day, that would cover the cost of his food. If every day he could also find even two or three good and rare stamps, that would not be bad. About ten thousand packs of foreign cigarettes were sold in Beijing daily. It would not be too hard for her to collect one percent of all the wraps. As for Xianggao, he would still concentrate on looking for letters of famous people or things that would sell better than stamps and wraps. Needless to say, he was already an expert, and needed no further guidance. She herself would do the heavy work. Unless there was a heavy rain, she would go out to collect paper, regardless of the burning sun or the sweeping wind. She would want to especially work during foul weather, because some of her competitors would then stay home.

Glancing at the sun through the window, she knew it was not yet two o'clock. She went to the outer room and put on her battered straw hat. Putting her head through the door, she said to Xianggao: "I still have to find out whether there's anything else being thrown out of the palace. You look after him at home. When I come back tonight, we'll discuss it again."

Xianggao could not stop her, so he let her go.

Several days went by in silence. But two men and one woman sleeping on one brick oven bed of course was very awkward. The institution of polygamy after all does not have too many adherents in the world, one of the reasons being that the average man cannot rid himself of his primitive concepts regarding his rights as a husband or father. It is from these concepts that our customs and moral codes are created. To be frank, in our society, only the parasites and exploiters observe the so-called customs and traditions; people who have to rely on their ability for a living actually do not have much respect for them in their hearts. Take Chuntao for instance. She was neither a matron nor a fashionable young lady. She would not go to a dance in the Building of Foreign Ministry, nor would she have any opportunity to play the hostess at a grand ceremony. No one judged or questioned her conduct. Even if they did, it would not hurt her deeply. Only the local policeman was checking on her, but he was quite easy to handle. And the two men? Though Xianggao had a bit of schooling and had some vague ideas of the precepts of the ancient feudal philosophers, he was not much different from Chuntao, except for some ideas about one's status. But his life, after he started to live with Chuntao, completely depended on her. Chuntao's words were vitamins going into his ears, which he must listen to because it was to his benefit.

Chuntao told him not to be jealous, so he would have to eliminate even the seeds of jealousy. As for Li Mao, if Chuntao and Xianggao would let him live there for one day, he would then live for one day. If they were willing to treat him as a relative, he would be quite satisfied. Being a soldier, one would always lose a wife or two. So Li Mao's problem was also one of reputation.

Nevertheless, although Xianggao was not jealous, many other disturbing things kept coming between the two men.

The summer days were still stiflingly hot, but Chuntao and Xianggao were not the sort of people to go to vacation resorts like Tangshan or Beidaihe. They had to go on making their living during the day. At home, Li Mao was beginning to learn the trade. He could already distinguish between which paper should be sent to Wan Liu Hall or Tian Ning Temple[26] to make rough paper and which he should keep for Xianggao to come home and appraise.

When Chuntao came home, as usual it was still Xianggao who waited on her. One day it was already late. When she smelled incense burning in the outer room, she called out to Xianggao under the arbor: "When did we ever burn mosquito-repellent incense? If you aren't careful, it'll be a wonder if the house doesn't burn down."

Before Xianggao made a reply, Li Mao said: "We aren't trying to drive away the mosquitoes. We are just purifying the air. I asked Brother Xianggao to light it for me. I plan to sleep on the floor in the outer room. It's too hot inside. With three people sleeping together, it's really uncomfortable."

"Say, whose red card is it on the table this time?" Chuntao picked it up to have a look.

"We talked it over today. You belong to Xianggao. That's the contract of sale." The voice came from the brick bed.

"Oh, you were discussing how to settle me! But I cannot let you boss me!" She walked in the inner room with the red card in her hand, asking Li Mao, "Was this your idea, or his?"

"It's our idea. Otherwise, I would be sad, and he would also be sad."

"You've talked and talked and it is still the same old thing. Don't either of you think we are husband and wife, all right?"

She tore the card to pieces and was breathing a little hard.

"How much did you sell me for?"

"I wrote down less than a hundred just for the luck of it. If one gives a wife away for nothing, he is good for nothing."

"But if he sells her, is he good for something?" She walked out to Xianggao and said, "You've got money now and can afford to buy a wife. If you were a little richer . . ."

"Don't talk like that, don't talk like that," Xianggao stopped her. "Chuntao, you don't understand. The last couple of days, the people in the trade have been just laughing at me—"

"What are they laughing about?"

"About . . ." Xianggao could not say it. As a matter of fact, he did not have a mind of his own. Nine cases out of ten, he did whatever Chuntao wanted him to do. Even he himself did not understand what power she had. Behind her back, he was thinking that this should be done in such way and that should be done according to his will. But as soon as he saw her, he was like the last Qing emperor meeting his mother, and had to do everything according to her order.

"Oh, so you've gone to school for a couple of days, and you are afraid to be cursed and laughed at."

From ancient times on, what really has ruled the people does not seem to be saints' teachings, but only whips that beat people and tongues that curse people. Curses and blows are what have maintained our customs. But in Chuntao's heart, she already seemed to have the attitude of "a curse for a curse, a blow for a blow." She was no weakling, and she did not beat or curse anyone, but she would not be beaten or cursed either. Let's just hear how she scolded Xianggao and we'll see.

"If anyone laughs at you, why wouldn't you hit him? What are you afraid of? What we do is nobody's business."

Xianggao did not speak.

"Let's not talk about this any more. Let's the three of us go on living as we have. Isn't that all right?"

The whole house was quiet. After supper, Xianggao and Chuntao sat beneath the arbor as usual, only they were not as talkative as they used to be. They did not talk even about their business.

Li Mao called Chuntao into the house, trying to persuade her to become Xianggao's wife. He said she did not understand a man's heart. No man wanted to be a cuckold; nor was wife-stealer a good name. Taking from his waistband a red card that had already turned dark brown, he handed it to Chuntao, saying: "This is our marriage certificate. When we fled that night, I took it from the shrine and put it in my shirt. Now you can take it and then consider us not a couple."

Chuntao accepted the card from him without a word, staring only at the torn mat covering of the bed. She helplessly sat down near the handicapped man, saying: "Mao, I cannot accept this. You take it back. I'm still your wife. One night of marriage, a hundred days of bliss. I cannot do something morally wrong. Am I still a human being if I throw you out when I see that you cannot walk and do heavy work?"

She placed the red card on the brick bed.

Hearing what she said, Li Mao was deeply moved. He said to Chuntao in a low voice: "I see that you like him a great deal, so I think it would be better for you to live with him. When we have a little money, you can send me back to the country, or to a home for disabled soldiers."

"To be frank with you," Chuntao replied in a low voice, "these years we've been living together just like a couple; everything was fine and all was well. If he were to go, I wouldn't be willing to let him. It would be better to ask him to come in to talk, and see what ideas he has." She called from the window, "Xianggao, Xianggao." But there was not a sound. When she came out to look, Xianggao was not there anymore. This was the first time he had ever gone out at night. Staring for a moment, she then called toward the house: "I'm going to look for him."

She expected Xianggao to go no other place. So she went to the lane's entrance to ask Old Wu. But Old Wu said that he went over to the main street. She went to all of his usual haunts, but Xianggao was nowhere to be found. It was very easy to lose a person. Once a person was out of sight, the world would be a place too vast to search. It was almost one o'clock when she returned home.

The oil lamp in the room was already extinguished.

"Are you asleep? Has Xianggao come back yet?" She went in the house and took out a match to light the lamp. Looking at the brick bed, she saw that Li Mao had hanged himself from the window lattice. He had used his own belt. Although she had in her heart the natural panic and fear of a female, she had the courage to get up there and untie the belt to lower him. Fortunately, the time had been short and it was not necessary to call others for help. As she gently touched him, he gradually came around.

Taking one's own life for the sake of others is the spirit of a knight. If Li Mao still had his two legs, he would not have had to resort to such a measure. Yet for two or three days he had felt that he did not have much hope, and it would be better to destroy himself and let Chuntao live well. Although Chuntao did not love him, she had a strong sense of duty to him. She comforted him with many words until the sky turned light. When he fell asleep, she got down off the brick bed and saw on the floor some charred ashes and the remains of a red card. She recognized them as the marriage certificate that Li Mao wanted to give her. She stared at it in a daze.

All that day, she did not go out the door. In the evening she sat on the brick bed to keep Li Mao company.

"Why are you crying?" she asked him when she saw Li Mao's tears rolling down.

"I'm unfair to you. What did I come here for?"

"Nobody is complaining about your coming here."

"Now he's gone, and I have no legs. . . ."

"You mustn't think like that. I think he'll come back."

"I hope he comes back."

Thus another day passed. When Chuntao got up, she picked a couple of cucumbers from the arbor for a dish. She made a big griddle cake without much care, and brought it with the cucumbers to the inner room for them both to eat.

As usual, she donned her battered straw hat and put the basket on her back.

"You are not too happy today; don't go out," Li Mao said to her through the window.

"It's even more depressing to sit around the house."

Slowly she walked out of the gate. Working was in her nature. Even though her heart was depressed, she still wanted to work. The Chinese woman seems to care only about living but not about love. Life is what she pays attention to. Love is only the agitation inside in her purposeless and depressed state of mind. Naturally, love is only a feeling, whereas life is tangible. The art of talking learnedly of love while reclining in a silken net or sitting in a secluded wood is a knowledge brought over on the ocean liners of queens and presidents. Chuntao had never been a sailor treading waves or a student in a school run by blue-eyed foreigners. She did not understand love and could only feel inexplicably confused.

She passed one lane and then there was another. Endless dust and endless roads engulfed the downcast woman. She sometimes called out, "Matches for scrap paper!" Yet at times she did not even collect from the roadside a pile of newspaper for which she did not have to trade. Sometimes when she was supposed to give two boxes of matches in exchange, Chuntao gave five. After muddling through the day, she returned home along with the black-cloaked ravens, which were good for nothing but cawing loudly and fighting for food. At the gate she saw the newly pasted residents' identification card, on which were written the residents' names as Liu Xianggao and his wife Mrs. Liu. This made her heart more depressed.

Just as she stepped into the yard, Xianggao hurried out of the house.

She stared, saying only: "You are back . . ." Her speech was continued with tears.

"I can't leave you. Everything I have, I owe it to you. I know you want me to help you. I cannot be ungrateful and cold-hearted," Xianggao said. In fact, for two days he had been wandering the streets, not knowing where to go. When he was walking, his feet seemed to be fettered with a heavy iron chain, the other end of which was fastened to Chuntao's hand. To make things worse, he saw everywhere the cigarette ad "Still This Is Better" and his feelings were stirred more constantly, so that he did not even know when he was hungry.

"I have already talked it over with Xianggao. He is the resident in charge. I'm the live-in."

Xianggao helped her lower the basket as usual, at the same time wiping the tears from her face. "If we go back to the country," he said, "Li Mao will be the resident-in-charge and I'll be the live-in. You are our wife."

She did not speak anymore but went into the house, hung up her hat, and took her ritual bath.

Once again the business talk began under the arbor. They decided that after they sold the paper from the Imperial Palace, they would set up a booth for Xianggao in the public market, or perhaps they could find a somewhat better house in which to live.

Inside the house, a moth, flying into the house from the arbor, snuffed out the oil lamp's tiny flame. Li Mao was fast asleep, for the Milky Way was already low in the sky.

"Let's go to sleep, too," said the woman.

"You go lie down first. I'll massage your legs in a while."

"It isn't necessary. I didn't walk very far today. We have to get up early tomorrow. Don't forget to take care of that business. We haven't been doing business for days."

"Say, I forgot to give it to you. On the way home today, I made a special trip to the Tianqiao Market and bought you a hat that's practically new. Look!" He groped for the hat in the dark, and wanted to hand it to her.

"How can I see it now? I'll wear it tomorrow."

The yard became all quiet. Only the scent of the tuberoses wafted in the air. In the room the dialogue of "Wife" and "I don't want to hear it; I'm not your wife" could scarcely be heard.

NOTES

1. Chuntao—The two Chinese characters in her given name mean "Spring Peach"; it is a very common name, possibly because of its youthful and beautiful connotations.

2. Zongbu Lane—a street in Beijing where foreign embassies used to be housed.

3. This sentence indicates an old belief a lot of Chinese had about beef and milk, that one would smell if one consumed beef and dairy products.

4. Zhuozhou County—a county in Hebei Province, not very far from Beijing.

5. Desheng Gate—Literally, it means "Victory Gate," a gate in Beijing's old city wall that still existed at the time of the story.

6. ". . . comparable to the romance of a couple of mandarin ducks"—Mandarin ducks are believed to be extremely faithful in their love affairs. When two mandarin ducks are "in love" and separated for whatever reason, they are believed never to form another couple again.

7. Tianqiao Market—A big business district in Beijing that used to include people of all trades, but was mostly a market for the poor.

8. "Old Li in the small market"—The small market refers to a market in an obscure location and is mentioned in comparison to greater places, such as big stores or decent hotels.

9. ". . . the local matchmakers could easily have passed her off as a young widow of twenty-three or twenty-four, still worth at least a hundred dollars or eighty"—It was not uncommon at that time to sell oneself into a marriage, especially in the case of desperate young women from the countryside.

10. Houmen Arch—It means the *back door* in Chinese.

11. Shenwu Gate of the Palace—The palace is the Forbidden City in the center of Beijing.

12. ". . . a big pile of red and yellow paper"—Those two colors were often exclusively reserved for the use of the emperor or his immediate family.

13. Using foreign newspapers as wrapping paper was probably an indication of the adoration for foreign things at that time in China.

14. Donghua Gate of the Palace—one of the side doors of the Forbidden City.

15. "Brick oven-bed"—In northern China, beds were often made of bricks with a special oven underneath to keep them warm in cold weather.

16. ". . . a humorous painting of Eight Fairies"—The Eight Fairies are eight legendary figures in Chinese folklore. They have some whimsical and distinguishing habits, features, and special abilities, and there are many interesting stories about their adventures.

17. "Still This Is Better"—This was an advertisement for the Camel Cigarette Company in China.

18. Rui Fu Xiang—a high-priced fashion store in Beijing.

19. Ten Monastery Lake—a park in Beijing.

20. "Brother Mao"—Notice how she is addressing her husband and the distance now between them, because one calls only a friend "brother" in Chinese culture.

21. Shenyang—an industrial city in the Northeast of China, which was Manchuria.

22. The Volunteer Army—It was an army organized by the people in the Northeast of China to fight against the invading Japanese after the Nationalist troops had withdrawn from the whole Manchurian area under the order of Chiang Kai-shek.

23. Haicheng—a county in the northeast province of Liaoning.

24. Pinggu—a county not far from Beijing, now a distant suburb of Beijing.

25. "the pouch in his belt"—It was a habit for cautious Chinese to sew or wrap a pouch in their cloth waistband to keep money and valuable things.

26. "Wan Liu Hall or Tian Ning Temple"—two paper mills in Beijing.

BIBLIOGRAPHY

Hsia, C. T. *A History of Modern Chinese Fiction*. New Haven, CT: Yale University Press, 1971.

Xu, Dishan. "Spring Peach." *Literature* (Wen Xue) 3.1 (1934): 56–68.

Zeng, Qingrui, and Zhao Xiaqiu, Eds. *Notes on 240 Writers in Modern Chinese Fiction*. Guilin, Guangxi: Lijiang (Lijiang Chubanshe), 1985.

Zhao, Xiaqiu, and Zeng Qingrui. *A History of Modern Chinese Literature*. Beijing: Chinese People's University Press, 1984.

CHAPTER 5

"The Class Teacher"
(Ban Zhuren)

Liu Xinwu (1942–)

Introduction to the Author

Liu Xinwu was born on June 4, 1942, in the city of Chengdu in the southwest province of Sichuan. He was the youngest of the five children in the family. In the most difficult years of the Anti-Japanese War, his parents were like the rest of the nation in their desperate efforts to survive the economic hardships. Because of family hardships, he was almost aborted by his mother, who was already trying hard to raise four other children. This Liu Xinwu tells without much bitterness in a 1984 magazine article.

When he was eight years old, in 1950, he moved with his parents to Beijing, the capital of the newly founded People's Republic of China, because his father was relocated there. He started writing in high school and some of his works were published when he was just sixteen. After high school, he took the college entrance examination and was accepted by Beijing Teachers' Training School, now known as Beijing Normal College. At nineteen, fresh out of the training school, he began teaching at Beijing Number Thirteen High School, where he would remain a teacher for many years to come.

While he was teaching high school, he continued writing until the outbreak of the Cultural Revolution in the mid-1960s. But what he wrote during this period was insignificant and not representative of his talent, which was revealed in later, more mature works. His writing came to a halt after the outbreak of the Cultural Revolution, which violently disrupted and discontinued normal life in China for ten years. Although he was not persecuted during the Cultural Revolution (1966–1976), he came close to being a victim of the massive upheavals and the anarchist student movement because of some short newspaper articles that he wrote at the time.

It was after 1976, when the Cultural Revolution ended, that he started writing stories and novellas of some importance. In 1977, he published "The Class Teacher," a short story that shocked the nation and attracted a great number of readers. This story, along with a story called "The Scar" by Lu Xinhua, started the literary school known as the Scar Literature. The major theme or purpose in the works of this school was to reveal the mental distortion, spiritual damage, and social disorder brought to the whole nation by the ultra-leftist Communist leaders of the country after 1956, especially in the years of the Cultural Revolution.

After he published "The Class Teacher," his writing flourished and many of his stories, novellas, and novels gradually were published. He left his teaching job and became an editor, first at the literary magazine *October* and later at the most prestigious, if not the most liberal, literary magazine, *People's Literature*. Before the crackdown on the student movement in 1989, he had become the editor-in-chief of *People's Literature*. But he was fired soon after he made public his support for the student movement. Although he still writes and publishes a great deal, nothing he creates now is as sensational and overwhelming as "The Class Teacher," partly because of the present restrictions for writers under the tight control of the government and partly because, as I noted in the introduction, written literature in China has been gradually but steadily losing its popularity and audience to television and films.

"The Class Teacher" has proven difficult for me to translate. Its language is politically charged and its tone is unmistakably didactic. Some expressions in the story simply have no equivalents in the English language, and there are whole paragraphs that sound like political lectures. Some patience may help in reading this important story. I only hope that the odd juxtaposition of words in this translation will serve to remind us that, even though the story was a breakthrough in Chinese fiction at the time, it was heavily influenced by the political language created by the government.

The Class Teacher

[1978]

1

Would you like to meet a young hooligan and spend every day with him? I think you surely would not like it. You might even blamefully question why I raise such a strange question.

But, in the office of the Communist Party Branch of Guangming Middle School, when the dark and slim but sturdy Branch Secretary Old Cao looked with trust at Zhang Junshi, the class teacher[1] of Junior High Grade Three Class Three, and raised the same question in a different way, Teacher Zhang did not find it odd or strange. He only thought about it very seriously for about a minute, and then answered firmly, "All right! I am willing to make his acquaintance. . . ."

It was like this: A few days earlier, the Public Safety Bureau[2] released Song Baoqi, a young hooligan, from a detention center. He had been arrested because he was involved in a gang criminal activity. But during the questioning, facing the great power of the proletarian dictatorship[3] and under the influence of its policy, he sweated all over and his lips trembled as he made a fairly thorough confession and also informed the bureau about the key crimes committed by the leader of the gang. So, with special consideration for his case, the Public Safety Bureau released him after educating him, because his crime was not serious, his confession and information were fairly good, and, besides, he was not yet even sixteen. Feeling that it would be hard to be around old neighbors any longer, his parents therefore moved by chance to the area of Guangming Middle School by means of trading their residence with some other people.[4] According to the method used in the last few years of "going to a school nearby," his parents applied to have him transferred to Guangming Middle School. Song was of the age to join Junior High Grade Three, and Junior High Grade Three Class Three happened to have a vacancy. In addition, Teacher Zhang had more than ten years of experience as a class teacher and was the only Party member among all the class teachers in this grade. So, after the Party Branch Committee discussed it, they accepted Song Baoqi's transfer request. Old Cao was delegated to find Teacher Zhang and tell him directly the situation, so he asked him: "How about it? Would you please accept Song Baoqi?"

Just as you already know, as soon as his pensive eyes met Old Cao's eyes, which were filled with expectation and encouragement, Teacher Zhang agreed.

2

What kind of person is Teacher Zhang?

Let's take a closer look at him as he cycles toward the Public Safety Bureau in the dusty spring wind to find out more about Song Baoqi.

Teacher Zhang could not have been more ordinary. He was thirty-six years old, of medium height, and slightly overweight. His clothes were obviously old but clean and tidy, with every button done up neatly; even the collar clips of the jacket[5] were flawlessly fastened. His face was oval; he had three rather deep wrinkles on his forehead; his eyes could not be said to be big, but they could look at a person with a shine. Students who lied were especially afraid of his eyes looking at them that way. But what students feared and admired the most was his mouth. People always say that thin lips could talk, but Teacher Zhang had a pair of thick lips, which were often dried into cracks by the wind in spring or winter. The words spilling out from this pair of thick lips were always so warm, lively, and fluent. Like a seed planter that would never rust, he sowed in the heart of the students seeds of revolutionary thoughts and knowledge. Also like a big broom, he endlessly and mercilessly swept away the dust on the hearts of the students. . . .

All the way to the Public Safety Bureau, Teacher Zhang's facial expression seemed quite calm. Only after he heard descriptions of the comrades in the Public Safety Bureau and thumbed through the files did his face show a strong expression—it was hard to describe. It was neither complete anger, nor without disgust and scorn. But gradually a determination seemed to have the upper hand, even though his concern and gloominess were still perceptible.

It was already three o'clock in the afternoon when Teacher Zhang returned to the school from the Public Safety Bureau. Wiping the sweat from his forehead with a neatly folded handkerchief, he walked into the office for the teachers of his grade. It was obvious that all the teachers in his group knew that Song Baoqi was to join his class the following day. Mathematics teacher Yin Dalei was the first to meet him and thus created the first ripple about Song Baoqi.

3

Teacher Yin and Teacher Zhang were the same age. Graduating from the same teacher's college, they were assigned at the same time to teach at Guangming Middle School. Often they taught the same grade. They had always been frank with each other. Even when they had an argument, they would never resort to insinuation or underhandedness. Instead, they would pour it all out at once, leaving nothing to hide.

Teacher Yin was slender in build, and his features were pinched close to each other, thus unavoidably giving him a childish face. It was only the thick glasses for nearsightedness on his nose that enabled him to maintain his dignity as a mature person in front of his students.

This was the spring of 1977. Teacher Yin felt in his heart a patch of splendid sunshine. He was filled with bright hopes for the future education of the country, for his own school, for the courses he was teaching, and for his classes. He felt that all irrational things should and could be reshaped rapidly. He believed that, as the Gang of Four had been arrested, it should not take very long to clear away the poisonous residue left by the Gang of Four in the educational system and thus create the ideal environment therein. But lately he had been a bit less patient. He wanted everything to be as smooth as floating down a spring river on a fast boat, but never did he expect that there would still be a series of problems to deal with.

As soon as he heard the news that Song Baoqi was about to "descend" upon them, he could not help burning with indignation. Once Teacher Zhang stepped into the office, he poured out all his "bewilderment" to his longtime colleague. Standing face to face with Teacher Zhang, he questioned: "Why did you accept it? Right now, when the situation our whole grade faces is to diligently work on the quality of teaching, you bring in a little hooligan and dig yourself into the hole of working with him individually. Where can you find the energy to work on the quality of teaching? Even worse, you could even have 'the one dropping of a mouse ruin the whole pot of porridge.' Oh, why didn't you think about it with a cool head before you agreed? It is really impossible to understand. . . ."

Some teachers in the office agreed with the views of Teacher Yin, but did not like his harsh attitude; some did not agree with his views, but nonetheless felt that he spoke them out of good will. Some were not sure what to think, but had sympathy and compassion, seeing that Teacher Zhang was, out of the blue, placed with such a heavy load. . . . Therefore, although all of them stood or sat watching Teacher Zhang, no one spoke for the moment. Even the fake ears used in biology-hygiene classes seemed to stretch up taller than usual to wait attentively for Teacher Zhang's answer.

Teacher Zhang felt that Teacher Yin's views were certainly a bit radical, but he nonetheless thought that there was some truth in what he said. He pondered silently for a minute, answered as if in defense: "There is no reason at the present to send Song Baoqi back to the Public Safety Bureau; nor is there any need to let him go back to his original school. Since I am the teacher of a class, then, if he comes, I will start to work with him. . . ."

These are indeed plain and flavorless words. Had he overbearingly rebuked Teacher Yin, an explosive argument might have been ignited. But, unexpectedly, he made a reply like that. Teacher Yin, instead, seemed to have acquiesced. Other teachers were also quite touched, and some even could not help but ask themselves secretly: "What would I think if Song Baoqi were assigned to my class?"

Teacher Zhang should really have started his work right away, because, right at that moment, the Youth League Secretary in his class, Xie Huimin, came to look for him.

4

Xie Huimin was taller than most boys. She always kept her back straight, appearing healthy and strong. One time, when she walked by outside the fence of the Amateur Athletic School, she caught the attention of the basketball coach at his first glance. The coach invited her in warmly, thinking for sure that he had discovered a hard-to-find athlete to build up. Unbeknownst to him, this girl with an oval face and big eyes was unusually disappointing after she tried to run up to shoot the basket—it turned out that she could hardly jump and that the joints in her wrist and elbow also seemed too stiff. Upon questioning, she did not have any interest in playing any ball games.

Indeed, Xie Huimin almost did not have any hobbies other than going to the movies and singing the periodically recommended songs[6] with the others. Her grades were average, and sometimes her homework was not done on time, largely due to the energy and time taken up by her social work[7]—thus she was understandably forgiven by her teachers and classmates.

Last summer, when Teacher Zhang took over as the class teacher, Xie Huimin was already the Youth League Secretary. Not long after, it was time for this class to go to the countryside to learn from the farmers.[8] On the day when they returned from the countryside and when they were already two li[9] away from the village, Xie Huimin suddenly discovered that a boy was twirling a head of wheat in his hand. She rushed over with surprise and anger to criticize him: "How could you take away the wheat of the poor and lower-middle-class peasants? Give it to me! It should be sent back!" That boy, unconvinced, retorted: "I want to take it home to let my parents have a look, and let them know how well the wheat here is growing." Thus a dispute resulted, with the majority of the students siding against Xie Huimin. Some said that she was single-minded, and others said that she went too far. Eventually, it was naturally Teacher Zhang's turn to speak his mind. Her hands firmly clutching the head of wheat and her mouth slightly open, Xie Huimin looked at Teacher Zhang with hope. To the surprise of many students, Teacher Zhang agreed with Xie Huimin's plea to send the wheat back. Hearing the sounds of many loud arguments and whispered disputes and looking at the distinctive figure of Xie Huimin rushing back to the village on the wet and muddy road after the rain, Teacher Zhang, touched by her action, was thinking: The question is not whether the little head of wheat should be dealt with this way; look, the Youth League Secretary who assumed her post three months ago was protecting the belief to "never let the poor middle peasants suffer the loss of even one grain of wheat." She possessed such a precious and shining quality.

But, after that and until the Gang of Four was ousted, thick clouds covered the vast landscape of our country. The shadows of the clouds were naturally cast on the small Junior High Grade Three Class Three. The city's Youth League Committee, controlled by the sinister female member of the Gang of Four, already sent to Guangming Middle School a liaison, was said to have come to cultivate some "role models." Whether to target Junior High Grade Three Class Three was already under consideration. Naturally Xie Huimin was constantly asked to have a talk with them. However, Xie Huimin could not thoroughly understand their "teachings," because she did not have the slightest opportunistic mentality; she was innocent and honest. But, from then on, there appeared to be some kind of seemingly unexplainable conflict between Teacher Zhang and Xie Huimin. For example, Xie Huimin came to report on some students, saying that when the Youth League was having a function, two out of the five League members were dozing off. Teacher Zhang did not criticize the two misbehaving League members; instead, he suggested to Xie Huimin: "Why should the

Youth League function always be reading newspapers? Next time, wouldn't it be all right to have a mountain-climbing competition? I guarantee that they will not doze off!" Xie Huimin stared with her eyes wide open, hardly believing her own ears. Only after a little while did she protest: "Mountain climbing, what League activity is that? We were reading the articles criticizing Song Jiang . . ."[10] For another example, one day it was as hot as the inside of a food steamer. When the class was over, the girls ran to the windows to get some fresh air. Teacher Zhang pulled Xie Huimin aside, looked her up and down, and said: "Why are you still wearing a long-sleeved shirt? You should set an example by changing into a short-sleeved shirt. And, it would be only right for you girls to wear skirts!" Although Xie Huimin was puffing for air in the heat, her face turned red all over in surprise. She could not comprehend what kind of lifestyle Teacher Zhang was promoting! In the whole class, only Shi Hong, the League committee member in charge of propaganda, wore a short-sleeved shirt with the pattern of little scattered flowers and also a kind of pleated short skirt. All this, to Xie Huimin, was the manifestation of having been "tainted by the lifestyle of the bourgeoisie."

After the Gang of Four was ousted, all the conflicts between Teacher Zhang and Xie Huimin naturally could be explained clearly, but they had not all been eliminated.

Now Xie Huimin had come to Teacher Zhang, reporting to him: "All the students in our class know that Song Baoqi is coming. Some boys say that he was the so-called 'Number Four in Caishikou'[11] and was particularly ferocious. Some girls are frightened and say that if Song Baoqi came tomorrow for real, they would not come to school!"

Teacher Zhang was startled. He had not expected all this. Now that these things had happened, he felt he especially needed the cooperation of the Youth League committee. So he asked Xie Huimin: "Are you afraid? What do you say we should do?"

Xie Huimin shook her short ponytail and said: "What am I afraid of? This is class struggle! If he dares to get crazy, we will fight against him!"

Teacher Zhang's heart was suddenly warmed. For a moment, the figure that rushed along the muddy country road jumped into his memory. He said to Xie Huimin amicably: "Go get all the people on the Youth League committee and the class committee.[12] Let's have a cadre meeting in our classroom!"

5

At about four twenty, the meeting for the cadres was over. All the other cadres had left. In the classroom only Teacher Zhang, Xie Huimin, and Shi Hong remained.

Shi Hong sat directly facing the window, and the afternoon sun was shining on her round face, making her red cheeks even rosier; her cheek rested against the hand holding a pen, her eyes wide open, the shining pupils floating around slowly, and her full chin slightly raised. This was the expression that her math teacher liked and was familiar with when she thought up an even more clever solution to a math problem. Presently, however, she was not trying to solve a math problem; she was pondering on how to write the "bugle poem"[13] that would greet the class—including Song Baoqi—early next morning.

Teacher Zhang and Xie Huimin were talking to each other near her. The work to be done to receive Song Baoqi had all been assigned. The boy cadres went to talk to the boys, telling them that Song Baoqi was not the so-called "hero" who put Caishikou in awe, but a person who made mistakes and needed help. They should be neither curious nor awestruck, and they should not discriminate against him either. All of them should work together for the common goal of helping him. The cadre girls would divide themselves up and go talk to those girls who announced that they would not come to school the next day due to either a lack of courage or a sense of defiance. They would explain clearly to their parents that the school would guarantee that the girls would not be bullied by Song Baoqi. For a hooligan like Song Baoqi, passively avoiding him could only encourage his bad habits. Only when the students were united and stood up to fight against him and educate him could anything harmful be rendered harmless, and, furthermore, be gradually made beneficial. Teacher Zhang himself wanted to visit Song Baoqi's home, gather some initial information about him and his family, and conduct the first talk on ideology.[14]

When Shi Hong's poem was about finished, the talk between Teacher Zhang and Xie Huimin was also about over. Teacher Zhang gathered together several items on the desk that had been shown to the cadres. These were things Teacher Zhang brought over from the Public Safety Bureau, found on Song Baoqi when he was arrested: a bicycle lock that was used for fighting, a deck of cards that were torn and greasy, a chromed cigarette box that had a built-in lighter, and a novel without its covers. The little cadre members winced and twitched their mouths at those items in disgust. Xie Huimin suggested: "Tomorrow the Youth League committee should organize an on-site meeting. The active students could also participate. These items should be displayed and criticized without mercy." All agreed to that, and Teacher Zhang also nodded, saying: "Good. We should make use of this opportunity and further our education against corruption."

Unexpectedly, when Teacher Zhang was gathering up these items, a conflict suddenly arose, and the situation even became quite uncompromisable.

When all the other things were put in a book bag, only the novel was left. Teacher Zhang had not had time to carefully examine the novel before. When he picked it up to have a look, he couldn't help but utter an "Uh!" It turned out to be the novel *The Gadfly* that was published before the Cultural Revolution by the Chinese Youth Publishing House.

Xie Huimin felt that Teacher Zhang looked a bit strange and quickly asked for the book to look through it. She had never heard of, let alone seen, this book. When she saw that there were illustrations of foreign men and women courting each other, she could not help screaming, "Oh! So pornographic! Tomorrow we should criticize this pornographic book hard!"

Teacher Zhang frowned and pondered. He remembered his middle-school days. At that time, the Youth League committee recommended the novel to the students in the class. . . . They sat together around a campfire, everyone taking turns to read it aloud with their youthful voices. Leaning against the

battlements on the Great Wall, they would discuss heatedly the
merits and shortcomings of the character "Gadfly". . . . This
work, written by the English writer Voynich, used to excite the
Teacher Zhang of that time and also his generation. They used to
draw the power to make progress from the descriptions of the
hero in the novel . . . Maybe, in those years, the shortcomings of
the novel were not criticized enough? Maybe, in those years, the
essence of the novel was not understood accurately enough or
deeply enough? . . . But, no matter what—thinking of all this—
Teacher Zhang could not help opening his mouth to argue with
Xie Huimin:
    "This book *The Gadfly* can't be categorized as porno-
graphic. . . ."
    Xie Huimin's two eyebrows almost flew off her face. She
opened her eyes wide and stared at Teacher Zhang, questioning
vehemently: "What? Not a pornographic book? If books of this
kind are not pornographic, what are pornographic books then?"
In the mind of Xie Huimin, there was already an ironclad logic
that if any books were not sold in the bookstores[15] or could not
be checked out from a library, they were all bad and
pornographic. Actually, she could not really be blamed for this.
It just happened that the years when she started to read books
were also the worst time of the fascist cultural totalitarianism
that was practiced by the Gang of Four. The lovable yet pitiful
Xie Huimin innocently worshiped everything in print. But in
those years when the mass media were controlled by the Gang of
Four, the newspapers and magazines she read with piety were
filled with numerous "gang"[16] articles spitting venom that
would poison countless young people. How wonderful it would
have been if one of the people closest to Xie Huimin had in
timely fashion pointed out that the two articles proclaimed as
"important articles" which "elaborated the proletarian dictatorial
theory" were at best highly suspect, and that the huge articles by
the likes of "Liangxiao" and "Tang Xiaowen"[17] were by no
means the "authoritative works" on Marxism and Leninism! But
due to various subjective or objective reasons, no one pointed
this out to her. Her parents always advised her and her brother
and sister to listen to Chairman Mao, listen to the radio
earnestly, and read the newspapers diligently; they asked them

to follow regulations and respect their teachers; they also wanted them to study well. . . . Xie Huimin had benefited greatly from such family teachings and was equipped with strong proletarian feelings and the qualities of working-class offspring. Yet in the environment of struggling against the capitalist and revisionist white-bone demon turned beauty,[18] it was easy to be trapped into being credulous and blindly obedient. And the "white-bone demons" just depend on the credulity and blind allegiance of some people to peddle their treacheries! It was under such circumstances that Xie Huimin, a girl in her prime who was wholeheartedly devoted to becoming a good revolutionary and was intending to strive for the realization of communism, was led by the Gang of Four to become narrow-minded and confused about right and wrong. It was not only *The Gadfly* that she would regard as poisonous. When this story was taking place, *The Song of Youth*[19] was already being reprinted, but Xie Huimin still kept the habit formed before the Gang of Four was ousted—she would regard those students as "tainted with bourgeois ideology" who were enthusiastic about exchanging "news in the fine arts," such as what new movie was being shown and what new song the radio station just aired. Only a few days ago, she found that Shi Hong was reading a thick novel during a self-study session.[20] As soon as the class was over, she confiscated the book. It was a copy of *The Song of Youth*, published in 1959. She casually turned the pages with her own heart thumping— feeling for sure that it was a "pornographic book"—and just as she wanted to turn it over to Teacher Zhang, Shi Hong snatched the book back from her with a smile, and, while snapping the cover of the book, said: "Really exciting! You should take a look, too!" They ended up having an argument. Later, she was in a hurry to go to a meeting at the school's Youth League Com- mittee, so she forgot to report it to Teacher Zhang. She therefore never expected that today Teacher Zhang would be even worse than Shi Hong—claiming himself that this foreign pornographic book was not "pornographic"! To Xie Huimin, foreign pornographic books must be more pornographic than Chinese pornographic books. Facing such a teacher, she thought of the many small conflicts before. Hence the respect for him that used to dominate her other feelings suddenly took a dive. She pouted slightly and the eyebrows that almost flew away came back to form a tight knot.

At this moment, Shi Hong had finished writing the "bugle poem" and was ready to read it to Teacher Zhang and Xie Huimin when she heard Teacher Zhang saying: "You can't say *The Gadfly* is a pornographic book. . . ." Only then did she know that the torn book was *The Gadfly* and she hurried to stand close by Xie Huimin to take a look. Right after Xie Huimin loudly questioned Teacher Zhang, Shi Hong warmly shook Xie Huimin's arms and said: "Don't say that! I heard my father and mother say that *The Gadfly* is worth reading! These last couple of days, I have been reading *How Steel Was Tempered*.[21] In the novel, Pavel Korchagin is a proletarian hero, but he especially admires 'the gadfly'. . . ." Shi Hong had long wanted to find a copy of *The Gadfly* to read, but had not been able to borrow one. So when she snatched the book from the hands of Xie Huimin, the strong desire for knowledge was boiling in her heart: When did the events narrated in the book take place? Where did the story take place? What kind of person is the "gadfly"? Is there really anything in him to admire? . . . When she returned the torn book to Teacher Zhang's hands, she could not help asking: "When I read this book, what should I pay attention to? What should I learn?" Xie Huimin bit her lips, narrowed her eyes and looked at Shi Hong with resentment, while her heart jumped wildly.

Teacher Zhang was turning the pages of *The Gadfly*, which had seen better days. He had wanted to explain to Xie Huimin patiently why it could not be regarded as a "pornographic book," but this book had been found on Song Baoqi. What was more, look, whenever the heroine appeared in the illustration, she was savagely smeared with a mustache. How could you know that Song Baoqi and his fellows did not read it as a "pornographic book"? The phenomena of life were complicated. The encounters of this copy of *The Gadfly* were bizarre enough. Children like Xie Huimin who were still quite naive would need ample time and a proper place to understand the exceedingly complicated life and the literary works that included both treasures and trash.

Thinking about these, our Teacher Zhang put *The Gadfly* in his book bag and said amiably to Xie Huimin: "About the book, let's talk about it tomorrow. Look, it's almost five o'clock. Let's listen quickly to Shi Hong's 'bugle poem.' Then we will go ahead according to our plan."

Not a single line of the poem read by Shi Hong made its way to Xie Huimin's head. She watched the mottled tree shadows on the desks with pain and bewilderment. She respected Teacher Zhang very very much, but his strange attitude toward such a book inevitably made her ask herself in her heart: "He is even a teacher; how could he react like this?! . . ."

6

Just a little after five o'clock, Teacher Zhang bicycled to the Songs' new residence. In the two rooms on the east side of the compound, things were not yet carefully arranged and they looked very disorderly. For instance, a pot of nopalxochia, just beginning to bloom, was inappropriately placed on a sewing machine that had a piece of plastic cloth casually thrown over it.

Song Baoqi's mother was a salesperson in a store. She had taken leave that day because of the move and was busily tidying up the house. Seeing that Teacher Zhang had come, she felt somewhat comforted, and then a bit ashamed. She hurriedly called Song Baoqi out from a room inside, asked him to bow to the teacher, and told him to pour some tea. We will not follow Teacher Zhang's eyes to check Song Baoqi. We will follow Teacher Zhang as he sits down to talk with Song Baoqi's mother and gather some general information about this family.

Song Baoqi's father worked at the nursery of the Park and Forestry Bureau. He worked a "regular shift," which means that he could come home right after six o'clock. Yet every day he usually would not come home until after eight or nine o'clock. Why? As she spoke, Song Baoqi's mother would sigh again and again. It turned out that over these years he had developed a bad habit: On his way home from work as he passed the Moon Temple,[22] he would prop up his bike and go to the little woods and sit down with a bunch of people to play cards and relax. Sometimes they would not break up even when it got dark. They would move under a street lamp and go on playing. Not until someone among them stood up and hurried to a night shift in a factory would they disperse.

Obviously, it was easy to imagine the lack of education and control over Song Baoqi from such a father, one who himself lacked a rich and meaningful spiritual life. As for the mother, from her complaining talk, it was not hard to see how she suffered from her own bitter fruit of pampering and indulging her only son.

Never assume that such a family was necessarily terrible. Teacher Zhang noticed that, although they still had a lot of cleaning and arranging to do to make the room spotlessly clean, the framed picture of Chairman Mao[23] was already up on the northern wall. And a small portrait of Premier Zhou was put in a homemade frame encircled by patterns of silvery plum blossoms, and placed solemnly in the middle atop the little dresser. This showed that in the hearts of this common couple of nearly fifty also surged the same emotional tides felt by millions of people.[24] Then, apart from the flaws in themselves, who should be responsible for the poverty in their spiritual life? . . .

At a quarter to six, Teacher Zhang asked the mother to go on with whatever housework she had to do, then took Song Baoqi to the inner room and started his first talk with the little hooligan.

Now we can take a closer look to see how Song Baoqi looked. He had on a nylon tank top. His rippling muscles and rosy skin amply demonstrated that he was lucky to be living in this society of ours, one in which no one had to worry about food and clothes. How much nutrition he enjoyed and how full of energy his body was. Alas, that face of his made even Teacher Zhang, who was accustomed to looking his students in the eye, shudder with a chill throughout his body. It was not that his facial features were not properly positioned, but what chilled the heart was that you could immediately feel that a soul, deformed by brainwashing, was stripped bare in the spotlight, as was revealed in his facial muscles, from his upper lip that had been cut open in a fight but was later stitched back together, to the uncontrollable flares of his nostrils, and especially in his eyes that were filled with stupidity and emptiness, obvious at the first glance.

After about thirty questions and answers, Teacher Zhang came to the following judgment about the boy: a lack of basic political sense; a knowledge level at about that of Junior High Grade One;[25] actually not good at any sports, even though he had a muscular body. Teacher Zhang thought that some people who were content to criticize Song Baoqi would accuse him of having "a brain full of bourgeois ideas." But after further questioning, Teacher Zhang more and more deeply felt that to make the ambiguous claim that hooligans like Song Baoqi had bourgeois ideology was like shooting arrows without taking aim, and it would be useless even if he were led to the right path.

Song Baoqi did have serious bourgeois thoughts, but what kind were these?

The bourgeois class flaunted "freedom, equality, and fraternity," stressed "individual endeavor" and "fame as an authority," and used hypocritical "humanism" to cover up their crime of exploitation and oppression. But what about Song Baoqi? Ever since he had been trapped in that ring of hooligans, he had been placed in tight restrictions at all times, and he had been many times scorched in the back of his head with a cigarette butt by the head hooligan "Jug Ear Eggplant."[26] Did he get angry? Did he rebel? No, he had neither acted to seek "personal liberation" and called for "liberty and equality," nor did he ever think about "fraternity"; on the one hand, he superstitiously believed in "brotherhood" and was willing to be the "tool" of the bigger hooligans; on the other hand, he took the greatest pleasure in slapping the younger hooligans on the face. As to "being an expert or specialist in something," he never thought of it, because when he started to understand things, all specialists—scientists, engineers, writers, and professors—were relegated to being the Stinking Number Ninth[27] by Lin Biao and the Gang of Four. When so ranked, the specialists seemed to be below the hooligans. To him, what was there to admire about the experts and specialists? Where was the need to strive for something? One of the typical bourgeois concepts was that "knowledge is power," but we are sorry to say that our Song Baoqi did not have such concepts either. What was the use of knowledge? The best thing was to "rebel" endlessly. It was said that Zhang Tiesheng[28] had scored a zero on his college entrance exam, and didn't he become an important official? . . . Therefore, Song Baoqi could not simply be labeled as a person with "a brain full of bourgeois ideas." The remedy should suit the illness. Those bourgeois concepts that existed in the rising period of capitalism[29] were few or nonexistent in his head. What he did have were the feudal "fraternity" and the kind of reactionary ideology like capitalistic hedonism in its declining period. . . . Please do not close your eyes or plug your ears when faced with Teacher Zhang's analysis of Song Baoqi. This was the fact. Moreover, regrettably, if you love our country, worry about our country, then you should acknowledge that the problems that were revealed about Song Baoqi are, to an extent, not isolated! Please take the attitude of solving practical problems and curing the ulcers on certain parts of the strong and healthy body of our country; let us be with Teacher Zhang, and think about how to educate and change young people like Song Baoqi.

Teacher Zhang took the much-abused novel out of his book bag, asking Song Baoqi: "What is the name of this book? Do you still remember?"

Song Baoqi had just gone through the stern questioning of the dictatorial apparatus, as well as imposing lectures that naturally felt far worse than the inquiry and education of a class teacher. Naturally, he replied with the most respectful and submissive attitude: "I remember. This is Niuwang." He did not know the word *gadfly*, and, according to his reading habit, he read only half of the word.[30]

"It is not Niuwang; it's 'Niumang.' Do you know what these two words mean?"

His face did not have any expression, and his two eyes stared straight at a butterfly that was fluttering outside the window. He rather frankly answered: "Don't know."

"Then, did you finish reading this book?"

"I turned some pages. I did not understand it."

"If you did not understand it, why did you keep it? Where did the book come from?"

"We stole it."

"Where did you steal it from? Why did you steal it?"

"Stole it from the library storage of our school. We heard the books in it were all books that could not be checked out or read. They were all bad books. We pried open the lock and stole two armfuls. We stole them to be sold."

"Why wasn't this book sold?"

"Later on none was sold. We heard that if we sold books bearing the seals of libraries, we would be arrested."

"Among the books you stole, what others were there? Could you name a few of them?"

"Yes!" Song Baoqi felt very happy that he could show he was not stupid or ignorant. For the first time, he had a concentrated expression. Blinking his eyes, he recalled with difficulty: "There was *The Red Cliff*,[31] and *Peace and War*, or maybe *War and Peace*. Oh, yes, it was *War and Peace*. Right, there was also a very strange book, called . . . called *The Lyrics of the New Wedding Carriage . . . .*"

That surprised Teacher Zhang. Having thought for a while, he took out a pen and wrote in the palm of his hand the characters *Selected Poems of Xin Jiaxuan*.[32] He extended his hand for Song Baoqi to look. Song Baoqi immediately nodded: "That's it! No doubt about it!"

Teacher Zhang felt pangs of pain in his heart. It was not really startling that several hooligans stole some books. The question was this: For what reasons were such valuable books all locked up in the storage and declared forbidden, when they were by no means poisonous grass but rather fragrant flowers?[33] Contrary to the logical thinking of everyone, one of the reasons for the degeneration of Song Baoqi and his fellow hooligans may not have been that they were poisoned by reading some harmful books. The reason was just that they believed they were great if they could cause trouble. They fell into a bottomless abyss of ignorance without reading any books!

As he turned the pages, Teacher Zhang asked Song Baoqi: "What kind of thing is it to draw mustaches on all the women in the illustrations? What were you thinking?"

Song Baoqi lowered his eyes, confessing his crime: "We had a competition. Each had a book in his hands and looked for pictures. We'd draw the mustache whenever we came upon a woman. Whoever drew the most mustaches was the luckiest. . . ."

Teacher Zhang stared at Song Baoqi with anger, speechless for a moment. Song Baoqi raised his eyes to steal a look at Teacher Zhang and, believing that he was not honest enough, he therefore added: "We were wrong. We shouldn't have read this pornographic book. . . . We were fortune-telling to see who'd be the first to find a girlfriend . . . we . . . I will never dare do that again!" He thought of the scene when he was being questioned in the Public Safety Bureau and his mother's two red eyes, mixed with both love and hatred, on the day when she came to get him out.

"We shouldn't have read this pornographic book"—this sentence was like a drumstick landing on a drum, making Teacher Zhang's heart jump in a "bong." Strange? Not strange— there was such a big gap between the good kids with good manners and nice qualities like Xie Huimin and the bad kids with bad personalities like Song Baoqi. But they happened to think the same when it came to firmly believing that *The Gadfly* was a pornographic book—furthermore, both came to the "natural" conclusion without reading the book. What a shocking social phenomenon this was! Who caused it? Who?

Of course it was the Gang of Four.

An inveterate hatred for the Gang of Four that he had never felt before erupted and burned like a volcano in the heart of Teacher Zhang. Up to now, in the history of human civilization, how many instances could one find that would resemble the act of the Gang of Four using the most revolutionary "logic" and slogans to cover up their most reactionary policy of obscurantism?

Song Baoqi was sitting on the bed, his head lowered, his two muscular arms pushing against the edge of the bed, and his two eyes idly looking at his two feet that were rubbing against each other in white-soled shoes. When Teacher Zhang looked at the person who refused to accept the useful knowledge and beautiful artistic fruits of human civilization, a shapeless force rushed to his throat, and he almost cried out loud—

Save the children damaged by the Gang of Four!

7

The days are short in spring. When the clock in the distant Telegraph Building chimed seven o'clock and the sound was wafted along by the soft spring wind, dusk had already enveloped the streets and lanes around Guangming Middle School.

Teacher Zhang pushed his bike and turned purposely into the little park that was admission-free and open day and night. He found a bench in a quiet place, propped up his bike, sat, and lit a cigarette. The tips of his eyebrows were trembling, and he intentionally let the tumultuous emotional waves in his chest gather up at the gate of reason and then flow out in proper channels so that they became actions of force and strength to carry out his duty as a class teacher.

The initial contact with Song Baoqi and his family happened to have so violently plucked the chords of both love and hatred in the heart of Teacher Zhang that he had difficulty controlling himself. He wished he could call together all his students right away and have a meeting right there in front of the bench. He had many deep and touching thoughts, many sincere yet grim notions, and numerous frank but serious entrustments, suggestions, criticisms, guides, and callings. And it was at such a moment that all these could be expressed thoroughly with the most unrestrained feelings and in the most appealing manner, including the use of many examples and metaphors that could come right out of his mouth and would be rich and exotic, easy for the young ones to accept. . . .

He felt, that he loved our dear country now more than at any other time. He thought about her future, her bright prospects, and the fascinating state of the first stage of the "Four Modernizations"[34] at the beginning of the next century. Thinking of this, he had a strong feeling that he would not allow anyone to humiliate or tease our country, and he would let no one strangle or suffocate our country's future. He thought about his duties—a people's teacher and the teacher of a class. What he cultivated were not just some students or some flowers,[35] but clearly the future of the country, the future that would allow the Chinese to live on and continue to develop strongly and prosperously on this land of nine million and six hundred thousand square kilometers, so that they could stand tall among the nations of the world.

He felt, more deeply than at any other time, that he hated the Gang of Four who had brought disasters to the nation and misfortune to the people. It was necessary to see not only the visible damage caused to the nation's economy by the Gang of Four but also the invisible filth the Gang of Four had poured on the souls of millions of people. It was also necessary to not only pay attention to the bunch of clowns like Zhang Tiesheng, as produced by the Gang of Four, who "had horns in their heads and thorns in their bodies," but also to note how many "deformed" Song Baoqis had already appeared. Moreover, even in kids like Xie Huimin, whose personality was pure and fine, there were the black markings left by the cruel obscurantism of the Gang of Four. The Gang of Four trampled not only on the present of the Chinese, but also even more so on their future!

The hatred for the wicked deepened his love for the people. And the love for the people then deepened his hatred for the wicked. When love and hatred were woven together, one would gain the boundless courage to fight for truths and also the endless strength to strive for victories without any fear of sacrifice.

Teacher Zhang suddenly stood up. He glanced at his watch: a quarter after seven. He thought of supper, not that he was hungry and should go home to have his meal. He literally forgot that he needed to have supper. He was planning on visiting several students at their homes to find out their reactions to Song Baoqi's arrival at Junior Grade Three Class Three. By now, the students must be home eating their supper. And visiting students at their homes during suppertime was not appropriate. He thought for a while, then joined his hands behind his back, and started pacing in the woods in the little park, deciding at the same time that he would leave at about seven thirty. . . .

The fragrant scent of the lilacs became stronger, wave after wave. The rich fragrance could make one think of pleasant and satisfactory things. Teacher Zhang thought about the Gang of Four who had already been swept away into the garbage can, thought of the fact that the Chinese Communist Party Central Committee had in the short time of half a year created a brand-new prospect, thought about how the country not only had a firm grasp of the present but also a future filled with hopes. Hence he felt that Song Baoqi might not be a piece of rotten wood that could not be carved. Then Xie Huimin's confusion and her misunderstanding and resentment toward him were far from being a piece of ice that could not be melted away when compared to the fine qualities and socialist enthusiasm latent in her character.

8

When Teacher Zhang was pushing his bike out of the little park, he met Teacher Yin, who was passing by the entrance of the park with a fully stuffed plastic bag.

Teacher Yin was greatly surprised: "Junshi, how can you still feel like strolling in the park?"

Teacher Zhang smiled a little but did not explain. He did not ask where Teacher Yin came from or where he was going. He knew that Teacher Yin had been persistently doing something for more than a month. Every day after four o'clock, other than organizing some students deficient in math to do extra learning, he would take turns going to their homes to conduct individual tutoring. Teacher Zhang was familiar with Teacher Yin's temperament, especially during the period when the Gang of Four was controlling all educational and cultural matters. He used to be full of complaints about the Ministry of Education, the officials in the school, the students, and the students' parents. An outsider, hearing such expressions of anger and seeing it on his face, would surely take him as a person who tended to shake off duties and was easy to offend. Actually, complaining was just complaining, and work was still work. No matter what time it was, no matter what attacks, obstacles, difficulties, or setbacks he encountered, he never gave up his diligent teaching. Even when the Gang of Four fanned the students' anarchism to the extreme and the classroom was usually as disorderly as a bowl of boiling porridge, even when he could bring his complaints to the point of saying "Let's have a teachers' strike," he would rush to the classroom immediately upon hearing the bell, and try his utmost to knock on the blackboards with his chalk and make his students listen to his formulas and polyhedrons by means of inducement, yelling, persuasion, or threats.

Teacher Zhang knew that Teacher Yin had just finished his tutoring and was on his way to the bus station outside the lane to ride the bus home. Now that he had done his work, his complaints would be easily touched off. Just as expected, before Teacher Zhang started speaking, Teacher Yin patted the seat of Teacher Zhang's bike and sighed a long sigh: "What kind of students have the Gang of Four created for us! Just think about it. I am teaching Junior Grade Three, but just now I was still talking to two students again and again about the Pythagorean theorem . . . and you are even 'luckier' than I am—to get assigned a 'new illiterate,' Song Baoqi! Frankly I cannot understand you. Right now, with all the neglected tasks waiting to be undertaken, there are so many things to do. But just this afternoon, you spent so much energy on the reception of a little hooligan; was it worth it? Let Song Baoqi get out of here! If the Public Safety Bureau does not want to keep him, let him go back to his old school! If his old school does not want him, then let him stay home! . . ."

Teacher Zhang said to him with sincerity: "Throughout this afternoon, I more and more consciously became aware that the problem is not whether to keep Song Baoqi here for sure—indeed, there may be a special school for kids like him, or we could group students like him into one class. Or, judging from the extent of his knowledge, we could relegate him to Junior Grade One to start all over again . . . but all this is not of primary importance. Where, then, is the problem? The things that happened one after another in relation to the reception of Song Baoqi were like a mirror that reflected the crimes of the Gang of Four in destroying our next generation. There are many detrimental and baneful influences left over from the Gang of Four that I did not recognize before or which did not seem so startling and shocking as today. I thought a lot, a lot. . . . Shilei, it is now the spring of 1977. What a beautiful and happy spring this is! Yet it is also the spring in which we face deeper struggles and put in more painstaking work. Therefore it is also a spring that demands more of us! Look forward, Shilei! . . ."

From these simple words, Teacher Yin couldn't possibly feel all that Teacher Zhang had already felt. Yet, when his eyes met Teacher Zhang's, which were replete with awakening, deep thinking, confidence, and strength, his complaints and agitated emotions suddenly disappeared. The evening spring wind in 1977 skirted by these two ordinary and unknown people's teachers. For a couple of seconds, they let their own thoughts fly away; it was quiet, and there was no talk.

Teacher Zhang was thinking that a few days later he would definitely find Teacher Yin to have a good talk about the simplicity in the logic of his thinking and also his problem of impatience: Feelings could never replace policies; earnest wishes for the revolutionary course to move forward could not simply be displayed in the form of impatience or complaints; when one keeps on fighting with perseverance, one should also have a corresponding positive attitude to wait for the development of things. Even the hatred for such little hooligans as Song Baoqi could be turned into sympathy and love for the budding young people who were damaged by the Gang of Four. . . . All in all, he should have a good talk with Teacher Yin on philosophy, on dialectics, about the present and the future, about love and hatred, about life and work, and even about *The Red Cliff* and *The Gadfly.* . . .

From the distance wafted along the chimes announcing seven thirty. Teacher Zhang reined in his vibrant thoughts, patted Teacher Yin on the shoulder, and said: "Let's find some other time to have a good chat. I am now going to some students' homes."

"Hurry over to Shi Hong's home then." Teacher Yin suddenly remembered something and told Teacher Zhang, "I just came out of their apartment building. I heard from a student in my class that Xie Huimin and Shi Hong had a fight. Go and find out about it."

Teacher Zhang's heart was shocked. He immediately got on his bike and dashed toward the building where Shi Hong's home was.

9

Shi Hong's father was a government official in the district, and her mother was a grade school teacher. Both had joined the Chinese Communist Party in the dynamic "Four Cleanups Movement."[36] Around the time they joined the Party, especially through the Cultural Revolution, they formed a very good habit, and that was their persistence in studying the works of Marx, Lenin, and Chairman Mao. On their bookshelves were light gray fingerprints on almost all the edges of the four-volume selections of Marx, Engles, and Lenin; the four-volume selections of Mao Zedong; and many monograph works of Marx, Lenin, and Chairman Mao. There were plenty of folds, underlines, and some other markings indicating their deep thinking. . . . Nurtured thoroughly in this environment of serious reading, Shi Hong had also become a little bookworm.

Shi Hong was a lucky one. "After supper" was a special term in her family. It meant that they would sit around the big square table, checking on each other's study of the works of Marx, Lenin, and Chairman Mao, and do their own things in an environment of mutual loving care for each other—her father would sometimes read the history books he loved; her mother would read students' assignments; and Shi Hong, her lips tightly closed, would be engrossed in thinking about a physics exercise or the solution to a formula in inequality. . . . Sometimes the whole family would analyze together current affairs or discuss works of fine arts. And pleasant but vigorous arguments would occur between father and mother, or between parents and daughter. Even when the Gang of Four was the fiercest at pushing for fascist cultural totalitarianism, standing tall on the bookshelves of this family were such books as *Violent Winds and Torrential Rains*,[37] *Red Cliff*, *The Collection of Mao Dun*, *The Selected Works of Gadiel*, *Eugenie Grandet*, and *Three Hundred Poems from the Tang Dynasty*. . . .

Once Teacher Zhang showed the students and their parents, along with two books of notes Shi Hong took, *The Communist Manifesto*, *The Three Origins and Three Components of*

Marxism, and the four-volume *Selected Works of Mao Zedong* that Shi Hong had read through. But what pleased him even more was that she could analyze some problems according to the principles of Marxism, Leninism, and Mao Zedong's Thought. Such thinking and analyses were usually fairly correct and they were also evident in her active actions.

On the day when our story took place, after Teacher Zhang knocked on the door of her family's apartment, he found that the room facing the door seated a roomful of people. Shi Hong was sitting by the dinner table in the middle of the room, reading a book aloud. There were five other girls, also from Teacher Zhang's class, who sat in different places in the room. One cupped her chin, staring at Shi Hong with her big eyes; one had her arms folded on the back of a chair, her head resting on her arms; one was toying with her ponytail with her head down. . . . Obviously, they were absorbed by the reading. According to Xie Huimin's report that afternoon, these turned out to be the few students who had announced, either due to fear or in a fit of resentment, that they would not go to class tomorrow if Song Baoqi also went.

Shi Hong was concentrating on the reading and therefore did not notice that Teacher Zhang had arrived. Two or three girls looked up and saw Teacher Zhang, only nodding to him with shy smiles without calling him "Teacher Zhang." Obviously, they had not forgotten their manners, but they did not want to interrupt the story they were engrossed in.

Shi Hong's mother, who had opened the door for him, led him to an inner room and seated him, explaining to him quietly: "The kids are reading 'Watch' translated by Lu Xun. . . ."

"The Watch" was written as a children's story by Pantaleyet not long after the October Revolution.[38] It describes the process of change of a street urchin in a Soviet Reformatory. Lu Xun once translated it with great enthusiasm. Although Teacher Zhang had not touched the book for many years, as soon as Shi Hong's mother mentioned it, many characters and segments of the plot at once surged into his memory. In these few short minutes, Teacher Zhang already had guessed the reasons why there was such a scene in Shi Hong's home. Just as he expected, Shi Hong's mother told him, "As soon as Shi Hong got home, she told me about Song Baoqi. During supper, she blinked her eyes frequently as she thought about something. When she was washing the dishes, she said to me: 'Mom, how about me inviting to our home Xie Huimin and those students who are afraid and resentful so we can read "The Watch"?' I agreed quite willingly. I said to her: 'When there is the Party to lead us, when there is the socialist system, and when the guidelines are correct, even little hooligans could be turned around as long as teachers and students make use of the unity of everyone!' Then she went to look for her classmates—only I don't know why Xie Huimin did not show up. . . ."

As they were talking, Shi Hong finished reading a paragraph and learned that Teacher Zhang had arrived. She went into the inner room and cried happily: "Teacher Zhang, you have come at the right moment! Please give us an analysis quickly!"

Teacher Zhang was dragged by her to the outer room, and several girls stood up and called "Teacher Zhang." Before he could speak, all kinds of questions were raised one after another:

"Teacher Zhang, may we read a book like this?"

"Teacher Zhang, how could the little hooligan in the book make you feel angry and sympathetic at the same time?"

"Teacher Zhang, Xie Huimin said that we are reading poisonous stuff. Could this book be called poison?"

"Teacher Zhang, have you seen Song Baoqi? Compared to the little hooligan in the book, is he better or worse?"

. . .

Teacher Zhang was in no hurry to answer them. Instead he asked them: "Why didn't Xie Huimin come along? Did Shi Hong have an argument with her? You should have worked together to make her come along."

With excitement, the little girls all answered his questions at the same time, creating a huge noise, and no one could be heard clearly. It was Shi Hong who quieted everyone down, explaining: "We weren't able to drag her here! Unless I publish an article in the newspaper proclaiming 'Watch' to be a good story. . . ."

It turned out that, when Shi Hong went to find Xie Huimin, Xie Huimin was quite happy to see Shi Hong so active with her work. But she became resentful as soon as she heard that they were to get together to read a foreign book. Shi Hong explained to her that the book was pretty good and that reading it could be enlightening to those few students. . . . Before she could finish, Xie Huimin quickly questioned: "Has it been recommended in the newspapers?"[39] That question froze Shi Hong, who could answer it only after a moment: "It hasn't been recommended." "Aren't you afraid to be poisoned if it has not been recommended? Right now we are in the middle of an anti-corruption movement, so we cadres should not lead the way of corruption! . . ." The alert look on Xie Huimin's face warned Shi Hong that not only would she refuse to participate in such an activity, but she would also advise Shi Hong not to "make a mistake. . . ." That offended Shi Hong and she had an argument with Xie Huimin. But when she was leaving, Shi Hong still tugged at her hand, begging her to "first just listen to it." Xie Huimin brushed her hand away. After Shi Hong left, Xie Huimin walked out of her house emotionally. The evening wind caressed her hot cheeks, and she was very pained, her upper teeth leaving some deep biting marks on her lower lip. . . .

At Shi Hong's home, what followed was a scene like this: Teacher Zhang sat at the table, and Shi Hong and the girls sat around him. The teacher and the students started a friendly and free talk, which ranged from "The Watch" to the changes in the Soviet Union, from the street urchin in "The Watch" to Song Baoqi, from how to reform little hooligans to why most hooligans could be reeducated. In the end, the talk shifted to the new situation the class would face tomorrow. Teacher Zhang asked those little girls with a smile: "Well, are you still boycotting the class?"

They exchanged glances with each other, and, all looking at Teacher Zhang, said almost at the same time: "We won't!"

When Teacher Zhang left Shi Hong's home, the stars all over the sky were glistening in the jade blue heaven.

Without even thinking, after he got on his bike, he naturally sped toward Xie Huimin's home. As a matter of fact, when he was having the discussion with Shi Hong and those other girls, Xie Huimin was always on his mind. He cared about Xie Huimin as a doctor cares for a strong child who unfortunately has fallen ill. He believed that, with the help of the kind of upright character and unadorned feelings like Xie Huimin's, the poisonous germs that the Gang of Four had planted in her could definitely be purged if only she were treated with undivided attention.

The closer he got to Xie Huimin's home, the heavier the guilty conscience weighed in Teacher Zhang's heart. In the past, faced with Xie Huimin's change into such a person, he had always felt that he was hardly responsible. Not long after he took over the class, he indirectly pointed out to Xie Huimin that she should not just study fragmented quotations, and that she should not have blind faith in articles paraphrasing the leader's thoughts,[40] but that she should earnestly study the original works and think independently. . . . But Xie Huimin did not comprehend. Today, Teacher Zhang had some new thoughts. He questioned himself: Although in the semester before October[41] there were dark clouds overhead, couldn't he, nonetheless, have been more courageous and relentless in fighting against the absurd and reactionary things? Couldn't he have talked to Xie Huimin more directly and more attentively and helped her to wipe her eyes clean and tell truths from lies? . . .

When he was close to the door of Xie Huimin's home, a plan had begun to outline itself in Teacher Zhang's heart: Today he would leave Xie Huimin *The Gadfly* in his bag, persuade her to read the book, and allow her to express whatever thoughts she might have after the reading. Then, starting from the analysis of the book, he would lead Xie Huimin to use the stand, the viewpoint, and the method of Marxism, Leninism, and Mao Zedong Thought to answer a series of interrelated questions: How to understand life? How to understand and know about history? How to view the fruits of civilization created by human societies? How to criticize the dross in the past civilization and in the meanwhile assimilate its remaining essence? How to look at a question dialectically and from all sides? How to tell fragrant flowers from poisonous grass? How to tell real Marxism from false Marxism? What kind of person should one make oneself? How should one fight for the country's "Four Modernizations" and the bright future of communism? . . .

Emotional tidal waves were surging high in Teacher Zhang's heart. When he put on the brakes and stood in front of the door of Xie Huimin's home, the plan in his heart became clearer: Not only would he help Xie Huimin, starting from this incident, to rid the baneful influence of the Gang of Four, but he would also use the guideline of unmasking and condemning the Gang of Four to launch guided reading activities in order to educate all the students in his class, including Song Baoqi. . . . He decided to get permission from the Party Branch Committee early the next morning. Would he get support? Before his eyes flashed the face of Old Cao speaking in the Party Branch Committee meeting with his eyes glowing: "Now is the time to enforce in earnest the education according to the system of Mao Zedong thought!" He wanted just to go all out "in earnest," and he would definitely obtain the support of the Party Branch Committee! Some questions other teachers might have also crossed his mind. Therefore he decided to try to speak at the teachers' meeting and explain his thoughts: Now, we should not only strengthen the teaching in class to enable the children to master the knowledge in the classes and textbooks, but also facilitate overall development in morality, intelligence, and physical fitness. We should not only continue to lead them to learn from the workers and the farmers so they could put theory into practice, but also we would guide them to look at a broader world to make them interested in the fruits of all human civilizations, equipped with higher analytic abilities, and thus become even stronger torchbearers of the socialist revolution and socialist construction. . . .

At this moment, the spring wind sent along a refreshing floral fragrance, and the stars all over the sky were blinking and smiling, as if conferring approval and encouragement to Teacher Zhang's beautiful thinking. . . .

NOTES

1. Class teacher—In Chinese high schools, as in Chinese grade schools and colleges, students in a grade (e.g., freshman, sophomore, etc.) are divided into classes in which the same students take classes and participate in various activities together. To each of these classes, one trusted teacher is assigned to take care of academic or other related matters, acting largely as a counselor to the students.

2. The Public Safety Bureau—the police department.

3. "... the great power of the proletarian dictatorship"—In China, under communist rule, the phrase "proletarian dictatorship" does not carry any negative connotations at all in governmental propaganda and is used proudly to refer to all the measures and organizations of the government to maintain stability and order.

4. "... by means of trading their residence with some other people"—At the time when this story took place, housing in Beijing and other large Chinese cities was not commercialized and was quite difficult to obtain for ordinary citizens. Therefore it was hard to change one's residence. For many people, the only way to change their residence was to swap residences with other people, which could be a slow, complicated, and aggravating experience.

5. "the collar clips of the jacket"—The jacket is what is often referred to in the West as the "Mao uniform," and collar clips are required to make the collars stand upright.

6. "the periodically recommended songs"—The government used to recommend to students certain songs, stories, movies, books, etc., and regarded other ones as inappropriate. This effort by the government was largely a brainwashing measure.

7. "... largely due to the time and energy taken up by her social work"—The social work here refers to the political activities she participates in, such as running the Communist Youth League branch in her class; it is not the kind of social work as defined in the West.

8. "... it was this class's turn to go to the countryside to learn from the farmers"—This was a practice in the 1970s in which high school classes were scheduled to work with farmers in the countryside or workers in a factory so that they could learn from the proletariat. When students were preoccupied with such activities, they had little or no time to study.

9. li—a Chinese measurement for distance, equivalent to 0.31 mile.

10. Song Jiang—the legendary leader of an uprising in the Song Dynasty (960–1279). A national movement was launched in the mid-1970s by the government to condemn the Chinese classical novel *The Heroes of the Marshes*, in which Song Jiang is a major character. The national movement was just part of a political maneuver in a struggle for power at the top.

11. Caishikou—a neighborhood in Beijing, known for its violence in those days.

12. These committees are usually made up of the most active students in a class; they are supposed to be the leaders in the class.

13. "... was pondering on how to write the 'bugle poem'"— Creative writing in those days was largely used for political propaganda; therefore poems were supposed to have the commanding power of a bugle call for battle.

14. "... and conducted the first talk on ideology"—Teachers were supposed to talk to students so that they could use the ideology prescribed by the government to control students' thinking. In times after the Cultural Revolution, as in this story, such a talk might not carry the negative note of brainwashing.

15. Bookstores and libraries were once strictly controlled by the government.

16. The word *gang* here does not refer to street gangs, but specifically to the Gang of Four, a radically leftist group of top Chinese leaders that included Mao Zedong's widow. They were arrested and sent to jail in 1976 by more moderate political leaders.

17. These names are pseudonyms, used by certain groups of political writers who worked for the government and wrote propagandistic articles to brainwash the population or help to start and shape a political movement.

18. "... white-bone demon turned beauty"—This phrase refers to Mao Zedong's widow Jiang Qing, who had once been a movie star but who was extremely merciless when she persecuted people against her. This sentence alludes also to a story in the classical Chinese fantastic novel, *A Journey to the West*, in which a white-bone demon is able to turn into a beautiful woman to lure and use people.

19. *The Song of Youth*—A novel published in 1958 by Yang Mo, a contemporary Chinese writer, it was once condemned by the government as corruptive and indecent largely because of certain detailed descriptions of romantic relationships in the novel.

20. The Chinese equivalent to "study hall" in high school.

21. *How Steel Was Tempered*—This novel about the growth of a young communist in the beginning years of the Soviet Union was once one of the most popular novels in China and was recommended to all young people by the communist government.

22. The Moon Temple—one of the four important temples in Beijing. The other three temples are the Sun Temple, the Earth Temple, and the Heaven Temple.

23. "the framed picture of Chairman Mao"—Almost in every home at that time there was a picture of Mao Zedong.

24. ". . . also surged the same emotional tides felt by millions of people"—When Zhou Enlai, China's Prime Minister for decades, died in 1976, he was mourned by millions in China. He was believed to be the person who held China together when the country went through disasters and turmoil.

25. ". . . knowledge level at about that of Junior High Grade One"—Junior High Grade One is equivalent to the freshman year in American high schools.

26. ". . . the head hooligan 'Jug Ear Eggplant'"—This nickname for the head hooligan may have come from an observation of some of his facial features and his large ears.

27. ". . . all specialists—scientists, engineers, writers, and professors—were relegated to being the Stinking Number Ninth"— Before and during the Cultural Revolution, intellectuals were ranked ninth in social importance and trust by radicals in the government, a position right along with the lowest people in society, such as the criminals and the crooks.

28. Zhang Tiesheng—During the Cultural Revolution, in a nominal college entrance examination that was easy for anyone to pass, Zhang Tiesheng scored zero. But he was admitted to college anyway because college education in China at the time was involved more in political activities than in education. Not only that, he was also used by the radical government as an example to illustrate the point that as long as one was loyal to the Chinese Communist Party and was politically active and correct, intelligence or knowledge was to be disregarded.

29. "Those bourgeois concepts that existed in the rising period of capitalism"—In the political propaganda during the Cultural Revolution, capitalism was regarded as being in its final moments. As an effort to explain away the concepts of freedom, equality, and fraternity in capitalism, these concepts were identified as the ideals of capitalism in its early stages, which the Chinese government claimed to no longer exist in twentieth-century capitalism.

30. "... according to his reading habit, he read only half of the word"—In Chinese, *gadfly* is pronounced as *niumang* and, in its written form, the second character in the word looks like *wang*, an easier and more common character. Therefore, the mistake in pronunciation ("niuwang" instead of "niumancy") comes from Song Baoqi's misreading of half of the word. In Chinese culture, to misread a word or to be able to read only half of a word is a shame and a sign of lack of education.

31. *The Red Cliff*—a popular novel (1961) in China about underground Chinese communists fighting against the Chinese Nationalist Party.

32. *Selected Poems of Xin Jiaxuan*—This is a situation similar to that in n. 30. The name of the poet Xin Jiaxuan, when written in Chinese, can be misread as "new wedding carriage."

33. "... which were by no means poisonous grass but rather fragrant flowers"—In those days, books approved by the government were called "fragrant flowers" and those that were not approved were naturally called "poisonous grass."

34. The "Four Modernizations"—This was a goal set in the 1970s by the Chinese government for the end of the century; and the four modernizations include modernization in industry, agriculture, defense, and science and technology.

35. "What he cultivated were not just some students or some flowers"—Flowers are often used to mean students, who are supposed to blossom and be fruitful in the future.

36. "Four Cleanups Movement"—One of the earlier political movements in the 1950s, the "Four Cleanups Movement" was launched to clean up the dissidents and solidify the rule of the Communist Party.

37. *Violent Winds and Torrential Rains*—a popular novel (1949) in China in those days about the Communist revolution and land reform in the Northeast of China in the late 1940s.

38. October Revolution—the Russian Revolution in 1917, which established the Soviet Union.

39. "Has it been recommended in the newspapers?"—Please note that all newspapers were strictly controlled by the government.

40. "the leader's thoughts"—The leader here refers to Mao Zedong.

41. "... in the semester before October"—The Gang of Four were arrested in October, 1976, and people use the month of October to mark

the end of the Cultural Revolution and the beginning of a more moderate political atmosphere in China.

Bibliography

Liu, Xinwu. "The Class Teacher." *People's Literature* (Renmin Wenxue) November, 1977: 16–29.

———. *Xiepo Wentan*. Shanghai: Shanghai Arts (Shanghai Wenyi Chubanshe), 1987.

Xu, Zidong. "On Liu Xinwu." *Studies in Literary Theory* (Wenyi Lilun Yanjiu) 4 (1987): 58–68.

CHAPTER 6

"Li Shunda Builds a House"
(Li Shunda Zaowu)

Gao Xiaosheng (1928–)

Introduction to the Author

Born in the county of Wujin in Jiangsu Province in 1928, Gao Xiaosheng began writing and publishing stories early in life. Yet his life would take some unexpected turns and his success and fame as a writer would not come until much later in life.

In his high school years, he quit school three times because of financial difficulties in the family. After graduating from high school in 1947, he entered the Economics Department in the Shanghai School of Law (Shanghai Faxueyuan), from which he did not graduate. Instead, in 1950, he graduated from South Jiangsu Journalism College. After graduation, he worked at various jobs, sometimes in the South Jiangsu Artists' Union and in the Cultural Bureau of Jiangsu Province. He was also once an editor for the arts section of the famous *Xinhua Daily* (New China Daily). During this period till 1957, he wrote works in different genres, but his moderate success and achievements were mostly in fiction. His first short story, "Collecting Tenant Fees" ("Shou Tiancai"), was published in 1950. His better known stories of this period were "Cancel the Engagement" ("Jie Yue") and

"Misfortune" ("Bu Xin"), which were published in the mid-1950s.

But because of his literary activities and his friendship with some other active young writers, his misfortune came not long after he published those stories. In 1957, he was categorized as a "rightist" in the notorious Anti-Rightist Movement, a poorly controlled movement launched by Mao Zedong to purge the country of dissenting intellectuals or anyone against the government. As a result, he was classified as a "dissident" and a "rightist," the humiliating title that made many a weak intellectual commit suicide, as did the famous Chinese writer Lao She and the not-so-famous writer Zhou Shoujuan. Having been given such a title, he was sent back to his birthplace to be reformed through labor. In the years to follow, he worked with the farmers, lived with the farmers, and finally became, to some extent, a farmer himself, knowing in detail how the farmers lived, what the farmers suffered, what they were thinking about, and how they felt.

Soon after the Cultural Revolution ended, Gao Xiaosheng started writing stories again. These stories are more often than not about the farmers he worked with side by side and the farming community in which he once lived. In numerous stories, he created such wonderful and famous characters as Li Shunda and Cheng Huansheng, not to denigrate them, but to reintroduce them to the whole country as never before. In 1979, he became known to the whole nation after the publication of his story "Li Shunda Builds a House," which was published in the July issue of the literary magazine *Yu Hua*. Later he would continue to publish such sensational yet well-crafted short stories as "Cheng Huansheng Goes to Town." Many characters from his stories, such as Li Shunda and Cheng Huansheng, were so representative of certain people in Chinese society that they became household names in China. Both "Li Shunda Builds a House" and "Cheng Huansheng Goes to Town" won the National Short Story Award in 1979 and 1980 respectively, and some of his stories were made into television feature movies.

Gao Xiaosheng still writes and publishes continuously. Although he may no longer enjoy the popularity he once did due to the present decline of written literature's status in China, his writings are still among the best of Chinese writers, and whatever he publishes now should not be neglected by any serious critic or student of Chinese literature.

"Li Shunda Builds a House" is about the small people in China who try to survive at the very bottom of the society. The story is filled with sarcasm and irony, which are often bitter. The story also has a keen sense of humor, but the humor is also quite biting. One caution about reading this story is that the author's attitude toward the Party Secretary Liu Qing is not negative, even though some passages about him may seem sarcastic.

Li Shunda Builds a House

[1979]

1

Farmers of the older generation always said that eating thin porridge for three years would buy one an ox. It seemed easy to say so, but it would be rather a feat to accomplish this. Just imagine, if even meals are begrudged for three years, wouldn't all the other expenses be tightened to the extreme? Not to mention that the saying is mostly idle talk! If one could not even afford meals, what else is there to save?

Li Shunda's family was like that before. So, before the Liberation,[1] he never had the dream of buying an ox. Yet, after the Land Reform,[2] he set himself a goal to build a three-bedroom house in the spirit of "eating thin porridge for three years to buy an ox."

To build a three-bedroom house, how many "three-year porridges" would it then take? He did not know. At any rate, it was different from before the Liberation, and as there was indeed some saving when the living was carefully calculated and managed, he had enough confidence.

At that time, Li Shunda was twenty-eight; thick short hair, dark red face, medium height, broad shoulders and thick chest, just like an iron tower. Among the four members of the family (himself, his wife, his sister, and his son), three were already working, and they were given six and eight-tenth mus³ of good land. He felt that the strength in his body was bigger than the sky, and it was even easy to poke a big hole in the earth with an iron harrow. Why would he worry about building a three-bedroom house? The firm determination was evident in his calm but not very smart eyes and in the straight and broad nose that pressed like a stickleback on his thick lips. This determination would not waver even if an ox had pulled on it.

To say nothing of oxen, not even a train would have pulled him off the course. Li Shunda's father, mother, and a one-year-old brother all died because they did not have a house. They were originally fishermen, fishing in the rivers south of the Yangtze River, wandering everywhere, not knowing themselves where they had initially come from. When the wooden ship was in the hands of Li Shunda's father, it was already quite old and in ruins. The nails' rust turned into holes and the sky could be seen through the torn reed-skin cabin top. It could no longer weather the wind and tides and they could not net fish and shrimp anymore. The family changed their profession. For a meal of porridge, some collected scraps; some traded candies for scraps; and some dug up snails. In 1942, when Li Shunda was nineteen, in a freezing month of the cold winter, their broken ship anchored in the river by the Cheng Village. That day, the clouds were dark and the wind was menacing. Li Shunda went ashore with his fourteen-year-old sister, one trading for scraps and one collecting scraps, and they went more than ten li⁴ away. On their return at dusk, the wind stopped and the clouds were gray, but the snow was all over the land and the sky, and they were lost right away. Fortunately they found a run-down temple and stayed there for the night. At daylight they hurried back to the Cheng Village, but the broken boat had already been sunk into the river by the snow. Their father, mother, and little brother were frozen to death at the gate of a farmer. It turned out that before the snow sank the boat, they came ashore to knock on people's doors for help. They knocked at the doors of a dozen families, but due to the turmoil and chaos of wars and the countless thieves, when they cried for help from outside, people thought that thieves had come to the village and nobody dared to open their door. As a result, they were literally frozen to death in the snow. The sky does not have eyes, and the earth does not have a heart. The sufferings of the poor are unimaginable and innumerable . . . without a house, alas!

Li Shunda and his sister cried till they passed out beside the bodies of their father and mother. Not one of the poor people in the Cheng Village was not sad. They dragged the sunken boat up to the shore and tore half of it apart to make coffins for the dead. The half that was left was turned upside down to become a little hut by the graves to let Li Shunda have a home.

After the Anti-Japanese War, the Civil War began. The Nationalist Party started their conscription, but no one wanted to go. The sheriff of the village received money from people who were conscripted, and, seeing that Li Shunda was an outsider without any relatives whatsoever, gave him three shis[5] of rice and forced him to sell himself to become a soldier.[6] He looked at the hut, which did not have a door, and he was afraid that when he was gone, his sister could be ruined by someone. He then used the money he sold himself for to build a little house of straws, wiped his tears away, and went to shoulder that "seven pounds and a half."[7]

There was no way that he was willing to give his life to the Nationalist Party![8] Three months later, as soon as the soldiers went to the front, he deserted and came back. The next year, the sheriff bought him again. All in all, he sold himself three times. The money he sold himself for the second time paid for the land of the straw house. The money for the third time paid for the cemetery lot for his parents. Oh, well, even if he sold himself three more times, the money would "probably" still all end up in other people's pockets.

Nonetheless, thanks to the little straw house, he eventually found a wife. When he was away being a soldier, his sister found a lonely and helpless beggar girl to live with her. The girl later became his wife. A year later a plump little son was born, who was not inferior in any way to other people's children.

The Land Reform gave him land but did not give him a house. There was only one landlord in the Cheng Village, and his house, built in the city, could not be moved to the village to be divided. Li Shunda had to find a way himself. He made a rough calculation. Two rooms for himself and his sister (he'd let his son live in one room if his sister got married), half a room each for the living room and the kitchen, and also a room for the pigs, sheep, and the fuel. It looked as if a family needed at the very least three rooms.

That was the goal that Li Shunda set himself to strive for after the Liberation.

2

For a liberated poor fellow, setting a three-bedroom house as his goal to strive for might be too shortsighted, and such an ambition might be too insignificant. But Li Shunda believed that it was because of the Communist Party and the People's Government[9] that he could have such an ambition and that there was the possibility of realizing the grandiose plan. Therefore he was truly willing in his heart to follow the Communist Party to the end. Up till now, his action from beginning to end proved this willingness. To him, to build socialism was to have "upstairs and downstairs,[10] electric lights, and telephones." The main thing was still building a house. He thought, however, that a two-story building was not as practical as two single-story houses. He would rather not have an upstairs and downstairs. He only wanted to build a single-story house, but did not know if single-story houses could be considered socialism. As for electric lights, he was for them. He had no use for telephones. He had no relatives or friends; what was the telephone for? If the kid broke it, it would take money to fix it. Wouldn't it be something to ruin a family? He had openly spoken these thoughts, but no one believed there was anything wrong with them.

The farmers in the Cheng Village had no disdain for his goal, but instead thought his goal a little too high. Someone used an old saying to begin his speech and said: "'A house of three bedrooms and ten mus of land, all over the world hard to find.' There is nothing easy about building a house in our area!" Some said: "Even if you could build a house, it would mean half a life of hard living." Some said: "The world after the Liberation is somewhat easier, but I am afraid it would take at least ten years of savings."

These words were rather frank. At that time, on both sides of the Shanghai-Ningbo Railway, with the town Benniu as the point of demarcation, the structures of the houses were entirely different: West of Benniu, eight out of ten houses were made of adobe bricks and a thatched roof. East of Benniu, eight or nine out of ten houses were made of gray bricks and a roof of tiles. The Cheng Village was a hundred miles east of Benniu, and the whole village had no house made of straw except Li Shunda's. Although he was poor, having lived in such an environment, Li Shunda was used to seeing good houses. Well, this honest fellow was really a bit ambitious, wanting to build a three-bedroom house. Could it ever be easy!

Faced with all the talk, Li Shunda always just laughed a little and said: "It wouldn't in any way be more difficult than the foolish old man moving mountains in the fable." When he spoke, his thick lips pulled the big heavy nose, looking as if he used a lot of strength. Therefore, the simple words he spoke nonetheless gave people the impression of carrying a lot of weight.

After that, the whole family of Li Shunda started a most difficult battle. It involved earning every grain of food by working with all their might using the simplest tools, and it involved saving every penny by using the most primitive management style. The earnings for their everyday labor were very little, but they completely understood that anything huge is the accumulation of innumerable small things, and so they displayed surprising optimism and a persistent, thrifty spirit. Sometimes, when the labor of the whole family would not even cover ordinary daily living expenses, they would then decide to go a little hungry, so, at every meal, everyone would eat half a bowl of porridge less, and they would regard the six bowls of rice saved as a surplus. There were even times when it rained or snowed for days and they could not work and became completely "unemployed." They then would lie in bed and not get up. The three meals were then combined into two meals, and they considered the one meal saved as an income. When they cooked porridge with vegetables, they would drop in some soybeans instead of cooking oil, because cooking oil itself was pressed out of soybeans. When they cooked snails, they would put in a scoop of rice soup instead of wine, because wine was, after all, made of rice. . . . They raised chickens all year long without eating the eggs;[11] the kilo of meat they bought on Memorial Day as sacrifice for their parents would not be eaten until near the Dragon Boat Festival when rice seedlings were planted.

Whenever he had free time, Li Shunda would take up his family profession, wandering about on city streets and in villages with a load of candies on a pole on his shoulders and trading them for such scraps as torn cloths, newspapers, old cotton waddings, and torn shoes. He would sort them into different categories to sell to the recycling station, and sometimes he could earn a very good profit. In the scraps there were often clothes and rain shoes that could be worn if mended. They would pick them out, mend them, and wear them for a while. When they could not be mended anymore, they would then be sorted into scraps. This also saved them a lot of living expenses. The candies they traded for scraps were manufactured by themselves out of malt sugar they bought, and the cost was very low. But Li Shunda's only son, Xiao Kang, did not know that it was sugar until he was seven, and did not know whether that thing was sweet or salty. At eight, he was encouraged by the kids in the village to go home and try a piece, but was caught by his mother as a thief. He was beaten on the behind and he cried like a pig being slaughtered. He was also forced by his mother to swear that he would reform himself from then on. His mother was still claiming again and again that he would be the black sheep of the family, saying that he would eat away the three-bedroom house his parents wanted to build, and that he would blame his father and mother if he could not find a wife.[12]

The most respectful thing was done by Li Shunda's sister Shunzhen. She was already twenty-three during the Land Reform in 1951. At that time, the government did not call on the people to marry late, and, according to the tradition, twenty-three was just the age to get married. She was not only hardworking, docile, and honest, but she also looked extraordinarily beautiful. Upon careful observation, she seemed to have the exact same look as her brother, only her nose was a little smaller and her lips were a little thinner. Just on these two little things, Providence revealed its greatness at being capable of anything, revealing an air of delicate beauty in the tall, slim, and oval-faced Li Shunzhen. At that time, more than a few young men from neighboring villages asked people to come and seek marriage.[13] But no matter what conditions they offered or how good their personalities were, Shunzhen said only that she was still young and refused them without exception. She had been brought up by her brother and she was determined to repay her brother's kindness. She knew that without her help, her brother's goal would be very hard to reach. If she got married, her brother would not only be without strong reliable help, but she would also take away the one and seven-tenth mus of land under her name. If so, her brother's economic base and workforce would be greatly reduced, and no one would know when in the world the three-bedroom house could be built. Therefore she willingly devoted the most beautiful time of her life—it could be said to be the youth of one's youth—to her brother's cause.

Not until the end of 1957, when Li Shunda had already bought all the building materials for the three-bedroom gray brick house, did Li Shunzhen eventually settle the matter, marrying as an old girl of twenty-nine to an old bridegroom of thirty in the neighboring village. The bridegroom was single till then because he had to shoulder the lives of two old parents and a handicapped sister, and therefore he possessed nothing other than the four walls of his house and had only clothes that had been mended many times. So, what was awaiting Li Shunzhen was still a hard life. But she was used to hardships and hence did not mind much.

3

When he was done with his sister's marriage, it was already the beginning of 1958. What else did Li Shunda need at this time? He still needed the wages for the carpenters and masons, and also the expenses for their meals. In one more year, the problem would be completely solved. Moreover, after the communization,[14] things were very much in Li Shunda's favor. All the land had become state property, so he could choose at will a most suitable piece of land to build his house on. Wasn't that ideal?

But Li Shunda was not a revolutionary after all. He was nothing more than a follower. As for heeding what Chairman Mao said or following the Communist Party, he was not only firm in action, but was also able to carry it out to the fullest. If any Party member said something to him, that would be like an order. One night, Li Shunda woke up from his sleep, suddenly hearing that all under the sky was the same and equal[15] and that there was no need to differentiate my things from your things. Eight years after the Liberation, there were indeed some possessions in people's hands. For example, don't you, Li Shunda, have the materials for building a three-bedroom house? Well, then, why don't we all put our things together to speed up our constructions? Our constructions are completely for all of us, and so we all should go all out to support such constructions. There is no need for any personal plans. In the future the life for all of us will be equally satisfactory. What is so important about that little pitiful private possession? Putting it in a great cause is the only glorious thing to do. There should be no worry. Everything is put together for the use of the collective unit,[16] and everyone is the same. Nobody will cheat any other person.

Such a theory, without any doubt, came out of concerns for the whole country. Li Shunda looked around, thought for a while, and felt that all stuffiness was cleared from his head and that he was happy and lighthearted all over. Although he was hurt and shed many tears when his bricks were taken away to build an iron-smelting furnace, his lumber was hauled away to make earth-moving carts, and, lastly, his tiles were put on the roof of the collective pigsty, he nonetheless felt extraordinarily happy and satisfied when he thought of the happiness in the future. His recent experience also changed his original thoughts. He believed that multistory buildings had more advantages than single-story houses because the grain stored upstairs would not rot and living upstairs would not give you eczema. It seemed better to live in the multistory building that he would be allotted. Why would he ask for trouble and always carry the burden of a house like a snail? So his mind was entirely liberated. No matter what the community wanted, he was happy to give. Even if they had wanted his broken bed, he would not have begrudged it: because both he and his wife did not grow up only lying in bed.

His wife, that girl beggar, was really shrewder than he was. But the twelfth degree typhoon[17] was already blowing everybody off their feet, and what could a woman like her do! More wisdom meant nothing more than added worries. She nonetheless hid an iron wok and did not send it to be melted in the iron furnace. So after the collective dining hall was dismantled, they did not have to line up to buy a wok.

Later on, not until there were no more funds to mess around with, did they come back to rebuild socialism. We are talking about our own dirty laundry, and so it becomes tasteless to talk too much about it. But before everything was torn down in the battlefields,[18] Li Shunda went really often to visit them. Looking at the collapsed iron-smelting furnace and the earth-moving carts deserted on the wild beaches, he opened his teary eyes and sobbed in the wind. He thought of his planning and sweat of six years, thought of the grain he saved by going hungry, thought of the candy he snatched from the mouth of his son, and he thought of his sister who sacrificed her youth. . . .

4

The government policy of paying compensations for the losses was, without any doubt, widely welcome. But it was not the government, but the collective unit, that took and spent all of Li Shunda's building materials. This collective unit should, of course, carry out a policy of paying compensations. But the collective unit was also turned into desperate poverty. Having no materials to give back and having difficulties in paying cash, the cadres[19] resorted to using all their power to work on the minds of the people to elevate the political consciousness of the people like Li Shunda and ask them for self-sacrifices so that they could carry out the compensation policy at the lowest price.

Li Shunda's loss was not small, but his political consciousness had indeed been raised, because never before had anyone given him such a serious and careful ideological education. The Party Secretary of the District,[20] Comrade Liu Qing, a leader of good moral integrity and high popular trust, made a special trip to come and see him, talking to him knee to knee. He explained that his things were not lost in any corruption, nor were they wasted away purposely by someone who hated him. The intentions of the Party and the government were all very good, with the pure purpose of speeding up the socialist construction to let everyone enjoy the happy life a little earlier. For this purpose, the investment of the country and the collective unit was infinitely bigger than Li Shunda's contributions, and therefore it was impossible to estimate their losses. Now, no matter how big the losses of the government and the collective unit were, they still decided to compensate the losses of the individuals. Other than the Communist Party, who would have done such a thing? There had been no such precedent in history. Only the Communist Party was able to care about farmers like us. It was hoped that he would be able to understand the difficulties of the Party, and, setting as priorities the interests of the country and the collective unit, he would share some of the losses. After these years, the Party and the government had learned their lessons and accumulated experience, and development in the future would be much faster. When the economy of the country and the collective unit turned for the better, your personal things would be easier to accomplish, too. It now looked really difficult to build the three-bedroom house you wanted, but in the future it would be easier. He should not be disappointed. In the end, Comrade Liu Qing helped him to get in touch with the Supply and Marketing Cooperative,[21] asking the cooperative to supply him with malt sugar even in the most difficult situations, so that he could trade for scraps to make a little more money.

Li Shunda's emotions were easy to stir. When he heard the teachings and advice of Comrade Liu Qing and his specific help, his tears were already rolling down. Without saying anything else, he fully agreed between sobs.

There were still the twenty thousand tiles that the brigade took away to roof the seven-and-a-half-room pigsty. Now they were still all on the roof and should be returned all together. But, if they were taken down and new tiles were not bought to cover the roof in time, the pigs would have to be raised outdoors. Tiles were also fragile things and many would be damaged if they were taken down and moved around. So it was better not to take them down. After negotiations by the two sides in order to solve each other's problems, they decided not to move the tiles. Instead, the brigade would clean out two pigsty rooms to let Li Shunda live there for a time. When Li Shunda built his new house, the brigade would return the tiles and he would move out of the pigsty. Even the pigsty was better than the straw hut he was living in then. There were two rooms, spacious enough. The roof was quite high; only the part in the back was lower than a person's height. But as the residents did not have the need to straighten their chests to look majestic, that posed no big problems. Besides, Li Shunda used to stay in boat cabins when he was young, so he naturally did not mind this.

The compensation problem was thus solved. Although Li Shunda wholeheartedly accepted the advice of the cadres, he learned a special lesson from this event. Before all this, he was thinking about the inflation in the Old Society,[22] when cash in one's hands was not reliable. So whenever he had extra money, he would buy something and store it up. Now he had some new experience, feeling that in the New Society it was not reliable to store things. It was safer to hide the cash under one's pillow. Frankly, in this kind of thinking, the especially sensitive "leftists" could certainly smell the "anti-Party" scent.

From 1962 to 1965, because of the "Sixty Item Document,"[23] relying on the malt sugar that Comrade Liu Qing gave special allowance for, Li Shunda accumulated about enough cash to build a three-bedroom house. But he made up his mind that he would not buy anything: He would either buy nothing at all or buy everything at the same time and build the house at once. He wanted to avoid a long delay that could incur many hitches and thus avoid the previous losses.

This Li Shunda, just like many other peasants, had only the limited smartness of looking backwards. Therefore, just when he thought he was sure that he would not suffer the previous losses again, he would tumble down right away on the road ahead. To tell the truth, helping such people move forward gives one's hands some real pain.

At the time, materials were plentiful and everything was supplied without limit, but he just would not buy anything. A few years later, when materials became scarce and it would be hard to buy anything without some connections, he suddenly thought about buying everything all at once. Didn't he make a fool of himself! Actually, it would not be right to blame him. Who can be a Zhu Geliang?[24]

5

Under normal conditions, Li Shunda felt that he would be capable of being a follower, his feelings true, his heart sincere, and his emotions not in the least unnatural. But after the start of the Cultural Revolution, it was hard for him to keep up. Even when he wanted to follow someone, he did not know whom to follow, when in all directions someone was yelling: "Only I am correct!" After all, who was right and who was wrong, who was good and who was bad, who was red and who was black?[25] His head was ringing and he was confused. He had to squat down and was unwilling to follow. "Every heart has the ability to tell the right from the wrong." This claim is overly self-confident, but actually it is quite naive because whoever says it did not go through the Cultural Revolution. You cannot just watch what is being sung up on the stage, but must also see what is being practiced behind the stage. But it would be reasonable to say that "everyone has the heart capable of being both good and evil." Li Shunda was just a little unhappy. This unhappiness was closely related to his desire to build a house. He saw that the tumultuous momentum was different even from that of 1959. In 1959, it was nothing more than destroying a few things. This time it would destroy some people. A life could be done within one move. Right now the house could no longer be built, and who knew what it would be like tomorrow? For this he was really a bit disgusted. Then again he felt fortunate that he had moved to the pigsty, which was in the center of the village. If he were still living in the straw hut by the river, the money under his pillow, he was afraid, might be stolen.

What Li Shunda was thinking was too outdated. In the civilized age, civilized people did not need to use any barbarous means. Under the blue sky, the head of a Rebellion Faction came to visit Li Shunda, a pistol worn on his waist and a little red book hanging from his shoulder, and he was accompanied by the head of the production team. It turned out that he was the Director of the Cultural Revolutionary Committee in the brick and tile plant of the commune. Being keen on brotherhood and having heard that Li Shunda could not buy bricks to build his house, he made a special trip to help him solve the problem. He cursed a great deal the capitalist-roader Liu Qing, who did not work for the benefits of the poor and lower-middle peasants.[26] Now it was his turn to be the savior. As long as Li Shunda could give him 217 yuan, he would take the responsibility of buying ten thousand bricks for him, and the bricks could be picked up the following month. Such a promise was made too beautifully, and should usually be suspect. But Li Shunda thought that, since they lived in the same brigade, saw each other now and then although they were not friends, and since he had not heard of any bad deeds by this person, now that he was out to join in the revolution, he would want to do something good and would not cheat people right away. Moreover, he was accompanied to Li Shunda's house by the production team leader, and he had a gun and a little red book with him. Therefore, there was friendship if you wanted it; there was faith if you liked it; and there was authority if you asked for it. Although Li Shunda deserted as a soldier three times, he had not seen a situation like this when carrots and clubs were applied at the same time. He was frightened, and he was softened, so he counted out 217 yuan with trembling hands.

Come next month, the goods could probably be delivered. But unexpectedly, Li Shunda courted with misfortune and was summoned by the commune's dictatorship apparatus,[27] which asked him to confess these few things: (1) Where did you come from? What kind of class did your original family belong to? (2) You were a soldier three times, so quickly give out your guns. (3) Confess your counterrevolutionary talks (for example, he once said such things as "multistory buildings are not as practical as single-story houses, and one cannot afford to fix broken telephones," and that was a vicious attack on socialism).

The things that happened later need not be mentioned; everyone knew them. He did not talk much about them either after he was released. But there were two things that were rather unique. The first thing was that while he begged for his life when he could not stand it any longer, the Director of the Cultural Revolutionary Committee of the brick and tile plant came to his rescue. To repay the deed, they decided between themselves that they would never again mention the 217 yuan. The second thing was that the house he was locked in was quite firmly constructed. For the first time in his life he studied architecture in there and had a very clear outline of the house he was to build.

When he was freed, he walked home leaning against the shoulder of his son (already nineteen years old). His tearful wife and sister asked him why he was locked up and what miseries he suffered. His hoarse voice uttered only two puzzling short phrases: "Them vicious! My house!"

For a year after that, he could not work and he did not feel good inside his back. When it was cloudy or rainy, his bones ached all over. He was a little curious. Although he had never been beaten up before, he had lived his life in poverty and hardships, so why was he now so fragile? Did he also become "revisionized"?[28] He was a little startled, feeling that it would be all right even if he had turned into a horse or a buffalo, but not a "revisionist." What was a "revisionist"? It was a black wok.[29] It could not cook rice, but could only be mounted on one's back as an ornament. It was a "family treasure" that was lifeless and therefore could not die and would be passed down from generation to generation. His son was nineteen years old that year; if he had this black wok on his back, where would he find a wife? And the house had not been built, so there was not yet a single favorable condition.

Li Shunda thought about this, and there was in his heart both panic and superstition. When he was little, he had heard many old stories, among which was the claim that men could turn into many different things. The storyteller would always say: "After one night he turned into such and such." And before the change, there were always some funny feelings, such as bones aching all over the body, the skin becoming hot and irritated, and so on. Therefore, whenever Li Shunda felt uncomfortable in his body, he was afraid of the dark night and feared falling asleep. He would always open his eyes wide to prevent himself from unconsciously turning into a black wok in his slumber. His alertness was always quite high, so till now he still had not turned into anything.

During those nights in which he feared falling asleep, to release the pains in his flesh, Li Shunda also thought of some pleasing recreational activities. He did not have a radio. He could not read, because he was illiterate. Besides, it would waste lighting oil. So the only way out was to recall the stories he had heard when he was young, the lines in the dramas he had watched, and the vulgar songs that the older generation had taught the children. Later when his health was better, he shouldered the candy baskets to trade for scraps and would often be singing a shady song to attract children. He claimed that these were the songs he recalled in those nights. From these songs we can tell what he was thinking at the time. He sang,

> Strange, strange, really strange
> An old man is trapped in a rocking cradle
> Strange, strange, really strange
> A table is put in a little pocket
> Strange, strange, really strange
> Rats bit open a cat's belly
> Strange, strange, really strange
> Lions are often bullied by lice
> Strange, strange, really strange
> Dogs send weasels to watch the chickens
> Strange, strange, really strange
> Swan meat fell into the mouth of a toad
> Strange, strange, really strange
> Big ships turned over in a sewer ditch
> Strange, strange, really strange
> Tall fellows become ladders for short ones
> Aha ha, the bald head wears a cap
> Clam shells hold a pot of pee
> The belly of a ball contains wind
> The bad god in robe is a hunk of mud
> Oh strange, oh strange, really strange
> Snakes wind into the belly of the Buddha for the winter
> Smelling the incense and pretending to be glorious[30]

This was indeed a children's song generally known for its load of "strangeness," and it was terribly old. But, the strangeness in everyone's load is different, because people would always put what they regard as strange in the load. If, however, he was questioned, Li Shunda would never admit that he added anything to it. He was no writer, and could not drop any black characters on white paper, so he was not afraid that any handle would fall into others' hands. Although he was not clever, he did, after all, go through the ordeal, and understood the people of that time—If those rebellious people in power and the powerful people in rebellion[31] wanted to ruin your luck, it would not be because of what you had done, but because they wanted to reach a certain goal, such as his 217 yuan.

One day, when he was trading candy for scraps in a neighboring village, he happened to run into the capitalist-roader who was being reformed there—the former Party Committee Secretary Liu Qing. He was both happy and sad, and was not willing to leave for a long time. In the end, Liu Qing begged him to sing for him once again the strange song. He started singing it without any hesitation. That miserable, heavy, and angry voice even made the air tremble while both men shed their tears.

6

After being sick for a year, Li Shunda was somewhat discouraged. He often thought, how many years could he live? Why would he take pains to build a house! The foolish old man made up his mind to move the mountains, and still he relied on his descendants to finish the work. So why should he have to build it himself! Besides, he had some savings, had thus made quite some contribution, and was not disgraceful. But he had not transcended his earthly existence, and his tainted heart was hard to cleanse. His son was already over twenty. If the house were not built, he would not be able to find a wife. Who would come and live in a bridal chamber converted from a pigsty? To find a beggar girl for wife as he did, there was no such good chance any more. That would not do. Without a daughter-in-law, how would there be a grandson? Without a grandson, how would there be a great-grandson? When communism was built in the future for a happy life, would it do to have no offspring of Li Shunda? It seemed that the house had to be built, and he should hurry up. Even so, his son might have to marry later than the late-marriage age as regulated by the government.

After some wavering, his decision became steadfast, and he acted on it immediately. He put on his shoulder the baskets for collecting scraps, slowly wandering from this town to that town, going through all the big streets and small lanes in the county seat, but he did not see any construction material for sale. He asked at certain stores and then found out that, even if he just wanted to buy a brick, he needed identifications from three administrative levels[32] and there was no room for idle talk. He knew that it would be useless to run around aimlessly, so he had to apply for permission from his production team, his brigade, and his commune. Luckily he brought his scrap baskets with him when he went wandering around. Although he did not buy any construction materials, the scraps he collected were sold for a dozen yuan, which was no waste of his work.

The next thing was naturally to ask for permission from cadres of the production team and the brigade. They said with a little laugh after they heard him: "What's the use of getting a permission? As for residential construction materials, sometimes there was just a little, and sometimes there was almost nothing. Even if we gave you the permission, you would not be able to buy any." Li Shunda was not willing to believe them, thinking the cadres were stonewalling him. But he did not dare talk back, because he was afraid of relationships turning sour. So he patiently hung around and refused to leave, putting on a quiet sitting demonstration in disguise. Unexpectedly, the others did not mind it that much. When at suppertime they found he had not yet left, they then said: "Go home. The door will be locked." He just had to go back home. The next day, he went back there to sit again. After three such days, the cadres became impatient, saying: "You would not take good advice, but just mess around. If you believe it's useful, we'll then give you the permission!" Indeed, the permission was written and he went gleefully to the Supply and Marketing Cooperative. The salesman looked at the permission, laughed a little, like the cadres in his brigade did, and said, "Can't help it. No goods to supply you."

"When will there be some?"

"Don't know," the salesman said. "When you're free, come often and ask."

From then on, Li Shunda was like a student going to school, going there six times in seven days. Half a year later, he still had not bought a single brick. That salesman was a kindhearted man. Although he secretly pitied Li Shunda's dull-wittedness, he was nonetheless touched by his spirit. Finally one day he told Li Shunda: "Why don't you save a bit of your time? Don't come here and ask. In these few years, the revolution[33] is revolving so fiercely that the earth is almost revolved out of things. When on a rare occasion a few things arrive, they are not even enough to give the cadres preferential treatment, to say nothing of giving you a chance. Even if there were something for you, it would be the leftovers after many times of picking and choosing by other people, but the price for it would be the same as what has been already picked away before you. You wouldn't get the value of it. I advise you to think of some other way."

Li Shunda heard the kind advice and was rather disappointed and also very grateful. Therefore he had to ask for wisdom: "What other way can you think of?"

The salesman quietly thought for a moment and said: "Do you have any close relatives or friends who are cadres?"

"No," Li Shunda said with heaviness and difficulty, "I only have a brother-in-law who is a farmer. No second relative."

"There is then no way out," the salesman said with sympathy. "Nowadays having money is not as good as having connections. When you don't have relatives and friends to depend on, what other way is there other than buying in the black market?"

Li Shunda believed that to be the truth and from then on wanted to find a way to buy black-market materials. Unbeknownst to him, the salesman did not have experience in this area either and did not know the complexity of the black-market dealings. Ten thousand bricks, priced at 217 yuan by the government, would sell for 400 yuan in the black market, and, for that price, payment had to be made first before the goods were to be delivered in a year or six months. Often one would run into con men. Li Shunda had been conned once already, and so the money would not leave his hands easily. Therefore, after walking a thousand miles and talking a ton of times, nothing was bought after three years. Still it was that salesman who was willing to help who bought for him a ton of lime[34] at the government price. The lime was originally allotted to be used in silkworm rooms. But in the last few years there was a continuous conversion of dry farmland into wet farmland and many mulberry-tree fields were changed into rice fields. How many silkworms could be raised on those few shabby mulberry trees that were left! There was thus no use for that large amount of lime. Instead it gave the salesman the opportunity, and Li Shunda found a bargain. For that, he wanted to buy a pack of good cigarettes to treat the salesman, but he just could not find any. Accidentally he ran into the former Director of the Cultural Revolutionary Committee of the brick and tile plant (now promoted to Director of the Revolutionary Committee[35]) and remembered that he was always smoking nice cigarettes. Since the former Director had once treated him unfairly, wouldn't he be willing if he asked him to buy a pack of cigarettes? So he unabashedly went up to him to renew his acquaintance. The Director was indeed straightforward, received his fifty cents, and took from his pocket a pack of unopened Big Qianmen.[36] But before he handed it over to him, he opened the pack without permission and took a cigarette to smoke himself, and said: "I have just this one pack. If it were not you, I wouldn't give it to anybody."

Li Shunda took the nineteen cigarettes to give the salesman, but he resolutely would not accept them. To show his respect, he smoked one cigarette. He forced Li Shunda to take those eighteen cigarettes home with him.

On his way home, Li Shunda thought that he did one inappropriate thing that day which he had never done before. He gave one cigarette to both his benefactor and his enemy. By suppertime he really became angry, scolding his son for being good-for-nothing, for being still dependent on his parents at home even at the age of twenty-five, and making his father suffer out there.

7

After many years of troubles, although Li Shunda still had not built a house, his name nonetheless became widely known.

Where there is faith, even stones and metals will crack open. He not only moved the salesman, but also the Almighty. This Almighty was none other than his future daughter-in-law, whose name was Xinlai. The girl Xinlai lived in the neighboring village and had already been seeing Li Shunda's son Xiao Kang, who was still dependent on his parents. She did not care if the house had been built. She had settled on the person, so it would be all right to build the house after she was married to him. But her dad objected to it, and, no matter what, would not marry his daughter into a pigsty. He used his own successes as examples to teach his daughter, because, although he was poor, he had managed to build a two-bedroom house to bring in a daughter-in-law. He ridiculed Li Shunda as a dumb fellow, a fool, and one who was not able to accomplish things. But unexpectedly, the Almighty liked to play tricks and enjoyed slapping those who boasted in the face. A year later, those in power in the commune overthrew the capitalist-roaders, and, in order to rearrange the mountains and rivers,[37] they felt very uncomfortable to see the course of a river winding like the spine of an old man. They simply summoned several thousand farmers and spent tens of thousands of work days to open up a straight model river, straight enough to let the advanced animals on Mars see it and praise the greatness of the earthlings. The new two-bedroom house belonging to the family of the Xinlai girl was right on the riverbed of the model river (of course, there were more things than that two-bedroom house), and it had to be torn down and moved. The commune paid a moving fee of 150 yuan in compensation for each room. After the move and the reconstruction, adding to it 300 yuan they had borrowed, they just managed to build a room and a half. Xinlai's father lost two-tenths of his weight and his hair became seventy to eighty percent white. Furthermore, the old man had to submit himself to the young and listen to his daughter's teachings. Xinlai suggested to him that he should learn from Uncle Li Shunda. Li Shunda was really smart and did not act rashly, hiding his cash beside his pillow, so that not a penny was lost. To build a house, one needed to be sure of the situation before one started! His words becoming weak, Xinlai's father had to admit defeat and so left his daughter on her own about her marriage.

Li Shunda not only got a daughter-in-law, but he also knew that his daughter-in-law fully confirmed in theory his practice. He was rather happy. Therefore, on the night of his son's wedding, after he drank a few cups of liquor, his mind clicked and he said some inspired words to the father of his daughter-in-law. He said: "Now it is the earth card eating the heaven card and the rotten and the dirty are both made lords.[38] You built your house in too great a hurry. There is an earthquake every day, and everyone is willing to live in a cowshed,[39] so what's the use for houses? The ten thousand bricks of mine were swallowed into the stomach of the kiln ghost, but it was less trouble than yours. . . ." He still wanted to keep on talking. Luckily his wife was more alert and to save him, she scolded him right away in front of the parents of their daughter-in-law: "You drink a bit of liquor, and then you act like someone who has eaten something filthy, and there is no guard on what you say. Forgotten are the days when your bones ached." This then ended the conversation and changed the subject. And everyone was happy.

From that time on, Li Shunda never again wasted his time to buy this and buy that. He shouldered the candy load, wandered here for a day and there for another day, collecting scraps for the country and earning a little living expense. But things were really strange; the people building houses were rather numerous. Seeing them, he could not help being envious and would usually ask people who was building which house and where they bought the materials. The answers he received were of all kinds. If told in detail, one could write a book about each house, but it would not attract people to read it either, because it would be nothing more than "big officials had things sent to them, small officials opened back doors, and the common people begged others." But those people who suffered limitlessly for their house admired Li Shunda instead and said that still he was clever and did not crawl into such bitterness, and he was deservedly the smart one knowing his time. One close acquaintance did not avoid the taboo and said to him angrily: "Not a single brick or tile of mine didn't come from the black market. To build the two-bedroom house, I used the money for a four-bedroom house. On the day when the beam was raised, the brigade leader who rose to that position through rebellion came to my dinner. And he said that without the Cultural Revolution, how could this house of mine be built? F--- his mother. This house of mine is not like his title; could it have been hammered out with a fist!"[40]

By that time, Li Shunda's knowledge of architecture was already insurmountable and could claim the acme of perfection. He did not expect that the sky was high and the earth was wide, and there was no limit to the things of nature. Things that could be written in huge volumes came rolling like the dirty torrents of the Yangtze River, and one could not bear not to look. I wouldn't talk about those trivial things, but it would be a pity to leave out the wonders that were worth voluminous descriptions. Take one brigade for example: All the residential houses were torn down to be grouped together at one place to build a one-row multistory building called "The New Countryside." The materials torn down were sold to the brigade at the government-set price. To live in the new building, one had to use money to buy it. When Li Shunda heard it, he was greatly excited, thinking that "upstairs and downstairs" would truly be realized. He impatiently put his candy load on his shoulder and rushed there at his own expense for a visit.

That place Li Shunda had often gone by before. When he looked at it this time, it indeed had quite a different look. In every village and street, there were people tearing down houses. The materials torn down were transported to a big field by the side of a road where the first row of buildings were being built. The families tearing the houses down had very lively discussions, even to the extent of being heated, all saying that ever since the sky and the earth were severed by Pangu,[41] there had never been anything like this. Hence some people shed tears, probably being overexcited. Some of the tiles that were moved down still had on them the coal dust from the kiln. They had obviously been put on the house without seeing any rain, but now they were liberated. Seeing these, Li Shunda felt that his twenty years of empty talk of building a house without really building one was the most correct thing he had ever done in all his life; however, thinking of all the efforts of the owner of the house, he could not help feeling tears stinging his eyes. Sighing, he walked away with his head bowed low, when suddenly he heard someone calling out: "Hey, candy man."

Li Shunda raised his head to look and saw an old man standing by the road watching the construction of the building with a little girl. The face was quite familiar, but he could not think of who it was. The old man said with a smile: "Why, don't you recognize me?"

Li Shunda suddenly recognized him and said in a hurry: "It is you, old secretary. Are you still reforming through labor?" He suddenly became sad. Having not seen him for several years, Li Shunda did not expect that the secretary was so old that he could not even recognize him. Obviously the old secretary was not happy at heart.

The old secretary laughed a little and said: "Still laboring, but not reformed yet. How about you? Coming here to collect strange songs again?"

"Well, well, old secretary, you are pulling my leg." Li Shunda said with embarrassment, "This is really 'upstairs and downstairs,' creating a 'new countryside.' Not till today did I understand that the division of old and new countrysides lies in the houses. It does not lie in collectivization."

The old secretary sighed lightly, saying: "Well, make yourself clear if you have things to say."

Li Shunda said with a laugh: "Naturally, it won't hurt if I say this to you. Of course I cannot knowingly break the law. But I said before that multistory buildings are not as good as single-story buildings, and that was criticized as reactionary talk. Now that I have seen this, I really have some thoughts. Really good houses, some of which are still new, are torn down and rebuilt, for what? With this energy, wouldn't it be good to grow the crops well? Such a thing people dare not talk about in this world, and in the netherworld, even the ghosts would roll their eyes when they see it."

Hearing such reactionary talk, the old secretary not only made no rebuttal, but even nodded his head and replied with seriousness: "'For what?' You asked the right question. Let me tell you, some people want to use this as the ladder to climb up to the sky. You are also smart, knowing that the basis of the new countryside is collectivization. But when some people started to roll backward, such an organization as the commune could still be taken advantage of. You should open your eyes even wider. Look, the poor and middle peasants suffered for twenty years to build a little house, and, come one order to tear them down, they have to be torn down. Do they care whether the people live or die? But the commune is still a commune."

Li Shunda listened. Although he had some understanding, he could not completely grasp it. He could only let his mouth hang open, open his eyes wide, respectfully look at the old man, and be silent.

The old man gave an angry snort and said no more. He looked down at his granddaughter and pointed at Li Shunda, saying: "Call him grandpa."

The little girl called him grandpa affectionately. Li Shunda was greatly touched and hurriedly knocked off a piece of candy to put in her little hand, proclaiming her to be the most well-behaved little girl. He was fifty-four that year and a scrap collector from elsewhere. But he was called grandpa for the first time by someone, and this gave him rather strong encouragement, diluting all the other thoughts in his mind.

From then on, he and the old secretary became friends.

8

At the Chinese New Year in 1977, only when Li Shunda brought a few pieces of candy to visit the old secretary did he find out that the old secretary was reinstated and was once again working in the district headquarters. Li Shunda was overjoyed. After giving the candy to the little girl and eating the pastry cooked by the little girl's mother, he rushed to the district headquarters with excitement. He felt that now that he had the district secretary as his friend, he could finally get some building materials.

When the old friends met, sure enough, it was very intimate. But when materials were mentioned, the old secretary became silent and hesitant, making Li Shunda's heart shudder with a feeling of apprehension. The old secretary slowly said: "Brother, your difficulties, I know them all. When you sang those strange songs before, I completely agreed with you. Now would you expect me to do those strange things?"

Li Shunda said in a hurry: "Old secretary, if others don't do it, I won't do it either. Now others are still doing it, so why should we be the only exception? Wouldn't that be our loss!"

The old secretary laughed and said: "After eleven years of turmoil, old habits are hard to change. Now wrongs should be made right. Otherwise, the plan to build our country would just be empty talk. We cannot do what other people do. As for all the cadres in the district, I should be the first one to change. As for the people, the change should come from the one who sang the strange songs. Would you say it is reasonable?"

At hearing this talk, all the pots of sweet-and-sour seasonings were knocked over in Li Shunda's heart.[42] On the one hand, he felt proud that the old secretary wanted to lead the rectifying efforts with him; on the other hand, he felt disappointed that although he eventually had a big government official as his friend, he could not take advantage of it for his personal matters. He had gone through the Cultural Revolution and had also learned to be smart. He thought for a moment and then said with confidence: "Old secretary, I agree with what you say, but let me say this first: If you do not want me to do those strange things, I will do according to your advice. But you cannot waver either. You cannot open the back door[43] when you meet people who are better friends with you and have more clout than I do, so that you won't let other people laugh at me for being friends with you for nothing. If that happens, I will rebel against you."

The old secretary laughed out loud, took out a pen and paper, and quickly wrote down what Li Shunda just said, saying: "Let me read this once. Listen." He read it, not a word different from what Li Shunda said. Then he said: "Take this and ask someone to copy it on a big piece of paper, and then put it up in my office."

Li Shunda said in surprise: "I won't. Wouldn't this make you look bad?"

The old secretary said: "Not at all, not at all. This actually helps me out greatly. I was really afraid that some big shot would come to me and open his stinking mouth! When you put this up, then I will not be in any awkward situation."

Li Shunda indeed did so with much gladness.

In the winter of 1977, Li Shunda's family suddenly got busy. The old secretary, Comrade Liu Qing, worked on the director of the brick and tile plant, who had been promoted from the Director of the Cultural Revolution, and asked him to give back Li Shunda's ten thousand bricks. The Revolutionary Committee of the commune also approved Li Shunda's application and agreed to supply him with eighteen cement beams. That kind salesman in the Supply and Marketing Cooperative also informed Li Shunda that the rafters were being supplied without limit. This time, Li Shunda would have the assurance of his house being built. To haul home so many things, the four members in Li Shunda's family were not able to make it. They had to ask for help from his sister, his brother-in-law, and the brothers and sisters of his daughter-in-law. Some rowed the boat; some pulled the cart. Even the aged father of his daughter-in-law gladly sweated a few times. It was a big moment of bustle and excitement.

Yet at the happy moment, a little unpleasant thing also happened. In the midst of hauling home the ten thousand bricks, Li Shunda encountered a little twist. When the big ship anchored by the brick and tile plant, the person there would not give him the supply and said to him with a fake smile: "You haven't bought your rafters. It would be useless, even if you haul the bricks home. Just wait a little." Li Shunda argued with him till his face turned red and his ears turned crimson, saying that the rafters had already been settled. But that person knew Li Shunda better than Li Shunda knew himself, absolutely claiming that he did not have rafters. Luckily the father of his daughter-in-law ran over, and relying on his own experience of brick purchases, secretly explained to Li Shunda what was meant by "rafters." Li Shunda then suddenly understood, immediately went over to the Supply and Marketing Cooperative, and bought two cartons of the best cigarettes to give to the person in the brick and tile plant. Then everyone was happy and the bricks were lowered into the ship. Later on when Li Shunda went to haul the rafters in the factory of cement products, he did not wait for them to open their mouths to ask and gave out a carton of cigarettes, so that they would not say that he still did not have any rafters.

Having done these things to corrupt other people, Li Shunda felt guilty in his heart and he did not dare tell the old secretary. But his soul could not find peace. Sometimes when he woke up at midnight and thought of all this, he would always blame himself: "Oh, well, I should become a little better!"

NOTES

1. "before the Liberation"—This is a phrase often used in mainland China to refer to the time before the founding of the People's Republic of China in 1949, because the birth of the New People's Republic has always been called a "Liberation" from the Chinese Nationalist government.

2. "the Land Reform"—Although there were land reforms on both the mainland and Taiwan in the middle of this century, this land reform refers to the one on the mainland in which almost all private land was confiscated from landlords and then redistributed fairly evenly to the peasants. But in a few years, the land was again collectivized by the state to form communes, which consisted of production brigades that were made up of production teams.

3. ". . . they were given six and eight-tenth mus"—Mu is a unit used to measure land in China and is roughly equal to .16 acre. The land was given to the family in the Land Reform.

4. li—a Chinese measuring unit for distance. It is roughly equal to .31 mile.

5. shi—a Chinese measuring unit for quantity. It is roughly equal to 2.75 bushels.

6. ". . . and forced him to sell himself to become a soldier"—This sentence refers to an old practice in conscription under the Chinese Nationalist rule, in which the poor people not drafted could join the armed forces for a drafted person for a certain amount of money.

7. ". . . and went to shoulder that 'seven pounds and a half'"—The sentence means that he went to become a soldier. A popular rifle at the time weighed seven pounds and a half.

8. "There was no way that he was willing to give his life to the Nationalist Party!"—It is only natural to expect such a judgmental sentence about the Nationalist Party in a story published in the Communist mainland. The truth, however, is that most people did refuse to fight for the Nationalist Party in the Chinese Civil War in the late 1940s, in which the Chinese Communists forced the Nationalist Party to retreat to the island of Taiwan.

9. "... the Communist Party and the People's Government"— The People's Government refers to the People's Republic of China. The two terms in this sentence are often used together even though they are supposedly different apparatuses, but since the Chinese Communist Party literally controls the government, the two are often regarded as interconnected or integrated.

10. "upstairs and downstairs"—refers to a two-story house, a standard prescribed by the government as a sign of having reached communism.

11. "They raised chickens all year long without eating the eggs"— More affluent peasants could afford to eat the eggs, but Li Shunda might be selling them somewhere for money.

12. "... he would blame his father and mother if he could not find a wife"—Since many or most marriages in the Chinese countryside at the time were arranged, a young man could naturally direct his blame toward his parents if he did not get married at the appropriate age.

13. "... asked people to come and seek marriage"—The traditional way of courting or seeking a marriage in the Chinese countryside was usually initiated with the help of a matchmaker.

14. "... after the communization"—Not long after the Land Reform (around the late 1940s and early 1950s) in which private land was confiscated and divided among the peasants, the communization started, taking back in one way or another the land from the peasants to form collective farming units, such as communes or state farms. The communes are made up of production brigades, which are then divided into production teams that vary in size and population.

15. "... suddenly hearing that all that under the sky was the same and equal"—refers to the time of the Great Leap Forward, in which the government absurdly called on all the people in the country to start living the life of communism and sharing as much as possible their personal possessions.

16. "the collective unit"—refers to the community or organization one was in, be it a factory, a production team, a business, or any other organization.

17. "the 12th degree typhoon"—Literally, it refers to the worst measurable hurricane possible. The phrase is often used symbolically to indicate an adverse situation that is uncontrollable.

18. "the battlefields"—does not refer to military battlefields, but to the sites of iron-smelting furnaces and other foolish projects of the time. The word is used to indicate the heavy costs and losses that resulted from such useless projects.

19. "the cadres"—In China, government officials at any level are often referred to as cadres.

20. "The Party Secretary of the District"—A district is often made up of several communes. In each district, there is a Communist Party Committee that governs almost everything, and the head of such a committee is called a party secretary.

21. "... the Supply and Marketing Cooperative"—Such cooperatives functioned in China as the country stores do in America. The difference is that such cooperatives were owned by the government in China, and for a long time they were the only place where the farmers could shop in the countryside.

22. "the Old Society"—refers to the time before the founding of the People's Republic of China in 1949. Hence "the New Society" refers to the time after 1949.

23. "the 'Sixty-Item Document'"—This was a special executive document from the central government, part of which was an order for organizations to pay back partially or fully individual contributions in the Great Leap Forward.

24. "a Zhu Geliang"—Zhu Geliang was a legendary military advisor in the Three Kingdoms Period (A.D 220–280) and his name is still synonymous with wisdom.

25. "... who was red and who was black?"—Red is symbolic of the good, and black represents the bad.

26. "He cursed a great deal the capitalist-roader Liu Qing who did not work for the benefits of the poor and lower-middle peasants"—A capitalist-roader was anyone who was deemed as being against the socialist doctrines. During the Land Reform, all farmers were classified into landlords, rich farmers, middle peasants, lower peasants, and poor peasants. "The poor and lower-middle peasants" were the ones to be trusted.

27. "the commune's dictatorship apparatus"—In Chinese, this phrase does not necessarily have a negative connotation, because the

phrase "dictatorship apparatus" comes from "proletarian dictatorship apparatus," which refers to the law enforcement agencies of the state.

28. "revisionized"—A very negative Chinese word, used to refer to any attempt at deviating from the orthodox communist theories or practices as prescribed by Marx, Lenin, or Mao Zedong.

29. "It was a black wok"—A black wok means a bad name.

30. These ridiculous lines pair up things that are supposedly contradictory to each other, implying the abnormal social conditions of the time, but to Western readers, some of them may not seem typically contradictory.

31. "rebellion"—This word was used during the Cultural Revolution to refer to any drastic action against an establishment or organization. Although destructive, these actions were regional and containable in most cases, but they proved to be costly and disastrous because the government controlled by Mao used such rebellions for their power struggles.

32. ". . . he needed identifications from three administrative levels"—These three levels refer to the production team, the production brigade, and the commune.

33. "the revolution"—the Cultural Revolution.

34. "lime"—not the fruit, but calcium oxide, a white substance obtained from limestones; often used in China to whitewash walls.

35. "Director of the Revolutionary Committee"—In the Cultural Revolution, besides the Communist Committees that already existed everywhere, a Revolutionary Committee was established for every Communist Committee. At times when things went out of control the Revolutionary Committees were more powerful than the Communist Committees.

36. "Big Qianmen"—a popular brand of cigarettes produced in Beijing that is of higher quality than local products and, therefore, also more expensive.

37. "rearrange the mountains and rivers"—In order to gain more arable land in the Cultural Revolution, there were many irresponsible and wasteful projects to blow away mountains and redirect rivers for more farm land.

38. ". . . and the rotten and the dirty are both made lords"— Although incomprehensible as a whole sentence, the words used in this sentence indicate the chaotic times and the unstable situation in the country.

39. "... everyone is willing to live in a cowshed"—This refers to the political movement to send dissenting intellectuals to the countryside to reform through labor, because many of those intellectuals were assigned to live or work in cowsheds. At the time, it was a great risk for anyone to talk about it or make fun of it in public. Hence next comes, in the story, his wife's effort to shut him up.

40. "... could it have been hammered out with a fist!"—meaning the use of violent physical force, as in a rebellion in the Cultural Revolution.

41. "Pangu"—a legendary figure in Chinese mythology who was said to have created the earth and the heaven by slashing the universe with an axe.

42. "... all the pots of sweet-and-sour seasonings were knocked over in Li Shunda's heart"—an idiomatic Chinese saying that indicates the complex feelings or emotions one experiences.

43. "open the back door"—It is the Chinese phrase indicating corruption, especially in the government, when personal connections are used to gain something not legally and easily attainable.

BIBLIOGRAPHY

Note: Please also see the chapter 3 bibliography for more references.

Decker, Margaret Holmes. *The Vicissitudes of Satire in Contemporary Chinese Fiction: Gao Xiaosheng.* Dissertation Abstracts International 48: 11 (1988). 2875A–2876A.

Fan, Boqun. "Another Discussion on Gao Xiaosheng." *New Literature Forum* (Xinwenxue Pinglun) 1 (1984): 42–57.

Gao, Xiaosheng. "A Discussion with Scholars in Foreign Literature." *Contemporary Foreign Literature* (China) 2 (1985): 202–203.

———. "Li Shunda Builds a House." *Rain Petals* (Yu Hua) (Nanjing, China) July 1979: 4–15.

Shi, Hanren. "Gao Xiaosheng and 'Lu Xun' Style." *Literary Criticism* (Wenxue Pinglun) (China) 4 (1984): 37–46ff.

Xie, Yongwang. "Raising a Unique Flag" (Du Shu Yi Zhi). In *A Selection of Articles on the Literature of the New Period.* Ed. Theory Institute of the Association of Chinese Artists. Shanghai: Shanghai Arts (Shanghai Wenyi Chubanshe), 1986. 557–69.

Ye, Gongjue. "Three Figures in Literature." *Contemporary Literary Scene* (China) 8 (1985): 34–38.

Yi, Qi, Ed. *Selected Works of Gao Xiaosheng*. Zhengzhou, China: Yellow River Arts (Huanghe Wenyi Chubanshe), 1987.

CHAPTER 7

"Ah, Xiangxue!"

Tie Ning (1957–)

Introduction to the Author

Tie Ning ("Tie" is pronounced like "tear" without the "r" sound) was born in the city of Baoding in Hebei Province in 1957, the year in which the Anti-Rightist Movement started. When she graduated from high school, the Cultural Revolution, although in its waning years, was still going on, and college education in China at the time was at best a political practical joke. Because college education was almost nonexistent, very few high school graduates went to college; those who did had to be either politically active or have connections, but they did not have to be exceptionally intelligent. Even if one went to college in those days, little was taught or learned in the classroom, because political movements and activities occupied most of the students' time. So like millions of other high school graduates, Tie Ning went to "settle in the countryside," a measure launched by Mao Zedong intended to solve multiple problems, both in the city, such as unemployment and disorder, and in the countryside, such as lack of education and lack of machinery. The high school graduates were called "Zhishi Qingnian" or "Intellectual Youths," and they lived and worked in the countryside like farmers, although sometimes they received preferential treatment from the native farmers. Most of these "intellectual youths" would return to the city after the Cultural Revolution, because, after all, life in the countryside in China was and is still far less comfortable than life in the city. But many of the intellectual youths would learn the most important lessons about life, about their country, and about themselves during those years working in the countryside, and one of these young people was Tie Ning.

Tie Ning published her first story, "The Sickle That Could Fly" ("Hui Fei De Liandao"; 1974), at age sixteen. From then on, she continued writing and publishing stories, but her success as a writer came a little later. After working and living in the countryside for some years, she came back to the city in 1978 to work as an editor at a magazine in the city of Baoding. It was about this time that her writing flourished. In 1979, when she published her short story collection *Evening Road*, she had already won the approval of a more famous writer, Sun Li, who highly praised her in his preface to her collection. She also garnered praises from Xie Binxin, another famous writer who, like Sun Li, wrote many works on Chinese women. Both writers were especially impressed with her women characters and the poetic qualities in her works.

Tie Ning's real fame came in 1982, when she won the Chinese National Short Story Award (Quanguo Duanpian Xiaoshuo Jiang) for her story "Ah, Xiangxue!" ("Ah, Fragrant Snow," Fragrant Snow being the name of a village girl; hence the phonetic translation of the title—"Xiangxue" is pronounced as "shiaang-shueh"). Winning that award may not have been the sign of great excellence, because, after all, more than ten short stories are given this same national award each year in China, but when writers of the old generation started to openly applaud her works, her name became known to many people all over the nation and her works became widely read. Sun Li, the writer who had written a preface for her collection in 1979, later wrote an open letter to Tie Ning about "Ah, Xiangxue!" In the letter he claims that the story "is a poem from beginning to end" (Sun Li, p. 215) and refers to it almost as a classic when he compares it to one of the most famous ancient Chinese poems. Two years later, she became immensely popular in the nation, especially among young readers, for her novella *The Red Shirt without Buttons*,

which won her the Chinese National Novella Award (Quanguo
Zhongpian Xiaoshuo Jiang) and was made into a successful
movie.

Having worked and lived with farmers, she still tries to
stay close to the countryside. In Sun Li's open letter to Tie Ning,
he advised her also to go to the countryside often in order to
sustain the originality and freshness in her works. She seems to
have listened to the advice. In recent years, largely because of
her literary fame, she has sometimes been appointed to
important political and administrative positions, working as the
chief government official in a county and getting involved in
many other administrative or political activities. One hopes that
such responsibilities will not interfere with her writerly activities
and that she will be as creative and fresh in her other works as in
"Ah, Xiangxue!" and *The Red Shirt without Buttons*.

Ah, Xiangxue!

[1982]

If no one had invented the train, if no one had laid the
railway tracks through the depths of the mountains, you would
never have been able to discover this small village of Taier
Ravine. It and its dozen or so families of country people were
wholeheartedly hidden, from spring to summer and from fall to
winter, in a deep fold of the big mountains, accepting silently
both the warmth and the cruelty begotten by the big mountains
at will.

But two slender, shiny tracks extended over to this place.
They bravely encircled the waists of the mountains, and then in
silence tentatively reached forward. Bend after bend, turn after
turn, they finally wound up at the foot of Taier Ravine. From
there they dived into a dark tunnel, dashed toward yet another
mountain ridge, and rushed to mysterious lands far away.

Soon this railway officially started running. People
gathered at the entrance of the village and saw the long green
dragon[1] whistle by, bringing with it the strange, fresh wind from
outside the mountains. It hurried away, right by the poor and

weak back of Taier Ravine. It ran in such a hurry that even the sounds of its wheels on the tracks seemed to say: No stop! No stop! Oh, yes, what reasons would it have to stop at the foot of the platform in Taier Ravine? Was there anyone in Taier Ravine who wanted to travel far? Was there anyone from outside the mountains who would come to visit friends and relatives at Taier Ravine? Were there oil reserves or gold mines here? Taier Ravine, from any perspective, did not have the power to press the train to stop by.

Yet at some vaguely remembered time past, a station called "Taier Ravine" was nonetheless added to the train schedule. Maybe travelers on the train requested it, or some influential person among them was a relative of Taier Ravine folks. Maybe it was the cheerful male train attendant who found that at Taier Ravine there were a group of beautiful girls between the ages of seventeen and eighteen. Whenever the train sped by, they would stand in groups at the entrance of the village, their chins raised, looking up at the train greedily and intensely. Someone would point at the cars, and now and then, one or two coquettish screams could be heard as they hit and pounded each other. Maybe there was no reason for it at all, but simply because Taier Ravine was too small, so small that it made people feel sorry for it. Even the huge train made of iron and steel could not march forward haughtily, but had to stop. Anyway, Taier Ravine was listed on the train schedule, and every night at seven o'clock, the train from the capital to Shanxi stopped here for one minute.

This short minute broke up the usual stillness of Taier Ravine. Before this, the people at Taier Ravine used to finish their dinner and then go to bed, as if they all heard an order from the mountains at the same moment. Therefore the small cluster of stone houses all became still at the same time. The stillness was so heavy and sincere that Taier Ravine seemed to be silently telling the mountains of its piety. Now the girls at Taier Ravine began to panic just as soon as they picked up their rice bowls at dinner. They would absentmindedly and carelessly eat a few mouthfuls and throw down their bowls to start dressing themselves up. They would wash away the yellow dirt and dust of the day to reveal their coarse, red faces, comb their hair until it shone, and then put on their best clothes to vie with each other. Some would put on the clothes that they would wear only at the New Year, and some would even secretly put some makeup on their faces. Although it would be dark already when the train arrived, they still painstakingly chose their makeup and clothes at their own will. Then they would run toward the entrance of the village, where the train would pass. Xiangxue[2] would always be the first one to step out of her house; her neighbor Fengjiao would be the second one to come out, right after her.

At seven o'clock, the panting train glided toward Taier Ravine. Then there was a series of irregular clanking sounds. The body of the train shuddered once before it came to a standstill. Their hearts beating, the girls swarmed forward, and as if watching a movie, leaned on the train windows to look in. Only Xiangxue stayed behind, her two hands covering her ears. When going to watch the train, she ran at the very front. Yet when the train came, she withdrew to the very back. She was a little afraid of that giant locomotive. The locomotive was spurting white mist in such a majestic manner that it seemed it could suck Taier Ravine into its belly in one breath. Its earthshaking thundering also frightened her. In front of it, she was like a rootless little blade of grass.

"Xiangxue, come here! Look at the gold ring on that woman's head. What do you call that?" Fengjiao pulled Xiangxue over and asked her while leaning against her shoulder.

"How come I don't see it?" Xiangxue asked, slightly narrowing her eyes.

"She's just the one further inside, that big round face. Oh! Look, her watch is even smaller than a fingernail." Fengjiao made another new discovery.

Xiangxue nodded her head without a word or a sound. She finally saw the gold ring on the woman's head and the watch on her wrist, which was smaller than a fingernail. But she also quickly found something else. "A leather book bag!" She pointed at an ordinary brown student bag of man-made material on the luggage rack. This was the kind of student bag that could be seen everywhere in small cities.

Though the girls had always been uninterested in what Xiangxue noticed, they still crowded over.

"Ouch, d——! You stepped on my feet!" Fengjiao screamed, complaining to a girl who had just piled over. She always liked to create a scene.

"What are you fussing about? Do you want the little white face[3] to start a conversation with you?" The girl that was blamed did not want to give in.

"I'll tear your mouth apart!" cursed Fengjiao, her eyes nonetheless looking toward the door of the third car.

That white-faced and clean-cut young train attendant really got down from the car. He was tall and big, his hair jet black. And he spoke with a beautiful Beijing accent.[4] Probably because of this accent, the girls secretly called him "Beijing Accent." "Beijing Accent" folded his arms and stood neither too far nor too close to the girls, saying, "Hey, say you little girls, don't lean on the windows. Dangerous!"

"Ah, we are little. Are you then old?" Fengjiao boldly made a reply.

The girls burst into loud laughter. Somebody pushed Fengjiao forward, and she almost bumped into him. This, however, gave Fengjiao more courage. "Say, don't you get dizzy when you stay in the train all the time?" Again she asked.

"That thing like a blade on the ceiling, what's that for?" another girl asked. She meant the fan in the car.

"Where do you boil your water?"

"What do you do when you get to a place without any road?"

"How many meals do you city people eat everyday?" Xiangxue also asked, right after the girls.

"How unruly!" "Beijing Accent" was trapped in the circle of girls, muttering to himself, at a loss.

It was not until the train was about to leave that they made way for him to go. He looked at his watch while he ran to the car door. When he got to the door, he turned to them saying, "Next time, next time I will tell you." His two long, thin legs agilely leaped, and onto the train he went. Then there was a series of clinking and clanking noises; and the green door closed heavily in front of the girls. The train dived into darkness, leaving them by the cold railway tracks. For a long time, they could still feel its diminishing trembling.

Everything resumed its silence, so silent that it made people feel listless. On their way home, the girls would always argue endlessly about something trivial: "Those nine golden rings were bound together and then put in the hair."

"No, they were not!"

"Yes, they were!"

Someone teased Fengjiao: "Fengjiao, why aren't you talking? Still thinking about . . . that 'Beijing Accent'?"

"Get out of here. Whoever talks about him is actually thinking of him." Fengjiao clasped Xiangxue's hand as she said this, meaning to ask for her help.

Xiangxue did not speak. She was flustered and blushing. She was only seventeen and had not yet learned how to speak in support of others on such things.

"I think you miss him but don't dare tell us. How white his face is." After a moment of silence, the same girl continued to tease Fengjiao.

"White? That is just because he stays inside the green train. Let him try to stay at Taier Ravine for a few days," someone said in the dark.

"Isn't that just so?! The city people just have to stay indoors. Talk about being white, compare them to our Xiangxue. Our Xiangxue was born with a good face. If she curls her hair like the girls on the train, hnh! Sister Fengjiao, don't you think so?"

Fengjiao did not answer and let go of Xiangxue's hand. It was as if they were really putting down someone related to her. She indeed felt in her heart indignant for him. Somehow, she was sure that his face was white not because he stayed indoors. He was born with it.

Xiangxue quietly put her hand in Fengjiao's hand again. She meant for Fengjiao to take her hand, as if asking for forgiveness, as if she had wronged Fengjiao.

"Fengjiao, are you mute?" It was still that same girl.

"Who's mute? No one's like you. You only try to see if the face is white or black. If you all like him, why don't you follow him!" Fengjiao had a sharp tongue.

"We aren't worthy of him."

"How can you be sure that he doesn't have a girlfriend?"

...

No matter how rowdy the arguments got, the girls became friendly when they parted, because an exciting notion rose again in their hearts: Tomorrow, the train would pass here again. The girls would have another beautiful minute. Compared to that, what's a little argument?

Oh, the colorful one minute, how much happiness, anger, sadness, and cheer you hold for the girls of Taier Ravine.

As time went by, the girls added new contents to this one minute. They began to carry with them willow baskets filled with walnuts, eggs, and dates. They stood beneath the windows and hurriedly did their polite business with the travelers. They stood on tiptoe, both arms stretching straight out, lifting baskets full of eggs and dates to the windows, to exchange for the machine-made noodles and matches that were rare in the valley, along with hairpins, scarves, and even colorful nylon socks that the girls liked. Of course, when they went home with the last few items, they ran the risk of being scolded because they did it purely of their own accord.

Fengjiao seemed to have been assigned to that "Beijing Accent" by the girls; every time, it was she who went to see him with a basket. The business between her and him was quite interesting. Often she would intentionally proceed slowly and would not give him the eggs until the train was about to leave. Before he had time to pay her, the train would already start to move. He would gesture to her from the train, the basket in his arms, explaining something. She was down on the platform, quite amused. That was what she wanted. Of course, the young man would bring her the money next time, or bring her some noodles, a couple of scarves, or something else. If there were ten kilos in the bundle of noodles, Fengjiao would surely take one kilo out and give it back to him. She felt that only in this way would she be worthy of associating with him. She wanted this sort of association to be somewhat different from just ordinary business. Sometimes she thought also of what the other girls had said: "How can you be sure that he does not have a girlfriend?" As a matter of fact, it was none of Fengjiao's business if he did. She did not plan to go with him. But she was willing to be nice to him. Did one have to be his girlfriend to be nice to him?

Xiangxue usually spoke little and had little courage. But when she did business, she was the smoothest one of the girls. The travelers liked to buy her goods because she looked at them with such trust, her crystal-clear eyes telling them that the girl standing below the window did not yet know what cheating was. She still did not know how to bargain, saying only: "Just give me what you see fit." When they looked at her clean face that looked like it was born a minute ago, when they looked at her lips that were as soft as red satin, a beautiful feeling would rise in their hearts. They would not have the heart to play any tricks on such a little girl. In front of her, the stingiest person would become generous.

Sometimes she would also use the time to question them about things in the outside world, asking if the universities in Beijing wanted any students from Taier Ravine, asking what was "musical poetry reading." (She happened to read about it in her deskmate's book.) One time she asked a middle-aged woman with glasses about a pencil box that could close on its own. She even asked about its price. But before the woman could answer her, the train had already moved. She ran to follow the train for quite a distance, but when the whistle of the autumn wind and the screech of the train wheels started to sound by her ears, she stopped running, realizing how laughable her behavior was.

In the twinkling of an eye, the train was out of sight. The girls gathered around Xiangxue. When they found out why she was chasing the train, they felt it was funny.

"Silly girl!"

"It ain't worth it!"

They patted her shoulders as the elderly would.

"All because I was too slow. I asked too slowly." Xiangxue nonetheless did not think the whole thing was not worth doing. She blamed only herself for not making the best use of time.

"Hey, couldn't you ask about anything else!" said Fengjiao as she picked up Xiangxue's basket.

"You can't blame her. Our Xiangxue is a student." Someone else spoke also for her.

Maybe it was just because Xiangxue was a student. She was the only one from Taier Ravine who had passed the exam to go on to high school.

There was no school in Taier Ravine. Every day Xiangxue had to walk to the commune⁵ seat seven kilometers away. Although it was her nature not to speak much, she still had things to talk about when she was with the sisters of Taier Ravine.

In the high school at the commune seat, she did not have so many sisters. Although there were many girls in the school, their talk and behavior, even just an expression in their eyes or a little laugh, seemed always to remind Xiangxue that she was from a small place, a poor place. The girls would ask again and again, "How many meals do you eat where you come from?" She did not understand their intention, answering every time earnestly: "Two meals." Then she would look at them in a friendly manner and ask: "How about you?"

"Three meals!" Every time the girls would answer her with assurance. Then they would feel pity and anger about Xiangxue's insensitivity in this regard.

"Why don't you have a pencil box when you come to school?" again they asked.

"Isn't that it?" Xiangxue pointed at the corner of her desk.

Actually they already knew that the small wooden box at the corner of the desk was Xiangxue's pencil box. But they still pretended to be surprised. At such a time, Xiangxue's deskmate would play with her own big plastic pencil box, making a lot of clicking noises. Hers was a pencil box that could close automatically. Much later, Xiangxue got to know that the pencil box could close itself because a magnet was hidden inside it. Xiangxue's small wooden box, oh, was made by her carpenter father when she passed the high school entrance exam. In Taier Ravine, it was the one and only pencil box. But here, compared to her deskmate's pencil box, why did it seem to be so awkward and old-fashioned? In the series of clicking noises made by the plastic pencil boxes, the wooden box recoiled to the corner of the desk with some shyness.

Xiangxue's heart could not be calm any longer. She seemed suddenly to understand why her classmates asked her again and again about those things and about how poor Taier Ravine was. For the first time, she realized that the place was not glorious. It was because she was poor that her classmates dared to question her again and again. She stared at her deskmate's pencil box, guessing that it must have come from some big and faraway city, thinking that its price must have been extraordinary. Could it be traded for thirty eggs? Or forty? Fifty? Then her heart sank: Why did she think of such a thing? Mother collected the eggs from the chickens' nests not for her to plan on such a thing! But why did the enticing clicking noise keep sounding in her ears?

In late autumn, the mountain wind gradually became biting. It got dark earlier and earlier. But Xiangxue and her sisters would wait for the seven o'clock train without exception. They could now put on their cotton-padded coats printed with flower patterns. Fengjiao put on her head a pink plastic hairpin. Some of the girls put some silver rubber bands at the end of their braids. These things they had traded for from the train passengers with eggs and walnuts. They imitated those city girls and dressed themselves and lined up along the railway, as if they were waiting to welcome some distinguished guests from far away, but also as if they were ready for an inspection.

The train stopped, giving out a heavy sigh, as if complaining about the cold in Taier Ravine. Today it showed its rare indifference to Taier Ravine: All the windows were closed, and the passengers were drinking tea and reading newspapers under the dim yellow light. No one looked out of the window. Those who had seen or traveled often through Taier Ravine also seemed to have forgotten the girls of Taier Ravine.

As usual, Fengjiao ran to the third car to look for her "Beijing Accent." Xiangxue tied a purple scarf on her head, changed the basket from one hand to the other, and then walked forward along the train. She tried to walk on her tiptoes, hoping the people in the cars could see her face. No one in the cars noticed her all the while, but, on a small table piled with food, she found the thing she had desired for a long time. Its appearance made her want to go no farther. She put down her basket, her heart jumping, her two hands tightly clutching the window frame. She recognized that it was really a pencil box, a pencil box that contained a magnet and would close automatically. It was so close to her. If there had not been a window pane in between, she could get it with a reach.

A middle-aged female attendant came over and pulled Xiangxue away. Xiangxue continued to stand at a distance to observe. When she was sure that the pencil box belonged to the student-like girl by the window, she resolutely ran over and knocked on the window. The student turned her face and saw the basket on Xiangxue's arm. She apologetically waved to her, not meaning to open the window. Nobody told Xiangxue to do it, but the car door was open, and not knowing why, she ran toward the door. When she stood at the door, she grabbed onto the door handle in one grasp. If there was still some hesitation when she was running over, her confidence was reassured by the warm smell coming from the car, the special smell that only trains would have. She imitated "Beijing Accent" and agilely leaped onto the door step. She had planned to run into the car at the fastest speed, and trade the eggs for the pencil box at the fastest speed. Maybe it was simply because she had so many eggs that she could decide in a few seconds to get on the train. She had forty of them.

Xiangxue was finally standing on the train. She held on tightly to her basket, carefully taking her first step into the car. At this moment, the body of the train suddenly jerked. Then the door of the car was closed by someone. When she realized that she should hurry to get off the train, the train was already bidding its slow farewell to Taier Ravine. Xiangxue threw herself on the door and saw in a flash Fengjiao's face below the train. It seemed that it was not a dream. Everything was real. She had indeed left her sisters and was now standing in the train that was both familiar and strange to her. She pounded on the window, yelling to Fengjiao: "Fengjiao, what should I do? What should I do?"

The train dashed forward, mercilessly carrying Xiangxue all the way. Taier Ravine was left behind in a flash. The next station was Xishankou. Xishankou was fifteen kilometers away from Taier Ravine.

Fifteen kilometers, to a train or a car, is really nothing. The travelers arrived at Xishankou just in the midst of their idle chat. Here there were quite a few people getting on the train, but getting off the train was only one traveler. It seemed that some people on the train tried to stop her, but she still jumped off resolutely, as resolutely as she had leaped onto the train a moment ago.

In her arms there was no basket anymore. She had secretly put it under the seat of that female student. On the train, when she told the female student, with her face flushing, that she wanted to trade the eggs for the pencil box, the female student flushed, too, without knowing why. She insisted on giving the pencil box to Xiangxue and said that she ate at the cafeteria in school, so that even if she took the eggs with her, she had no way of eating them. She was afraid that Xiangxue would not believe her, and so she pointed at the badge on her chest,[6] on which there were indeed the words "Institute of Mining and Metallurgy." Xiangxue, however, felt that she was lying to her. Could she have no home other than her school? Xiangxue accepted the pencil box, but eventually left the eggs on the train. Poor as Taier Ravine was, she had never taken anything from others for nothing. Later, when the passengers knew Xiangxue wanted to get off at Xishankou, what was it that they said to her? They advised her to stay one night at Xishankou before going home. That warm "Beijing Accent" even told her that his wife had a relative who lived right at the station. Xiangxue did not want to look for his wife's relative. But his words made Xiangxue feel wronged, feel wronged for Fengjiao, and for Taier Ravine. Thinking about all these grievances, shouldn't she hurry off the train? Hurry off the train, hurry home. The next day when she hurried off to school, she would then boldly and assuredly open her book bag and put "it" on her desk. . . . So she said to those who again tried to stop her: "It doesn't matter. I am used to walking." Maybe they believed her. They had not seen how the whistle of the train frightened her, making her seem like a little deer who did not know what to do. They could not figure out how capable the girls from the mountains were. Her words made them believe that the people in the mountains did not fear walking at night.

Now Xiangxue stood alone at Xishankou, seeing the train off into the distance. The train finally disappeared from sight, and there was an empty vastness in front of her. A cold wind came upon her, sucking on her thin body. She tied on her head the scarf that had slipped to her shoulders and sat down on the tracks with her body huddled up. Xiangxue had experienced all kinds of fears. When she was little, she was afraid of hair. If she could not pick off a single hair on her body, she would be so worried that she would cry. When she was older, she was afraid to go to the yard of her house at night on her own, afraid of caterpillars, and afraid of being tickled (Fengjiao loved to take advantage of this). Now she was afraid of this strange Xishankou, afraid of the dark mountains all around, and afraid of the silence that could make one's heart jump. When the wind whistled in the little woods nearby, she was then afraid of the rustling noise of the little woods. Fifteen kilometers. All the way walking home, how many big and small woods she had to pass by!

A full moon rose, lighting up the silent mountain valley, the little gray roads, lighting up the dead grass of autumn, the coarse tree trunks, those bundles of shrubs and strange stones, and those lines of trees covering the mountains like soldiers. And also the shiny little box in Xiangxue's hands.

It was only now that she wanted to hold it up for a good look. She thought, Why didn't I take it out for a look all the way riding on the train? Now, under the clear and clean moonlight, she saw that it was light green, and on the cover there were two pure, white lotus flowers shaped like horseshoes. She carefully opened it, and then lightly patted the cover as had her deskmate. "Click," it sounded and closed tightly. She opened the cover again, feeling that she should immediately put something inside the box. She groped out of her pocket a small box containing ointment and put it in the pencil box. Then she closed the pencil box. Only then did she feel that the pencil box indeed belonged to her. She then thought about the next day when she went to school, how she wished that the girls would ask her those questions again and again.

She stood up, suddenly feeling very content in her heart. The wind had also become much softer. She found the moon to be very bright and clear. Showered in moonlight, the mountains were like a mother's solemn and sacred breast. The leaves on the walnut trees had been dried by the autumn wind, curling up like golden bells. For the first time at night, she heard them singing under the urging of the wind. She was no longer afraid. She took big strides on the railway ties, heading straight forward. The mountains were actually like this! The moon was indeed like that! The walnut trees were in fact like so! As Xiangxue walked, she seemed to recognize for the first time the valley that had raised her. Was Taier Ravine like this? Not knowing why, she hastened her steps. She was anxious to see it, feeling curious about it, as if she had never seen it before. Taier Ravine would certainly be like "this": In time the girls in Taier Ravine would not ask for help from other people, and they would not need to answer the repeated questions from others. The handsome guys on the train would all come to their doors for them, and the train might also stay longer. Maybe three minutes, four minutes, or maybe eight minutes, ten minutes. The train would open all its windows to Taier Ravine. If a situation like tonight should happen again, anyone would be able to get off the train in no hurry.

Oh, yes, such a situation happened in Taier Ravine when the train pulled Xiangxue away; why then did she recall all these things as if for amusement? Oh, yes, the forty eggs were also gone. What would her mother say about that? Didn't Dad always hope that every day some family would take in a daughter-in-law or marry off a daughter? Then he would have endless work to do; then he would bare his copper-colored back and make those chests, cabinets, and crates day and night, so that he could earn the school tuition for Xiangxue. Thinking about these things, Xiangxue stopped. The moon seemed to have dimmed, and the ties under her feet became fuzzy. What would she say when she got back? She looked around at the mountains, but the mountains were silent. She then looked at the willow woods nearby, but the willow woods rustled, not really telling her what to do. From where came the sound of flowing water? She looked and found a shallow creek several yards away from the railway tracks. She walked off the tracks, and squatted by the creek. She thought of the time when she was washing her clothes with Fengjiao. They met an old man selling sesame candies. Fengjiao urged her to trade an old shirt of hers for candies, and told her that she could tell her mother that the creek washed the shirt away when she was not watching. Xiangxue wanted very much to eat sesame candies, but in the end she did not trade the shirt for candies. She still remembered that the old man waited earnestly for quite a while. Why would she think of such a little thing? Maybe now she should tell her mother a lie, because sesame candies were not as important as a pencil box. She would tell her mother that this was a magic box. Whoever used it would have everything they wished, would be able to go to college, and go to many places on the train. They could get whatever they wanted, and then they would not be looked down upon by others. . . . Mother would believe it, because Xiangxue had never lied to anybody.

The singing of the little creek became louder. It ran forward cheerfully, smashing against the stones in the water, now and then spurting little white waves. Xiangxue had to be on her way, too. She scooped up some creek water with her hands to wash her face; then she used her wet hands to comb her hair, blown loose by the wind. The water was very cold, but she felt quite spirited. She bade farewell to the little creek and went back to the long railway tracks.

What was that in front of her? It was a tunnel, sitting there like a black eye of the big mountain. Xiangxue stopped again, but she did not turn back. She thought about the pencil box in her coat, thought of the surprised and admiring looks in the eyes of her classmates. Those eyes seemed to twinkle in the tunnel. She bent down to pull up a blade of dry grass and put the stem of the grass in her braids. Mother had told her that this would "ward off evils." Then she ran toward the tunnel. To be more accurate, she dashed forward.

The more Xiangxue walked, the warmer she became. She untied her scarf and put it on her neck. How many kilometers had she walked? She did not know. She heard only nameless insects singing in the grass; loose and soft wild grass caressed the bottoms of her pants. Her little braids were blown loose by the wind; she stopped to braid them together again. Where was Taier Ravine? She looked ahead. She saw right in front of her black specks wiggling one after another. When she looked closer, they were people, a crowd of people walking toward her. The first one was Fengjiao; behind her were the sisters of Taier Ravine. When the girls saw that it was Xiangxue in front of them, they suddenly stopped walking.

Xiangxue guessed that they were waiting for her. She wanted to run over quickly, but why did her feet become extraordinarily heavy? She stood on the ties and turned around to look at the straight railway tracks. Under the moon, the tracks gave out a subtle yet clear light. They calmly recorded the journey of Xiangxue. She suddenly felt a tightening in her heart, and without knowing why, she started crying. Those were happy tears, tears of contentment. Facing the stern yet good-natured mountains, she felt rising in her heart a sense of pride that she never had before. She wiped her tears with the back of her hands, took out the grass in her braids, and then, raising the pencil box high, she ran toward the crowd in front of her.

On the other side, the still crowd also started to flow. At the same time, the valley suddenly burst out with the girls' happy laughter. They were calling Xiangxue's name, their voice unbridled and passionate. They laughed, their laughter very untainted and unrestrained. The ancient mountains were finally so touched that they trembled, giving out echoes that were deep and clear, accompanying the girls' cheers.

Ah, Xiangxue! Xiangxue!

NOTES

1. "the long green dragon"—Chinese passenger trains were painted almost exclusively green.

2. Xiangxue—Although used as only a name in the text, it is a Chinese word meaning "fragrant snow," alluding to purity and innocence.

3. "the little white face"—In the Chinese countryside, because the farmers have to work endlessly under the sun and a tan is only the sign

of hard labor, a person with fair skin is surely from the city, and a whiter face may bear a certain superiority.

4. "And he spoke with a beautiful Beijing accent"—Although a standard pronunciation system based on the Beijing dialect is taught to all school children in the country, a pure Beijing accent carries a certain prestige because of the political importance of the city and also because the dialect is believed by many to be elegant.

5. Commune—the way farmers have for decades been organized by the government in the Chinese countryside. A commune is a large unit which is divided into several production brigades, which are then divided into several production teams. The population in different communes varies greatly. Chinese communes should be distinguished from such communes as formed in the 1960s and 1970s in the United States.

6. ". . . and so she pointed at the badge on her chest"—College students in China are given little badges with the name of their college on them for security and other purposes. Many college students wear them everywhere they go, and they did so especially in the late 1970s and early 1980s, when colleges were extremely hard to get into.

BIBLIOGRAPHY

Sun, Li. "Commenting on 'Ah, Xiangxue.'" In *A Selection of Contemporary Excellent Fiction with Comments*. Ed. Zhaoteng Wang. Beijing: Language (Yuwen Chubanshe), 1986. 214–15.

Tie, Ning. "Afterword." *The Red Shirt without Buttons*. Beijing: Chinese Youth (Zhongguo Qingnian Chubanshe), 1984: 295–96.

———. "Ah, Xiangxue." *Youth Literature* (Qingnian Wenxue) May 1982: 37–42.

Zhang, Mingyuan. *The Curve in the Life of the Chinese*. Beijing: Chinese People's University Press, 1989.

CHAPTER 8

"Buddhist Initiation"
(Shou Jie)

Wang Zengqi (1920–)

Introduction to the Author

A writer whose fame and success came late in life, Wang Zengqi was born in 1920 in the city of Gaoyou in Jiangsu Province. Not much is known of his life before his college years, because the writer seems unwilling or has had few opportunities to detail that period of his life in his writing. But his life in his hometown and the nearby area has certainly been a rich resource for his short story writing, which has produced many memorable characters and depicted the colorful folk culture of his hometown area.

In 1943, he graduated from Southwestern United University, a college made up of the best professors and intellectuals in China, who fled to the southwest region after the Anti-Japanese War broke out in eastern China in 1937. After graduation, he taught high school, worked as a museum staff member, and did other odd jobs.

He started to publish stories in 1940. He followed the style of the late Shen Congwen, a great writer well known in the 1930s and 1940s, who was his teacher at Southwestern United University in Chongqing. His first published story was an assignment from Shen Congwen, who recommended it to a magazine for publication. Wang Zengqi frankly and gratefully acknowledges the influence and teaching of Shen Congwen, but his own writing would later on cultivate a unique style—a style deceptively simple but emotionally rich and socially perceptive—that became immensely popular in China in the 1980s. During his residence in Shanghai in 1946 and 1947, he wrote some memorable stories that were collected in *The Accidental Meeting Collection* (1949).

In 1949, he joined the People's Liberation Army of the Chinese Communist Party and later was assigned to work as a magazine editor in Beijing, the capital of the new People's Republic of China. His creative writing did not quite pick up after he moved to Beijing, as he devoted most of his time to editorial work for various magazines of folk literature. It is important to note that according to his own autobiographical writings and other people's accounts, Wang Zengqi has always been a rather mild-tempered person with a fascination for Chinese folk culture; his personality and interests have some obvious impact on his fiction. But his editorial work was interrupted when political movements came sweeping over the nation in the late 1950s.

Although many other writers suffered greatly or died in the disastrous years from the humiliating and devastating Anti-Rightist Movement (1957) to the annihilating Cultural Revolution (1966–1976), Wang Zengqi's writing did not completely stop. But he was nonetheless labeled a "rightist" in 1958, instead of in the 1957 Anti-Rightist Movement, because in 1958 the magazine he worked for had to find enough "rightists" to meet the government quotas. After he became a "rightist" overnight, he was sent away from Beijing to work in the countryside to "reform" himself. From 1958 to 1960, he worked as a laborer at various jobs in a local agricultural research institute in a suburb of Zhangjiakou, a city not very far from Beijing. In 1961, he wrote the short story "A Night in the Sheep Shed," about young adolescents facing changes in life, which was followed by two other stories for children, and all these stories were collected in *Evenings in the Sheep Shed.*

In 1960, judging from his honest work and good attitude toward the policy of "reform through labor," the institute he worked for decided he was no longer a "rightist." Since there was temporarily no other organization or *work unit* (the term in China used to refer to almost any organization, company, factory, etc.) to employ him, he stayed with the research institute to assist in their research work or do whatever job was assigned him. Although he was not an artist by trade, his major responsibility there in those years was to draw all kinds of things, such as illustrations for agricultural exhibitions. For instance, on assignment from the research institute, he produced *The Picture Diagrams of Chinese Potatoes*, a work that he is still proud of. In 1962, he was relocated to Beijing's Peking Opera House and worked there as a scriptwriter until his recent retirement. As a writer at Beijing's Peking Opera House, despite harsh difficulties similar to those encountered by almost all intellectuals in the Cultural Revolution, Wang Zengqi was able to create such successful modern Peking Operas as *Sha Jia Bang*, an opera that is still widely appreciated for its witty dialogue and well-designed plot.

His creative writing flourished after the Cultural Revolution. Encouraged by friends, he started to write and publish stories in 1979. In 1980, he published in *Beijing Literature*, a monthly literary journal, the story collected in this chapter, "Buddhist Initiation." In 1981, he won the National Short Story Prize for the story "Memories of Danao," a story about love in adverse situations, which was also published in *Beijing Literature*. Although now in his seventies, he still writes and publishes a few stories and essays of a unique flavor and excellent quality. A lover of folk culture, he edited and published in 1990 a collection of essays about Chinese food penned by forty-five contemporary Chinese writers, including himself. Although the essays are nominally about food, they are actually writings about Chinese culture, history, and society. When it comes to Chinese culture, Wang Zengqi enjoys even the simplest things in life, and in his essays he sometimes expresses his admiration for the originality or wisdom in such little things as cleverly written public announcements or concise traffic-warning phrases.

It is therefore no wonder that "Buddhist Initiation," although largely a love tale, is also a story of local culture in the eastern region of China. The detailed descriptions of the temples, the people, the customs, and the villages and towns offer a wonderful panorama of the vibrant life in Eastern China in the early part of this century (probably around the early 1930s). Meant to create a positive and lively picture of Buddhist monastery life, the story may seem rather ironic to American readers. A little knowledge of Buddhist doctrines and customs may help one to understand the story.

Buddhist Initiation

[1980]

It had already been four years since Minghai became a novice.

He was thirteen years old when he came here.

The name of the place was a bit unusual; it was called Ahn Zhao Village. "Zhao," because the majority of the villagers had the same surname, Zhao. Though it was called a village, the houses were scattered far apart in twos and threes. Stepping outside a door, one could see the neighboring houses, but it would be a while before one could walk there because there were no big roads, only winding paths dividing the fields. "Ahn,"[1] because there was a nunnery. The nunnery was called Bodi Nunnery, but everyone mistakenly called it Biqi Nunnery.[2] Even the monks in the nunnery called it that. "Where is your precious residence?"—"Biqi Nunnery." Nunneries are for nuns. "Monks in monasteries and nuns in nunneries." But Biqi Nunnery was occupied by monks, probably because Biqi Nunnery was not big. The big ones are monasteries, and the small ones are then just nunneries.

When he lived at home, Minghai was called Little Mingzi. It was decided when he was little that he would leave his family for a monastery. In his hometown area, people did not call it "leaving the family," but rather "becoming a monk." His native village was known for its supply of monks, just as other places were famous for their pig castrators, mat weavers, coopers, cotton fluffers, painters, or prostitutes. Other families with several sons always sent one to become a monk. To become a monk, one also needed connections, and there were factions, too, among the monks. Some of the monks from this village went to faraway monasteries. There were those who went to Linyin Temple in Hangzhou, Jingan Temple in Shanghai, Jinshan Temple in Zhenjiang, and Tianning Temple in Yangzhou. Usually they resided in the temples of their own county. Minghai's family had just a little land, and his three older brothers could easily cope with the work. He was the fourth son. In the year when he was seven, his uncle, who was a monk, came home. Little Mingzi's father and mother consulted with his uncle and decided to let him become a monk. He was right there with them and felt that it was indeed reasonable and found no reasons to object. There were many advantages in being a monk. First, one could eat for free. Any monastery would supply meals. Second, one could save some money. Once one had learned how to perform the Buddhist rites, one would be given his part of the pay. When the money was saved, one could later return to the secular life and get married; if one did not want to resume one's secular life, he could buy a few acres of land. Yet it was not easy to be a monk. First one's face had to be as handsome as a full moon; second, he had to have a sonorous voice; third, he had to be intelligent and have a good memory. His uncle studied his face a little, asked him to walk a few steps forward and a few steps backward, and then asked him to sing a rice-threshing work song: "Ge tung de. . . ." His uncle said, "Little Mingzi can surely be a good monk. I'll guarantee it!" To become a monk, one had to make some investment—go to school for a few years. Where would you find a monk who could not read?! So Mingzi began to go to school. He read *Three Character Scriptures*, *A Hundred Surnames*, *Four-Character Assorted Words*, *Youxue Qonglin*, the two-volume *Analects of Confucius*, and *Mencius One*, *Mencius Two*. Every day, he had to copy a page of calligraphy. The people in the village all praised him for writing the characters well, all very dark characters.

On the appointed day, his uncle came back home again. He brought with him a Buddhist jacket which he had worn. He asked his elder sister to shorten it a bit for Mingzi to wear.

Mingzi put on this monk's jacket, the pair of purple trousers he used to wear at home, and a pair of new cloth shoes on his bare feet. He kowtowed to his parents and then walked away with his uncle.

He had a formal name when he went to school, called Minghai. His uncle said there was no need to change it. So "Minghai," his formal name in school, became his Buddhist name.

They crossed a lake. What a big lake! They went through a county seat. The county seat was really lively: the state-run salt shop, the tax bureau; in the butcher's shop hung full sides of pork; a donkey was grinding sesame seeds into oil, and the aroma of sesame oil filled the whole street; cloth shops; some shop selling jasmine powder and hair oil; sellers of velvet flowers, silk-thread vendors, peddlers performing martial arts to sell medicine patches, sugar-figurine peddlers, and snake players. . . . He wanted to see everything. His uncle kept on pushing him: "Hurry up! Hurry up!"

They arrived at a river, and there was a small boat waiting for them. In the boat there was a very tall and very slender man of about fifty, and at the head of the boat squatted a girl about the same age as Mingzi, breaking open a lotus seedpod to eat the seeds. Mingzi and his uncle sat in the cabin of the boat, and then the boat set off.

Little Mingzi heard someone talking to him. It was that girl.

"Is it you who's going to Biqi Nunnery to be a monk?"

Little Mingzi nodded.

"They'll burn incense scars on your head if you want to be a monk. Aren't you afraid?"

Mingzi did not know how to answer, so he shook his head uncertainly.

"What are you called?"

"Minghai."

"And what do they call you at home?"

"Mingzi."

"Mingzi! I'm called Little Yingzi! We are neighbors. My house is next to Biqi Nunnery—Take it!"

Little Yingzi threw him the remaining half of the lotus seedpod. Little Mingzi then began to break it open, eating the seeds one after another.

The man rhythmically rowed the boat with his oars. Only the sound of the oars splashing the water was heard:

"Hua—shu! Hua—shu!"

. . .

Biqi Nunnery was very well located. It was on a plateau. Around the area, this had to be the highest piece of land. The builders of the temple were good at selecting the location. In front of the temple was a river. Outside the gate of the temple, there was a large threshing ground. On three sides of the threshing ground were tall and large willow trees. Inside the main gate of the temple was a hallway. A statue of Buddha Maitreya was on the shrine, facing the gate. An unknown celebrity had written a pair of couplets:

His big belly bears all troubles unbearable to others,
His broad smile laughs at those who are laughable.

Behind Buddha Maitreya stood the statue of Skanda. Across the hallway was a large courtyard, and two ginkgo trees were planted there. On either side of the courtyard there were three chambers. Across the courtyard was the central hall of the temple in which the three magnificent portraits of Buddha Sakyamuni were worshiped. The portraits were only about four feet high, including their shrine. On the east side of the central hall lived the chief monk, and on the west side was the storage room. To the east of the central hall, there was a little door in the shape of a hexagon. On the white door in green characters, a couplet was carved:

A flower is a world
Three looks are three bodhis

Behind the door were a long and narrow courtyard, a rock garden, several pots of flowers, and three little rooms.

The daily life of Mingzi, the little monk, was leisurely. He would get up early in the morning, open the front door, and sweep the courtyard. The grounds in the nunnery were all paved with square bricks, making them very easy to sweep. He would burn a column of incense before the Buddhas Maitreya and Skanda. He would also burn a column of incense in front of the three images of Buddha Sakyamuni, kowtow three times, chant three times: "Nanwu amituofuo,"[3] and beat the inverted wooden bell three times. The monks of the nunnery did not have the custom of either morning or evening services; Mingzi's three beatings of the inverted wooden bell delegated all of those services. Then he would fetch water in buckets and feed the pigs, then wait for the abbot, namely his own uncle, to get up and teach him to chant sutras.

Teaching sutra chanting was like teaching a student to read. With a book in front of the master and a book in front of the apprentice, the master would chant one sentence and the apprentice would follow by chanting a sentence. It was chanting, indeed. While chanting, his uncle would use his hand to beat time on the table. One beat after another, the beat was loud, like teaching opera-singing. It was like teaching opera-singing, exactly like it, indeed. Even the names used were the same. His uncle said: "In sutra chanting, one, the beat must be accurate, and two, the notes should be correct." He said: "To be a good monk, one must have a good voice." He said: "In the twentieth year of the Republic,[4] there was a big flood. The Canal[5] broke loose. Finally the Canal was repaired at Qinglong Lake. Because too many people drowned, there was a grand Buddhist service. Thirteen masters—the thirteen monks in the upper seats—and all the abbots of the large temples in the county came. There were up to a hundred monks present below the upper seats. Who was to take the seat of honor? After deliberate consideration, it was, after all, Shiqiao—the abbot in Shanyin Temple! He sat up there, just like the Bodhisattva Ksittigargha, needless to say. Once he voiced 'Open the incense box,' silence reigned over the thousand people watching." His uncle said: "Voice has to be exercised. It is to be exercised even on the hottest days of summer and the coldest days of winter. You should learn to use the breath deep in your lungs." His uncle said: "Only when you taste the bitterest can you become the noblest!" His uncle said: "There are outstanding monks among monks! Attention should be focused, and no indulgence in playing is allowed." Such a big sermon by his uncle convinced

Minghai utterly, and so he followed his uncle to chant beat after beat:

> As soon as the incense is burned in the burner—
> As soon as the incense is burned in the burner—
> The holy world will be filled with its fragrance—
> The holy world will be filled with its fragrance—
> And heavenly Buddhas will appear in their golden
>   figures—
> And heavenly Buddhas will appear in their golden
>   figures—

. . .

After Minghai finished his morning sutra—he also had to learn to chant a section of the Buddhist scriptures before going to bed in the evening and that was called evening sutra—the older monks of Biqi Nunnery would begin to wake up, one after another.

The makeup of the population in this nunnery was simple, altogether six people. Including Minghai, five monks.

There was an old monk, over sixty years old, who was the teacher of Minghai's uncle. His Buddhist name was Puzhao,[6] but few people knew it, because few people would call him by his Buddhist name. They all called him Old Monk or Old Master. Minghai called him Grandfather Master. This was a very dull and lonely man, sitting in his closed room all day, the room by the couplet of "A flower is a world." He was not seen reading scriptures either, just sitting there without a sound. He was a vegetarian, except on Chinese New Year and holidays.

Ranking below him were his three students, who were named with the word *Ren*: Ren Shan, Ren Hai, and Ren Du. Yet outside and inside the temple, people called them "First Master" and "Second Master," or "Master Shan" and "Master Hai." The exception was Ren Du, whom no one called "Master Du," because it did not sound appropriate. Most people directly called him Ren Du. He deserved only that, for he was still young, just over twenty.

Ren Shan, Mingzi's uncle, was the manager of the temple. Being called "manager" instead of "abbot" had sound reasons, because he was indeed in a management position. In his room stood a desk for accounting. On the desk there were account books and an abacus. There were altogether three account books. One was a book for money received for the Buddhist service; one was an account of the rent; one was the book of loans. Monks needed to provide Buddhist services, and there were charges for the services—otherwise, what was the use of being a monk? The frequently performed ceremony was chanting sutras for the dead. A formal chanting of sutras for the dead required ten monks. One would sit in the leading seat; another would beat a drum, and there would be four more monks on both sides. If there were not enough monks, just three would do on both sides. Biqi Nunnery had only four monks. They had to cooperate with monks from other temples if a formal chanting of sutras for the dead was to be performed. There were such moments. Usually their ceremony would have only half a set of monks. One would take the leading seat, one at the drum, and one on either side. One reason for this was that it was troublesome to seek cooperation from other temples; the second reason was that there were not many families that could afford a formal sutra-chanting ceremony for the dead. Sometimes, when a family had a death, they would invite only two monks, or even just one, who would do no more than noisily chant sutras for a while and beat the inverted wooden bell a few times. Many families would not pay the sutra-chanting fee right away, waiting usually till after fall.[7] This had to be recorded as accounts. Besides, the pay for different monks was not the same. It was like singing an opera; there were different shares. The one in the leading seat would take the first share, because he had to chant in the lead and also chant in solo. During the chant there was a long section of "grieving over the skeleton." All the other monks would lay down their equipment to rest, while only the one in the leading seat would chant slowly, beat after beat. The second share would go to the drummer. Do you think that was easy? Ha, if one's hands did not possess the skill, just the "commencing drum" in the opening would demonstrate no speed or leisure, no pause or transition. The shares for the rest of the monks would be the same. This also had to be written down: month, date, which family had half a set of monks, who was in the leading seat, who was at the drum. . . . It would save the cursing when accounts were summed up at the end of the year. . . . The nunnery had a few dozen acres of land rented out to be farmed by others, and the rent had to be collected when it was time. The nunnery also gave out loans. The rent and loans rarely suffered any losses, because the people renting the land or borrowing their money were afraid that Buddha might be annoyed. Such three accounts would already keep Ren Shan busy enough. There were, alas, also candles, lamps, cooking oil, salt, and "sacrificial food," which all had to be recorded on time. On the wall in Master Shan's room, other than the account books hanging there, there was also a board on which were written four red characters: "Diligent recording saves recollection."

Of the three qualities Ren Shan cited for being a good monk, he actually did not possess any himself. His facial complexion needs only two words to describe it clearly: yellow, fat. His voice did not resonate like bells, but rather like the grunting of a female pig. Clever? Hard to say; he would always lose at card games. He never wore his Buddhist ceremonial garment in the nunnery; even his dark gray Buddhist robe was left aside. Usually he would throw on a short Buddhist jacket, exposing a yellow belly. Farther down, his bare feet shuffled along in a pair of Buddhist shoes—even if they were new he would still shuffle them. All day, with no proper attire or proper shoes, he would walk here for a while and there for a while, making a noise like that of a female pig: "Mm—mm—."

Second was Master Ren Hai. But he had a wife. His wife would come to live for several months between summer and fall every year because the nunnery was cool. In the nunnery there were six people, one of whom would be the wife of this monk. Ren Shan and Ren Du called her sister-in-law, and Minghai called her Mistress. This couple loved cleanliness, cleaning and washing all day. Around dusk, they would sit in the courtyard to cool themselves. During the day, they would shut themselves in the house, never coming out.

Third Master was a man who was smart and capable. Sometimes First Master would pluck the abacus for half a day for a certain account with no result, but Third Master would just roll his eyes around a couple of times and already he was totally clear in his calculation of the account. He was most likely to win when playing cards. After twenty or thirty cards were laid down, he would almost know for sure who around him had what cards. When he played cards, there were always people who loved to stand behind him to check on him. Whoever wanted to invite him to play cards would say, "I want to give away some money to you." He not only could chant sutras and perform rituals (there were not many monks in small temples who could perform rituals), but he had also learned the consummate skill of "flying cymbals." In July, some places would have open fairs at which a large Buddhist ceremony would be performed. Several dozen monks dressed in Buddhist garments would fly cymbals. Flying cymbals were thrown into the air, cymbals weighing dozens of pounds. When the time came, all Buddhist instruments would stop playing and pairs of cymbals, dozens of them, would begin to be pounded on rapidly. Suddenly hands would go up, and big cymbals would fly into the sky, spinning as they flew. Then they would fall and be caught. Catching cymbals was no ordinary catch; there were different stances, such as "rhinoceros gaping the moon" or "warriors bearing a sword. . . ." This certainly was not sutra chanting, but acrobatics. Maybe the Buddha in charge of earth loved to see such a thing, but the ones who were really made happy were people, especially women and children. This would be the opportunity for young and handsome monks to show off. After a big Buddhist ceremony, just as after a good drama troupe was gone, there would be one or two girls or young wives missing—they had run away with the monks. Ren Du was also capable of performing fancy Buddhist ceremonies. Some families, in which there were many unrestrained young fellows, would request the fancy version when the Buddhist ceremony was not a very sad event—like celebrating a birthday anniversary of a dead relative. The so-called fancy ceremony was to ask monks to sing ballads, play string and organ instruments, and clap clappers. Different songs could be requested. Ren Du could sing a whole night without repeating himself. Ren Du had been away for a few years, and he lived in the nunnery only for the last couple of years. It was said that he had a lover, maybe even more than one. Usually, however, he was quite well behaved. When he saw girls or young wives, he always behaved himself, not even cracking a joke with them, not even singing a ballad. One time, when cooling themselves off on the threshing ground, a bunch of people circled him and would not leave him alone till they made him sing a couple of songs. He felt compelled, saying, "All right, I'll sing one. I won't sing any song from around here. You are all familiar with the ballads from here. I'll sing one from Anhui Province."

> Girl and boy thresh wheat,
> One could not bear to hear what they speak.
> Listen you won't, then you will not hear,
> After they thresh wheat they thresh each other.

After the song, they all felt that it was not enough, so he sang another one:

> The girl is born so pretty,
> The two breasts are so bouncy.
> Feel like going up to touch them,
> But the heart is just a little jumpy.

. . .

In this nunnery, there were no such things as monastic rules. No one would even mention these two words.

Ren Shan smoked a water pipe and would even bring his water pipe with him when he was out performing Buddhist rituals.

They often played cards. This was a good place to play cards. The square dinner table in the main hall, when placed at the doorway in a diagonal way, would be the card table. When the table was set, Ren Shan would take the chips from his room, pour them onto the table with a crashing noise. They played paper cards less often than they played mah-jongg. Other than the three monks as regular players, the ones who often came were a person who collected duck feathers and a rabbit hunter who would steal hens on the side, both decent fellows. The duck feather collector would shoulder a pair of bamboo baskets, going from village to town, stretching his gravel voice to yell out:

"Duck feathers for ca—sh!"

The hen thief had a device—a copper dragonfly. When he laid his eyes on an old fat hen, he would drop the copper dragonfly and the hen would go up to give it a peck right away. At the peck, the spring in the copper dragonfly would jump open, cocking open the mouth of the hen, which could make no sound anymore. Just as the hen was quite puzzled over this, he would go up and snatch her.

Mingzi once asked this decent fellow to see the copper dragonfly. He went to try it in front of Little Yingzi's house. Yes, it was true! Little Yingzi's mother found out, scolding Mingzi:

"Wishing to die! Son! How come you came over to play the copper dragonfly at my house!"

Little Yingzi ran over:

"Give me! Give me!"

She also tried it. It really worked. The mouth of a black hen was popped open, and the hen froze.

On rainy or cloudy days, the two fellows would come to Biqi Nunnery, idling the day away.

Sometimes there was no one available, and the old master would be dragged out. At the end of the card games, usually the monk serving as the dealer would be filled with anger: "F— you! Lost again! Next round we'll quit."

They would not hide it when they ate meat.[8] At the end of the year, they would also kill a pig. The killing would take place right in the hall of the temple. Everything was the same as at the secular places: boiling water, wooden barrels, pointed knives. When the pig was tied down, it would also scream for its life. What was different from secular places was the added ritual of "praying for the afterlife" for the pig going to heaven. And it was always the old master who prayed, with very solemn expressions:

". . . all animals, vivipara, ovipara, or borne out of air, come from the void, and should go back to the void. Past life or afterlife, both should be happy. Nanwu amituofuo!"

Third Master Ren Du swished down with his knife, and bright red pig blood would spurt out with many bubbles.

. . .

Mingzi frequently went over to Little Yingzi's house.

Little Yingzi's house was like a little island, with the river on three sides. On the west side there was a little road leading to

Biqi Nunnery. A single household with a single door, there was only this family on the island. There were on the island six big mulberry trees, which each summer would bear big mulberries, with white mulberries on three trees and purple ones on the other three. There was a garden of vegetables, beans, and melons that were available in all four seasons. The lower half of the wall of their yard was brick, and the upper half was made of adobe bricks. The door had been painted with tung oil and was pasted with a couplet in long-lasting red paint:

> Spring stays with the estate facing the sun
> Surplus be with the family who are kind

Inside the door was a wide yard. In the yard there were the cowshed and the rice-hulling shed on one side, and on the other side the pigsty and the chicken coop. There was also a fenced-in area for ducks. On the open ground lay a stone mill. On the north side were living quarters, also with bricks in the lower half and adobe bricks on the top. The roof was half tile and half straw. The house had been renovated only three years ago, and some wooden structures still showed a white surface. In the middle was the family hall, where the gilding on the family Buddha had not yet turned black. On both sides of the family hall were bedrooms. In alternate frames of the windows was fixed a glass of one foot square, shiny and glittering—this was still rare in the countryside. Under the eaves on one side was planted a pomegranate tree, and on the other a cape jasmine tree, both as tall as the house. When they bloomed in the summer, one white and one red, they looked very pretty. The fragrance of the cape jasmine was so strong that it itched one's nose. One could smell it in Biqi Nunnery when the wind was blowing that way.

The family was not made up of many people. The head of the family was, of course, named Zhao. All together there were four members: Uncle Zhao; Aunt Zhao; two daughters, Big Yingzi, Little Yingzi. The old couple did not have a son. Because in these years no one was sick, the cows did not have any mishaps, and there was no drought or flood or locusts, their life was quite flourishing. They had their own land, which was enough to feed them, but they also farmed ten acres of the nunnery's land. On their own land they grew an acre of water chestnuts—this was partly Little Yingzi's idea; she loved to eat water chestnuts. On another acre were planted yams. The family raised a big flock of chickens and ducks. Just the chicken and duck feathers would cover the cost of a year's oil and salt. Uncle Zhao was a capable man. He was a jack-of-all-trades, not only an expert in everything in the fields, but also able to fish with a net, wash mills, make rice hullers with a chisel, fix waterwheels, repair boats, lay bricks, bake bricks, coop barrels, split bamboos, and weave jute ropes. He did not cough, and his back did not ache. Firm and strong, he was like an elm tree. He was friendly, quiet all day. If Uncle Zhao was a ready source of money, Auntie Zhao was then a treasure pot. Auntie was surprisingly energetic. At age fifty, her two eyes were still clear and bright. No matter at what time, her hair was combed slick and smooth, and the clothes on her were crisp and clean. Like her man, she would not stop all day, cooking food for the pigs, feeding the pigs, pickling vegetables—her pickled radishes were extremely tasty—making rice flour, milling soybeans for bean curd, weaving straw raincoats[9] and weed baskets. She also knew how to make paper-cuts. In this area, at weddings dowry items, including china pots and tin cans, would all be pasted with paper-cuts made of red paper with lucky designs, for luck and also for good looks: "two birds facing the sun," "being together till hair is white," "thousands of generations of offspring," or "long lives and endless fortune." People came from as far as twenty miles away to invite her: "Auntie, the chosen date is the sixteenth. On which day are you coming?"

"The fifteenth; I will come early in the morning!"

"Sure?"

"Sure! Sure!"

The two daughters grew up looking like they had been taken out of the mold of their mother. Their eyes were especially like hers, the white as clear as egg white, and their black pupils dark as a black "go" piece. When their eyes were still, they were like clear water, and when they were blinking, they were like stars. From head to toe, everything was in its proper place about them. Their hair was slick and smooth, and their clothes were crisp and clean. The custom here was that girls who were fifteen and sixteen years old would comb their hair in a bun the way a married woman would. What wonderful hair these two girls had! The roots of their hair were a healthy red and their hairpins were snowy white. When the mother and the two daughters went to a fair, the whole fair would turn to look at them.

The two sisters looked very much alike, but had different characters. The older girl was courteous, quiet, spoke little, and was like her father. Little Yingzi was even more eloquent than her mother, noisily chatting all day without a stop. The elder sister said:

"You are twittering from morning till dark—"

"Like a magpie!"

"You said it! Your babble makes my heart flutter!"

"Makes your heart flutter?"

"Makes my heart flutter!"

"Blame me for your heart fluttering!"

The younger sister was hinting at something in her talk. Big Yingzi already had a fiance. She had stolen a look at the young fellow, who was very honest, good-looking, and came from a well-off family. She was satisfied. The marriage had been promised, but the date had not been decided. For the last two years, she rarely went out of her chamber, sewing her dowry all day. She could tailor and cut designs, but she was not as good as her mother when it came to embroidering. But then again, she was not satisfied with her mother's old-fashioned designs. She saw some brides in the city and said that what was embroidered now were lively flowers and grass. This made it difficult for the mother. In the end it was Little Yingzi, the sparrow, who clapped: "I recommend a person to you!"

Who was this person? It was Mingzi. When Mingzi was reading *Mencius One* and *Mencius Two*, he somehow came upon half a set of *Jiezi Yuan*,[10] which he liked a great deal. When he came to Biqi Nunnery, he still often dug it out to leaf through it. Sometimes he would use the back of the account book paper to copy the designs. Little Yingzi said:

"He can draw! He draws them just like they were alive!"

Little Yingzi invited Minghai to come over to her house, and she ground the ink for him. The little monk drew a few sketches and Little Yingzi could not help liking them.

"That's it! That's it! These would be good for embroidering!" The so-called "perspective embroidering" was a kind of embroidery. After the first layer was embroidered, the stitches of the second layer would go between the stitches of the first layer. The colors then could go from deep to light without any traces of abrupt change. This was unlike the ordinary stitches her mother used to make silk flowers, where the borderline between dark and light colors was clear-cut with one line of shade after another. Little Yingzi was like a secretary and also like an advisor.

"Draw a pomegranate!"

"Draw a cape jasmine!"

She picked some flowers, and Minghai would draw them.

Later on, things such as garden balsam, China pink, indigo plant, henon bamboo leaves, fish pelargonium, and winter sweet, he could draw them all.

Auntie also liked the drawings when looking at them. She hugged Minghai's shaven head.

"You are really smart! Why don't you be my adopted son!"

Little Yingzi grabbed his shoulder and said:

"Call her Mother now! Call her Mother now!"

Little Minghai knelt down on the floor, kowtowed once, and from then on called Little Yingzi's mother Adopted Mother.

The three pairs of shoes that Big Yingzi embroidered became known for miles around. Many girls came either on foot or by boat to see them. After looking at them, they said, "Oh my, my, my, they look really good! How could this have been embroidered? This is a fresh flower!" They would come with paper to beg Auntie to ask the little monk to draw for them. Some asked him to draw for the fringe of a mosquito net; some asked him to draw door curtains and belts; and some asked him to draw flowers for the top of their shoes. Every time Mingzi came over to draw flowers, Little Yingzi would cook him something nice to eat: boil a couple of eggs, steam a bowl of yams, or fry some lotus root balls.

In order to let her sister sew her wedding dowry, Little Yingzi took care of all the minor chores in the fields. Her helper was Mingzi.

The work around this area was to transplant rice seedlings, pedal water to higher fields, uproot the weeds, and then harvest the rice stocks and thresh them. A family could not manage these heavy tasks all by itself. In this area, people tended to trade their labor. After work was properly scheduled, several families would take care of one family after another in turn. No labor fee was collected, but the meals were good. Six meals a day, in the first and last of which there would be meat. There was wine at every meal. When they were working, they would beat drums and cymbals and sing songs with much fanfare. At other times, each family worked on their own, and the work would then not be so intense.

When the fields were being weeded the third time, the rice seedlings were already pretty tall, hiding people if they lowered their head. In the patch of deep green a very crisp voice sings:

The cape jasmine blooms in petals of six
Right before the sister's door there is a bridge

Hearing this, Minghai would know where Little Yingzi was and would rush over in big steps. After he got there, he would bend down to weed. Leading the buffaloes to take a mud bath at dusk was Mingzi's job. Water buffaloes are afraid of mosquitoes. According to the custom around this area, after the buffaloes had been freed from their yokes and had drunk their water, they would be led to a pond of well-mixed muddy water to roll about by themselves and splatter, covering their bodies with mud. This way the mosquitos could not bite through the skin any more. When watering the lower fields, using only a waterwheel of fourteen scoops,[11] two people would be able to do the work in half a day. Mingzi and Little Yingzi would lean on the bar and pedal the waterwheel neither too fast nor too slow, lightly singing the folk songs of different places that Minghai had learned from Third Master. Then at the time of threshing, Mingzi could replace Uncle Zhao for a while, letting him go home to eat. The Zhaos did not have their own threshing ground, and every year they threshed their rice on the ground outside Biqi Nunnery. Mingzi raised the whip for the buffalo and started singing the work song for threshing:

"Ge tung de—!"

This work song for threshing had a tune but no words to it; yet when the tune twisted and changed, it was more pleasing to the ear than any folk song or other work song. At home, Auntie Zhao, hearing Mingzi's work song, would prick her ears.

"Such a voice this kid has!"

Even Big Yingzi would stop her needle work. "Really nice to listen to!"

Little Yingzi would very proudly say:

"Number one in all thirteen provinces!"[12]

At night they would watch the threshing ground together. The grain that Biqi Nunnery collected would also be dried in the sun on the same ground. They sat shoulder to shoulder on a stone roller, listening to frogs croak, winter snakes sing—the singing of crickets was mistaken for that of earthworms in this area, and earthworms were called "winter snakes"—grasshoppers weave around endlessly, and watch glow worms fly here and there, and the meteors in the sky.

"Oh! I forgot to tie a knot on my belt!" Little Yingzi said.

The folks here believed that, when a knot was made on their belt at the time meteors fell, the good things they were hoping for in their hearts would come true.

. . .

"Squeezing" in the mud for water chestnuts was the work that Little Yingzi loved the most. When the fall season was over, the field had been harvested and the threshing ground cleared. And the leaves of water chestnuts withered. The round and straight leaves of the water chestnuts were like onion leaves, but with little blocks in them. They would make snapping sounds when brushed with a hand. Little Yingzi loved most to rub them with her hands. The water chestnuts were hidden in the soft mud. The bare feet stepped around in the cold and slippery mud—oh, a hard one! One hand went down, and there was a purple-red water chestnut. She loved to do this work herself, but she also dragged Mingzi along. And she constantly stepped on Mingzi's bare feet with her own bare feet, on purpose.

She went home with a basket of water chestnuts on her arm, leaving on the paths among the fields a string of footprints. Minghai looked at the footprints and felt dazed. Five little toes, smooth sole, narrow heel, and an empty space at the arch. Minghai had in his body a feeling that he had never had before. He felt as if his heart were itching. This string of beautiful footprints had the little monk's heart stirred.

. . .

Mingzi went to town often on the boat of the Zhaos, buying incense candles, oil, and salt for the nunnery. When it was not the busy farming season, Uncle Zhao would row the boat; when it was busy, Little Yingzi would go and Mingzi would row the boat.

From Ahn Zhao Village to the county seat, there was a big stretch of reedy marshes along the waterway. The reeds grew to be very thick, and amidst them there was a waterway, and no one could be seen from all around. When they came to this place, Mingzi always felt nervous at heart for no reason. He would then row the pedals with much force.

Little Yingzi would yell out:

"Mingzi! Mingzi! What's wrong with you? Have you gone crazy? Why do you row this fast?"

. . .

Minghai was going to Shanyin Temple to be initiated.

"Are you really going to burn the Buddhist spots?"

"Really."

"Burn twelve holes on such a nice head. Wouldn't the pain kill you?"

"Grit the teeth. My uncle says that this is a big step toward being a monk. I will have to take it anyway."

"Wouldn't it be all right to not be initiated?"

"Uninitiated monks are homeless monks."

"What's good about being initiated?"

"Once initiated, a monk can travel all over the place, putting down his gear whenever he sees a temple."

"What is called 'putting down his gear'?"

"It means living in the temple. And dining whenever meals are served."

"No charge?"

"No charge. When there is a ceremony, they would also give the traveling monk the priority to perform it."

"No wonder everyone says 'It's easier for the monk from afar to get to chant the Buddhist sutras.' Just because of the burnt spots on top of the head?"

"He is also required to have a certificate."

"After all, initiation is just accepting the diploma of a qualified monk!"

"That's right!"

"I'll row you there."

"Okay."

Little Yingzi rowed the boat very early to the front door of Biqi Nunnery. For some unknown reason, she was quite excited. She was full of curiosity, wanting to take a look at the big Shanyin Temple and see what the initiation was like.

Shanyin Temple was the biggest temple in the county. Located outside the county seat's eastern gate, it faced a deep moat and was surrounded by tall trees on three sides. Because the temple was hidden among the trees, looking from afar one could dimly see only a bit of the golden, shining roofs and would not know how big the temple was. Everywhere on the trees was hung the sign "Be wary of fierce dogs." The dogs in the temple were known to be fierce. Usually few people went into the temple. When the temple was open to the public, people were permitted to tour around at will and the fierce dogs would be locked up.

What a big temple! The threshold at the gate of the temple was higher even than Little Yingzi's knees. Facing the door stood two big signs, one on each side. On one were written two huge characters, "Open Tour," and on the other was written "Loud Noise Forbidden." The temple indeed looked solemn and dignified and no one dared even to cough loudly when one got in there. Minghai naturally went to take care of registration, and Little Yingzi then went to different places to have a look. How impressive; the two guards and the four Vajras stood about thirty feet tall and they all looked brand new after recent repair. The courtyard was as big as two square mu, paved with blue stone slabs and planted with pines and cypresses. "Mahavira Hall" could indeed be called a "great hall." One would feel very chilly upon entering. Everywhere it was a dazzling golden color. Buddha Sakyamuni sat on a lotus flower pedestal. The pedestal seat itself was taller than Little Yingzi. Raising her head, she could not see his entire face but only his slightly closed lips and a fat chin. On each side was a big red candle, as thick as two arms' length. On the table of offerings in front of the Buddha were placed fresh flowers, velvet flowers, silk flowers, along with corallites, jade ruyi,[13] and a whole elephant trunk. In incense burners joss-sticks were burning. Little Yingzi came out of the temple, smelling fragrance in her own clothes. Many heavy embroidered streamers were hung. These streamers were made of some unfamiliar satin, very heavy and thick, and the flowers on them were very carefully embroidered. What a big inverted bell. It could hold at least ten buckets of water. What a big wooden fish.[14] It was as big as a cow, painted red all over. She then went to the hall of the Arhat. She also went to have a look at the Pavilion of a Thousand Buddhas. There were indeed a thousand little Buddhas. She also went with some people to have a look at the Pavilion of Buddhist Scriptures. There was not much to see in the Pavilion of Buddhist Scriptures, full of scriptures. Oh my! After this tour, her legs became sore. Little Yingzi remembered that she had to buy oil for her family, silk threads for her sister, cloth for her mother to make shoes, two silver butterflies to weigh down the belts on her skirt, and tobacco for her dad. So she went out of the temple.

After she took care of everything, it was noon. She went back to the temple to have a look and the monks were just having some porridge. What a "dining room!" It could seat eight hundred monks. There was protocol even when the monks ate porridge: In the front were placed two tin vases in which were inserted red velvet flowers. Behind the tin vases sat a monk dressed in a red Buddhist garment embroidered with golden thread. He had a ruler in his hand. This ruler was for beating people. If a monk made a noise when eating porridge, he would come down and give him a beating with the ruler. Yet he did not really beat anyone, but only made a gesture of it. It was really a wonder that there was not a sound when so many monks were eating porridge. She saw Mingzi among them and wanted to greet him but dared not. She thought for a while and did not care whether loud noise was allowed or not, so she called out loudly: "I am leaving!" She saw Mingzi slightly nodding his head without averting his eyes, and not minding all the people looking at her, she walked away leisurely.

On the early morning of the fourth day, Little Yingzi went to see Mingzi. She knew that Mingzi's initiation was at midnight on the third day. The burning of initiation spots could not be watched. She knew that old barbers were invited to shave the initiates' heads and their heads had to be shaved without any stubble to be felt by the hand. Otherwise, the burning could go awry, and the spots would become too big. She knew that a mixture made from dates was dotted on the head and then lit with a joss-stick. She knew that after the spots had been burnt, they had to drink a bowl of mushroom soup, to let the spots "rise." They could not lie down, but had to walk around constantly. That was called "discharging the initiation." These things Mingzi told her. And Mingzi had learned them from his uncle.

When she looked, the monks were really there "discharging the initiation" in the abandoned field at the foot of the city wall. One monk was here and another there, all wearing their new gray uniforms, and on all their bare heads there were twelve black spots. After these black spots fell off, the white and round "initiation scar" would appear. The monks were all laughing, appearing to be very happy. She saw Mingzi right away. With the moat between them, she called out:

"Mingzi!"

"Little Yingzi!"

"Are you initiated?"

"Initiated."

"Did it hurt?"

"Hurt."

"Does it still hurt?"

"Now the pain is gone."

"When do you go back?"

"Day after tomorrow."

"Morning? Afternoon?"

"Afternoon."

"I'll come to pick you up!"

"Okay!"

. . .

Little Yingzi met Minghai in the boat.

Little Yingzi wore a white linen blouse that day and also black cotton trousers. She had on her bare feet a pair of fine straw sandals. On one side of her head she had on a cape jasmine flower and on the other a pomegranate flower. Seeing that Mingzi had on the new gray uniform and that the white collar of his shirt stuck out, she said: "Take off the uniform. Aren't you hot?"

They each had an oar in their hands. Little Yingzi was in the middle of the boat and Mingzi was at the helm at the end.

She asked Mingzi many questions, as if she had not seen him for a year.

She asked, "When they were burning the spots, did anyone cry? Did anyone yell out?"

Mingzi said that no one cried, but they prayed endlessly. There was a Shandong[15] monk who cursed:

"F—— you! I won't burn any more!"

She asked if the look and voice of Abbot Shiqiao at Shanyin Temple were both outstanding.

"Yes."

"I hear his chamber is even more beautiful than a rich girl's room."

"It is. Everything was embroidered."

"Is it very fragrant in his chamber?"

"Very fragrant. The incense he burns is made of agalloch eaglewood, very expensive."

"I hear he can write poems, do paintings, and practice calligraphy."

"He can. The big characters carved in the beam at each end of the hallway were all written by him."

"Does he have a concubine?"

"He has one."

"Only nineteen?"

"I heard so."

"Pretty?"

"They all say pretty."

"Didn't you see her?"

"How could I see her? I was locked in."

Mingzi told her that an old monk in Shanyin Temple had told Mingzi that the temple had intended to select him to be the tail-Samir. But it had not been finalized and had to be discussed with the monk in charge.

"What is 'tail-Samir'?"

"When an initiation ceremony is performed, a head-Samir and a tail-Samir will be selected. A head-Samir has to be mature and be able to recite many sutras. A tail-Samir has to be young, smart, and good-looking."

"What is the difference between a tail-Samir and other monks?"

"Both the head-Samir and the tail-Samir can become the abbot in the future. After the present abbot retires, they will succeed him. The abbot Shiqiao used to be a tail-Samir."

"Will you be a tail-Samir?"

"It is still not certain yet."

"If you become an abbot, will you be in charge of Shanyin Temple? Be in charge of such a big temple?"

"Still too early to say."

Rowing for a while, Little Yingzi said: "You will not be an abbot!"

"All right, I will not."

"You will not be the tail-Samir either!"

"All right, I will not."

Rowing again for a while, they saw that stretch of reed marshes.

Little Yingzi suddenly put down her oar, walked to the end of the boat, leaned by Mingzi's ear and whispered: "I will be your wife. Do you want me?"

Mingzi's eyes opened big and wide.

"Say something!"

Mingzi said: "Mhm."

"What is that 'Mhm'! Want me or not, want me or not?"

Mingzi said loudly: "Want!"

"What are you yelling for?"

Mingzi whispered: "Wan—t!"

"Row quickly!"

Yingzi hopped to the middle of the boat, and the two oars rowed as if they were flying, gliding into the reed marshes.

The reed catkins were fresh and new. The grayish-purple catkins gave off a silvery shine, soft and slippery, like a string of silk thread. In some places cattails were ripe at the spikes, which were bright red all over, like little candles side by side. Green duckweeds, and purple duckweeds. Long-legged mosquitoes, water spiders. Water caltrops blossomed in white flowers with four petals. A lepwing (a kind of water fowl) was startled, and skidding right above the reed catkins, it flew away in a flutter into the distance.

. . .

NOTES

1. Ahn—This is a sound translation of the Chinese word "nunnery."

2. "but everyone mistakenly called it Biqi Nunnery"—*Biqi* and *Bodi* are two Chinese words that look quite similar to each other, but *biqi*, meaning water chestnut, is an easier word and is used far more often than *bodi*, hence the misreading.

3. "Nanwu amituofuo"—A standard phrase used in prayers, often shortened to "amituofuo" by some people. My translation is based on phonetic representation instead of semantic interpretation.

4. "the twentieth year of the Republic"—Please see n. 1 in Chapter One.

5. The Canal—This refers to the Grand Canal in China, the longest canal in the world. Because it links several rivers in China, it used to flood easily. When it was first constructed, the canal was used mainly to transport grains up north and to move massive numbers of troops. Although diminished in strategic importance, it is still in use today.

6. "Puzhao"—Though a name, it literally means "to shine all over the place." Note the irony in the contrast between the grand names of the monks and their behavior. The word *Ren* in the following paragraph means in Chinese "endurance" and "tolerance."

7. "Many families would not pay the sutra-chanting fee right away, waiting usually till after fall"—meaning after harvest, when the farmers would have sold their grains.

8. "They would not hide it when they ate meat"—Buddhist monks are forbidden to eat meat, because eating meat is equivalent to killing lives in Buddhism.

9. straw raincoats—In the Chinese countryside, when plastic raincoats were not yet available, farmers used to weave raincoats out of straw and other materials.

10. *Jiezi Yuan*—an old Chinese book containing a series of drawings, from which Mingzi evidently learned to draw.

11. "a waterwheel of fourteen scoops"—This is a device Chinese farmers have long used to transport water from one field to another, especially from a lower place to a higher one. A chain of wooden scoops is geared to a big wheel that turns when farmers use their feet to drive the axle by stepping on the pedals attached to the axle.

12. "Number one in all thirteen provinces!"—Though she may be referring to a specific group of provinces in the east of China, the expression is used to exaggerate his popularity.

13. ruyi—an ornament made of jade or other materials and shaped like a question mark. Though largely used as an ornament, it is generally regarded as a symbol of good luck and fortune.

14. wooden fish—a piece of wood carving shaped like the head of a fish, used to beat rhythms.

15. Shandong—a province on the northeastern coast of China.

BIBLIOGRAPHY

Chun, Rong. *Folk Literature in the New Period*. (Xin Shiqi de Xiangtu Wenxue). Shenyang, China: Liaoning University Press, 1986.

Li, Guotao. "A Descriptive Discussion of Wang Zengqi's Fictional Style" ("Wang Zengqi Xiaoshuo Wenti Miaoshu"). *Wenxue Pinglun* (Literary Commentary) 4 (87): 56–63+.

Wang, Mingfan et al. *A Contemporary History of Chinese Fiction*. Nanning, China: Guangxi People's press (Guangxi Renmin Chubanshe), 1991.

Wang, Zengqi. "Author's Preface." *Selective Short Stories of Wang Zengqi.* Beijing: Beijing Publishing House, 1987. 1–3.

———. "Buddhist Initiation" (Shou Jie). *Beijing Literature* (Beijing Literature) October 1980: 41–49.

———. *Wan Cui Wen Tan.* Hangzhou, China: Zhejian Arts press (Zhejiang Wenyi Chubanshe), 1988.